St. Louis' Big League Ballparks

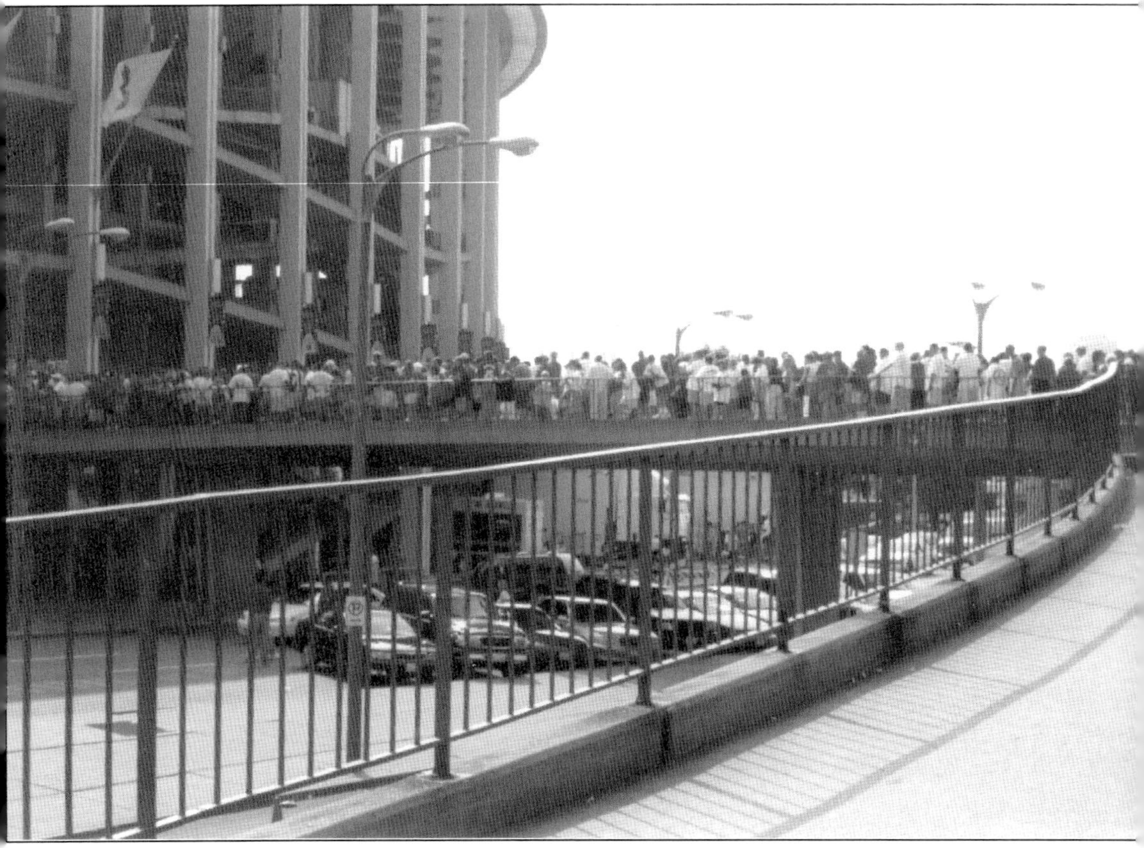

On September 27, 1998, baseball fans lined up across Stadium Plaza Drive. This familiar scene at St. Louis's downtown Busch Stadium was captured on the Sunday that Mark McGwire hit his 70th home run of the season. Many of these people attended church services earlier that day. Here they enter the city's cathedral of baseball to bask in the glory of the National Game.

ST. LOUIS' BIG LEAGUE BALLPARKS

Joan M. Thomas

ARCADIA
PUBLISHING

ISBN 978-0-7385-3265-3

Published by Arcadia Publishing
Charleston, South Carolina

Printed in the United States of America

Library of Congress Catalog Card Number: 2004103396

For all general information contact Arcadia Publishing at:
Telephone 843-853-2070
Fax 843-853-0044
E-mail sales@arcadiapublishing.com
For customer service and orders:
Toll-Free 1-888-313-2665

Visit us on the Internet at www.arcadiapublishing.com

This book is dedicated to my late father Leo Wendl, and every other lover of the National Game who never had the opportunity to attend a World Series game at a ballpark.

CONTENTS

ACKNOWLEDGMENTS

The images used in telling the story of St. Louis' Big League Ballparks are a combination of photos and collectibles provided by and/or with permission from the following individuals, companies and organizations. Providers of Private Collection images are listed under individuals. Photos other than collectibles, and captured after 1980, were taken by the book's author with two different cameras—a 35 mm Pentax MV and a Minolta Vectis 20 APS.

INDIVIDUALS

David Aitken, St. Louis Baseball Fan and Collector
Erma Bergmann, former AAGPBL pitcher and St. Louis Police Officer
Gary Thomas, New York Photographer and Collector
Joan and Bob Thomas, St. Louis Baseball Fans and Collectors

ORGANIZATIONS AND COMPANIES

Allied Photo, St. Louis
Fred Longshaw Postcards, Des Peres
Fru-Con Construction
Herbert Hoover Boys and Girls Club
Library of Congress, Photo Division
Mipakaco Sports Collectibles/Early Era Baseball Photos
Missouri Historical Society, St. Louis
National League St. Louis Baseball Cardinals
Missouri Secretary of State Archives
St. Louis City Hall Central File
St. Louis City Hall Recorder of Deeds
The Sporting News
VBBA Rock Springs Ground Squirrels
VBBA St. Louis Base Ball Perfectos

INTRODUCTION

A baseball park is just a place with a playing field. The very earliest versions offered no such accommodations as spectator seating. The first rules of the game of base ball (written as two words at first) differed somewhat from the modern sport. But today's Americans would immediately recognize the game, and spot the variances. Plus, they would find themselves just as drawn to it as they are to baseball as we know it now.

As base ball grew with the nation, the major leagues formed. With professional play came enclosed ballparks and a charge for admission. The first such parks, surrounded by wooden fences, offered simple wooden stands for seating. Over time, the stands grew to become grandstands and the ballparks became stadiums. The seating capacity grew and grew. And yet, what drew the crowd was basically the same game once enjoyed by gentlemen in the natural setting of the city parks.

As much or more than any other city, St. Louis became a baseball town. Over the years, a large part of the city's population developed an enthusiasm for following the home team. And each of its teams had a home park—a place. A place where one witnessed innumerable exciting, dramatic, and unforgettable events; where one shared those events not only with certain loved ones, but also with a group of strangers-become-comrades for a few memorable hours; and where one spent countless summer afternoons or evenings drinking in the multi-layered aura of the National Game. Eventually, the park, or the stadium, grew old and outdated and another took its place. But the memories created at the old parks were irreplaceable.

In 2004, St. Louis citizens, as well as baseball fans the world over, know about Busch Stadium. Many of those individuals hold precious their recollections of experiences at that majestic park. And, though the number of people who remember old Sportsman's Park continues to dwindle, a billboard now at the site of that centenarian of baseball informs passersby of its history. Only a sparse few fans are aware that five other big league baseball parks once existed within the boundaries of the city of St. Louis. For a two-year period, the city actually had a choice of three such places. To fully appreciate how St. Louis got to be a baseball town, one needs to visit all of these parks, including Sportsman's and Busch in the beginning, and learn about the people who built them and played there. It is the author's intent to act as the tour guide.

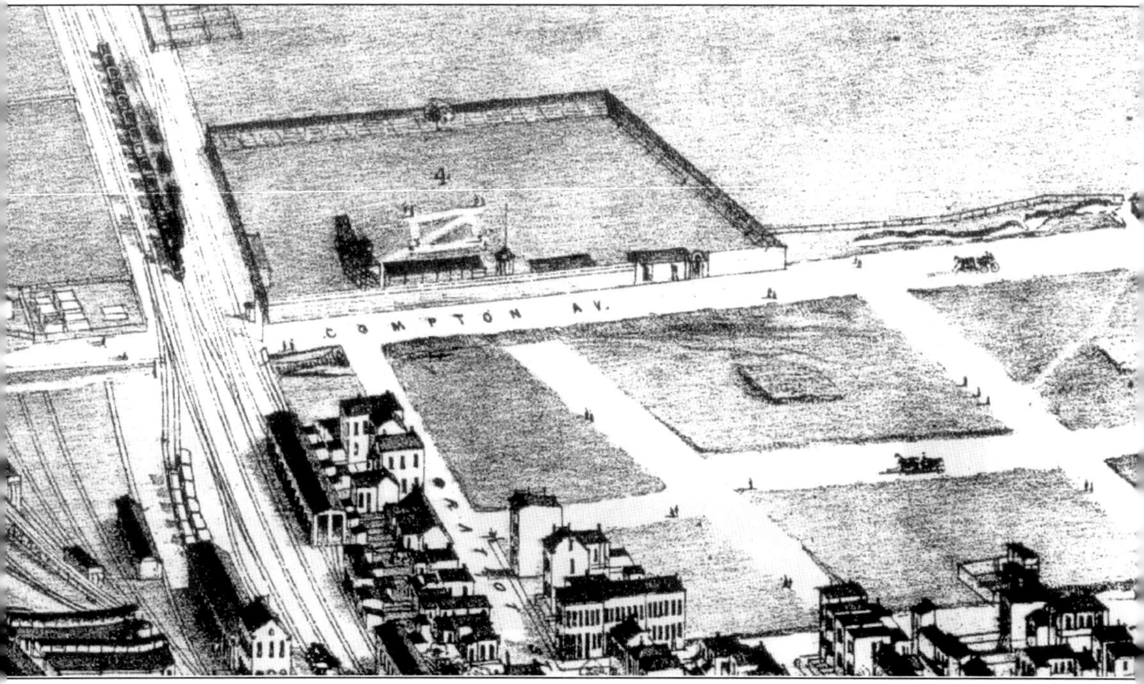

The Compton Avenue viaduct now spans the railroad tracks seen in this nineteenth century drawing. The simple wooden stockade-enclosed baseball park pictured here hosted the first fully professional baseball contest held in St. Louis. (Photocopy image from *Pictorial Saint Louis, 1875*, by Camille N. Dry, courtesy St. Louis Public Library.)

ONE

Baseball Grows with St. Louis

Historians cite June 19, 1846 and Hoboken, New Jersey as the date and place of the birth of baseball. Following the sport's natural evolution, the first recorded match played under the original rules set out by Alexander J. Cartwright occurred then and there. Base ball soon gained popularity throughout the country. The American Civil War, 1861–1865, contributed to widespread familiarity with Cartwright's rules. Soldiers mingling with those from divergent parts of the country learned the game from one another. One young man from Brooklyn, New York was posted to St. Louis while serving in the Union Army's Quartermaster's Corps. Having played with several amateur base ball clubs in Brooklyn, he shared his knowledge of the modern method of play with St. Louis base ball enthusiasts. As all legends are rooted in truth, this is the origin of Jeremiah Fruin's recognition as "the father of real baseball in St. Louis."

Fruin remained in St. Louis, and came to be referred to as the "stranger from somewhere in the East" who came onto the grounds of Lafayette Park, laid out a diamond, and showed the other young men how to play by the modern rules. But old news stories reveal that early St. Louis sports devotees played a form of a game called "base ball" as early as 1860. A local news item during the summer of that year reported that "the first regular game of base ball" would be played in the field immediately west of the Fair Grounds on July 9. That would be the same place that is known today as Fairgrounds Park.

So, the sport was not unknown to the Mound City when Fruin first arrived. When interviewed many years later, he dismissed the idea that he brought baseball to St. Louis. Yet he did admit that he may have been the first to show the local lads how to catch the ball by giving to it, how to trap the ball, make a double play, and other techniques. Captain of the St. Louis Empires Base Ball Club for four years, he promoted the game as a gentlemen's sport, discouraging the team's former propensity for engaging in fisticuffs when a game turned sour.

Regardless of the beginnings of countless "big innings" in the city, baseball ingrained itself in St. Louis culture long before its teams played within the confines of a stadium. Playing on grass in a woodland clearing with open sky for lighting, those early ball-tossers played without gloves. And they played just because they loved the sport. But it was inevitable that a game that drew so much interest would yield to commercial enterprise. The first professional league of baseball players in this country, the National Association, formed in 1871, and St. Louis acquiesced on the last year of that league's existence, 1875. By then, St. Louis had many amateur clubs. At the start of that season, the city had not one, but two professional baseball teams listed with the National Association.

Teams named for the color of their stockings then, the St. Louis professionals of 1875 were the Brown Stockings and the Red Stockings. Each club had its own ballpark consisting of wooden grandstands and a playing field surrounded by wooden fences. They were St. Louis' first big league ballparks—a far cry from the stadiums of today. Nevertheless, the game played in those parks then was not much different than what we see today.

The Brown Stockings were organized by a group of prominent St. Louis men. That club was based at the Grand Avenue Grounds, the same location that later became Sportsman's Park. Selling stock in the club for $50 a share, and recruiting ringers from all over the country, the owners anticipated a successful business venture. Yet, some local citizens frowned on the idea of bringing in outsiders. Consequently, an existing amateur club consisting of all St. Louis talent, the Red Stockings, turned professional and joined the league too.

The Reds played at a park built just for them the previous year. It happened that the first fully professional base ball contest in St. Louis took place at the Red Stockings Park on May 4, 1875. That day the St. Louis Reds lost 15-9 to the St. Louis Brown Stockings. The following week on May 11, the Reds lost to the visiting Chicago White Stockings (predecessors of the Chicago Cubs, not the White Sox). The significance of that game was the then unheard-of score. Though the local club lost, St. Louis fans reveled in the witnessing of the first 1-0 professional game recorded. However, the Reds faded from the league by mid-season. On the other hand, the Browns' fine performance that year convinced the city's baseball advocates that perhaps it wasn't such a bad thing to bring in outside talent to field a contender. That team continued to host games at the Grand Avenue Grounds, and became one of the first members of the National League that emerged the following year.

Though Red Stockings Park's use as a pro arena was brief, it continued to serve baseball and other popular sports until it was torn down in 1898. By then, it was just called the Compton Avenue Grounds. It lay just west of Compton and north of the railroad tracks. On a stretch of land once called the Veto grounds, it hosted base ball even before the simple wooden stockade enclosure and stands were erected for the Reds. Described as situated on six acres of smooth level ground, it was then easily accessible by public transportation. Railroad tracks running next to the southern edge of the field, the property was on land originally owned by David J. Ranken, an Irish immigrant who gained financial success in real estate. His moniker is now widely associated with St. Louis's Ranken Technical School.

As for capacity at the Compton park, it probably seated about 1,000. At least four times that many witnessed one game held there in June of 1883. Hosted by a champion St. Louis African-American club called the Black Stockings, it drew a sizable crowd of some "four thousand spectators," according to one newspaper accounting. Possibly some of the fans saw the game from the opposite side of the fence. At the beginning of the 1875 season, there were news reports of vandals cutting holes in the fence to see the game for free. That may have contributed to later use of the term knothole gang.

By the time of the dismantling of old Red Stockings Park, St. Louis had turned its attention to several local Major League teams, at several other ballparks. Though in 1913 the Compton site was considered as a possibility for the ephemeral Federal League Terriers' park, it never saw baseball again. Today, Bi-State Development Agency's Repair facility occupies the space next to the tracks where professional baseball began in St. Louis.

Busy commuters travel over the Compton Avenue viaduct daily, and it is a good bet that many of them are baseball fans. Yet time has erased all visible evidence of what happened there next to the tracks some 129 years ago. Only scratchy city directories, maps, documents, and newspaper stories preserved on microfilm offer positive proof that parks like this once existed.

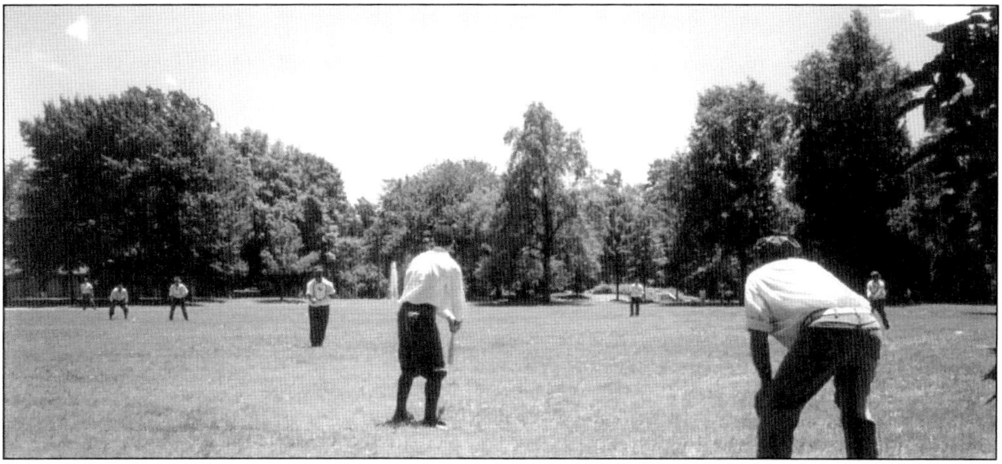

In June 2003, the Vintage Base Ball Association (VBBA) St. Louis Perfectos bat against the visiting team, the Rock Springs Ground Squirrels. With the Perfectos' home grounds in historic Lafayette Park, the teams simulate a scene of nearly 150 years earlier.

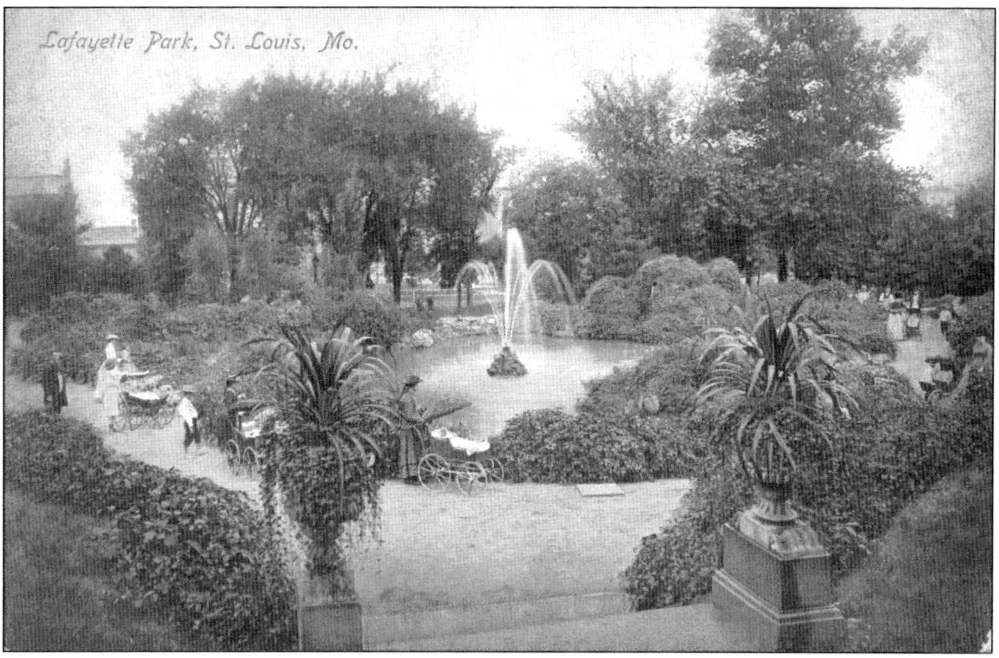

This pastoral nineteenth-century picture postcard rendering of Lafayette Park shows the same fountain seen in the background (to the left of the batter) of the above photo.

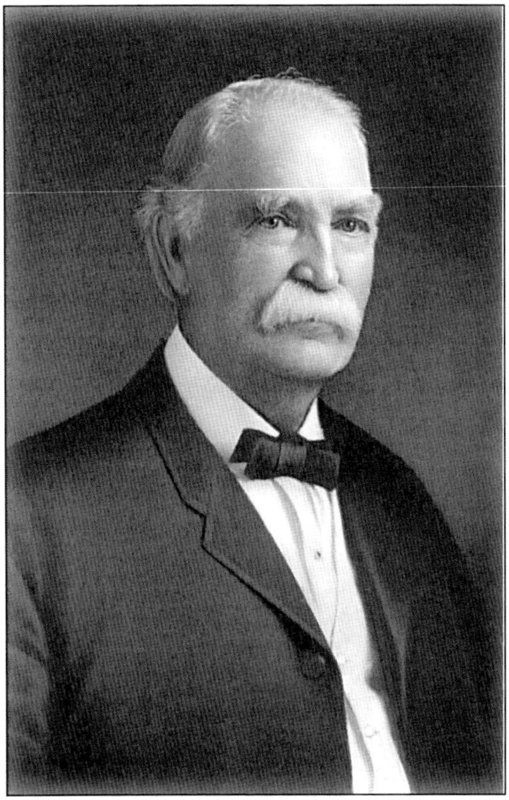

Born in Tipperary, Ireland in 1831, Jeremiah Fruin grew up in Brooklyn, New York. Arriving in St. Louis during the Civil War, he introduced the improved game of base ball to local lads playing in Lafayette Park. In 1872, he founded Fruin & Co. General Contractors. Over a century later, the game as well as the company, now called Fru-Con, thrive. (Photograph courtesy of the Fru-Con Construction Corporation.)

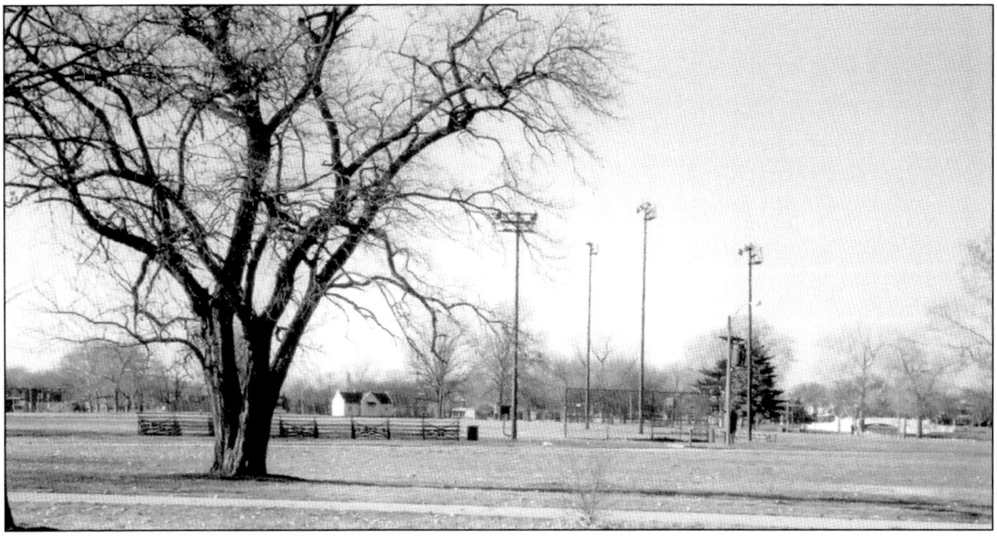

This photo, shot at Fairgrounds Park in north St. Louis on a bleak winter day in early 2004, shows one of several baseball fields in that public grounds. A large span of land originally used for an annual trade fair beginning in 1856, the park hosted a version of the game called base ball as early as 1860. The barren tree in the foreground seems to await another spring, when the crack of the bat will again resound.

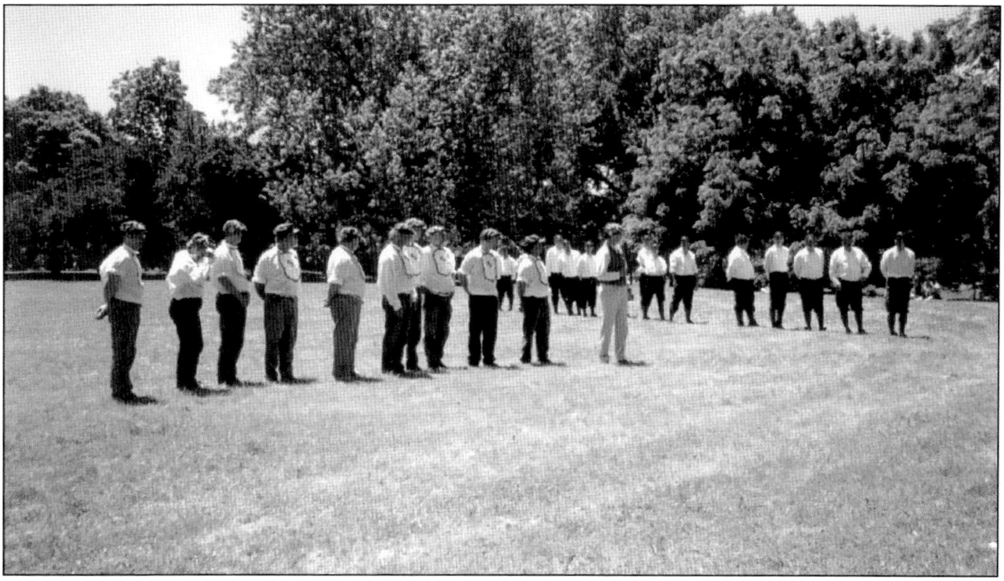

The VBBA St. Louis Perfectos and Rock Springs Ground Squirrels tip their hats individually during introductions prior to a 2003 game. The VBBA plays base ball by the earlier rules, which vary somewhat from those of today. They play it as a gentleman's game in the fashion of Jeremiah Fruin's Empire Base Ball Club.

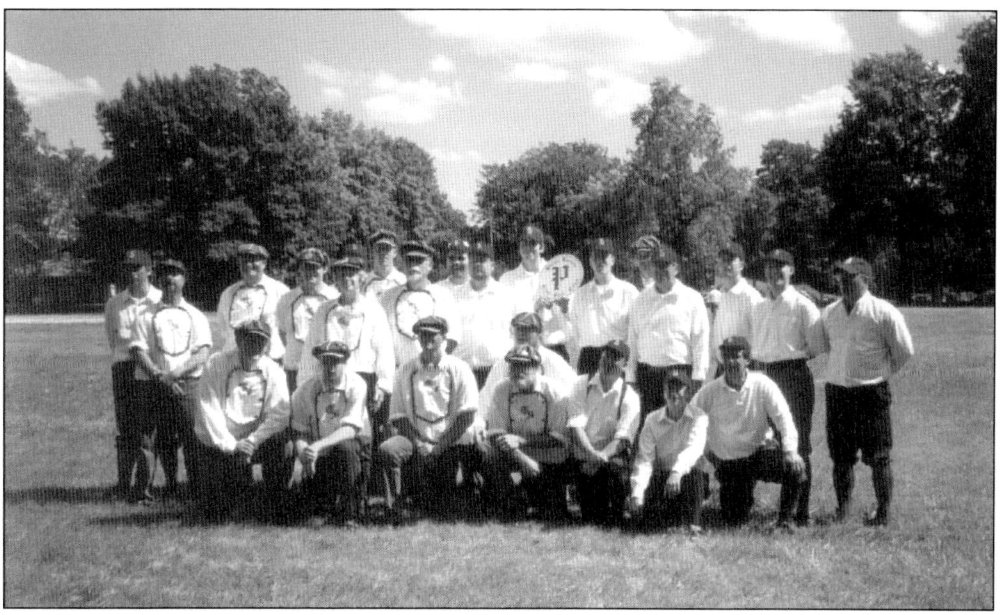

The Perfectos and Ground Squirrels pose for a group photo between games of a double header at Lafayette Park. The clubs not only adapt the earlier rules of the game, they also dress in nineteenth-century fashion. This kindles an image of the original base ball grounds: A pasture beneath the open sky, surrounded only by trees.

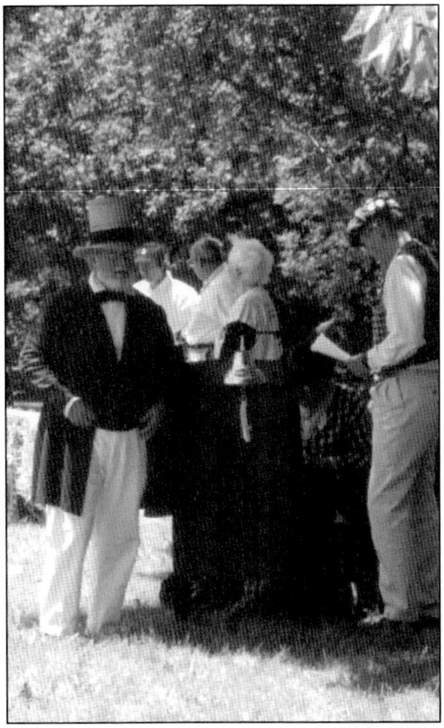

Not only the players dress in period garb for a VBBA game. Here the Ground Squirrels' Lee Slider in the role of team owner Joseph Trobaugh discusses the day's lineup with Honest Harold Longbons. One notable difference in the playing rules of yore, an out called with the batted ball caught on one bound off the ground, confuses modern fans.

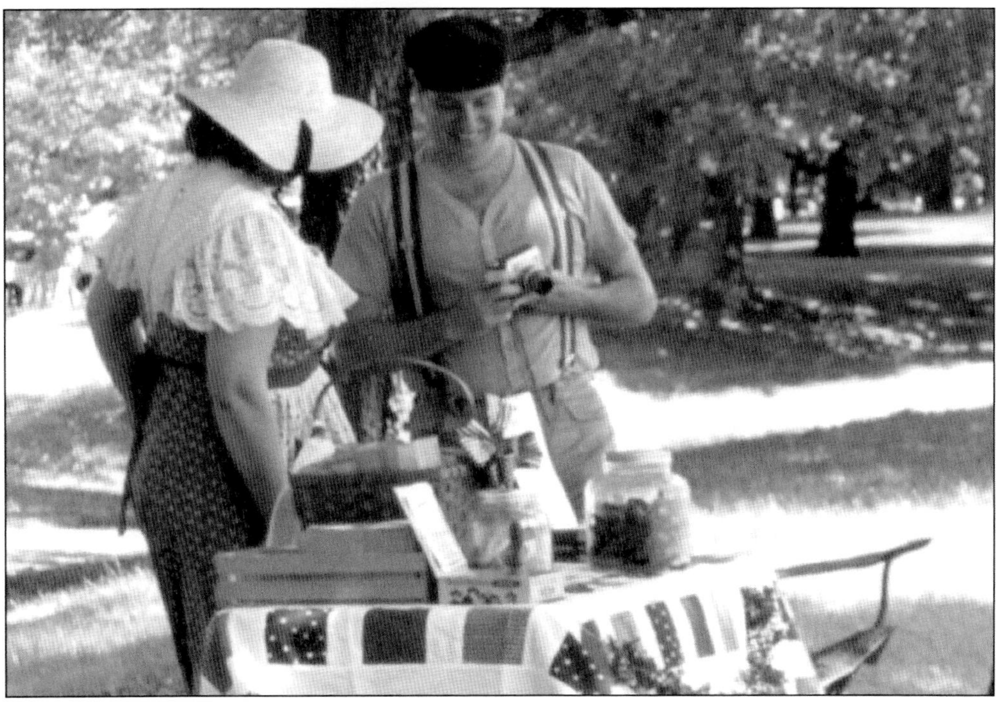

Renee and Joe Pellegrino man the concession stand during the Perfecto/Ground Squirrel match. Hot dogs were not introduced to St. Louis until the twentieth century, so the Pellegrinos stay with the vintage period, selling horehound candy and popcorn. Joe's modern camera belies the times.

VBBA clubs produce base ball cards similar to the earlier tobacco cards. In this example, Dan "Frenchy" Aubuchon appears much like an 1880s batter. (Card courtesy of the Perfectos Base Ball Club.)

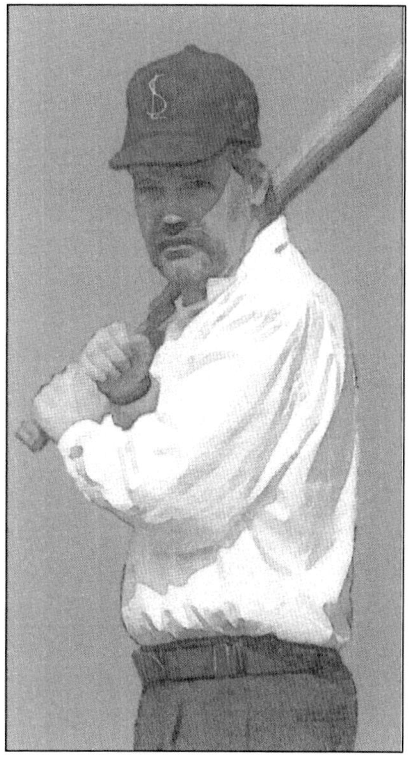

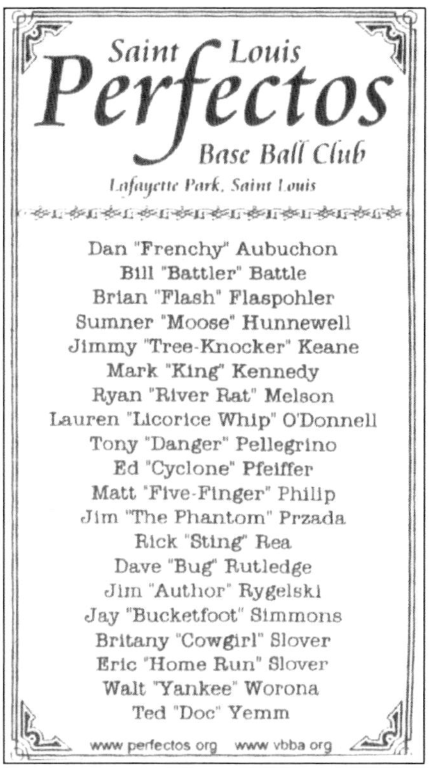

The reverse side of Aubuchon's base ball card lists the other members of the Perfectos. As in earlier times, each player has a nickname such as Frenchy. (Card courtesy of the Perfectos Base Ball Club.)

Parks.

BENTON PARK, es. Jefferson av. nr. Arsenal

BRIDGE SQUARE, 3d and Washington av.

CARONDELET PARK, Osceola and Minnesota av.

CARR PARK, Wash, Carr and 16th.

CONCORDIA PARK, 2d Cardt. av. sw. cor. Wyoming.

EXCHANGE SQUARE, North Market.

FOREST PARK, Olive St. rd. west of city.

GRAVOIS PARK, Louisiana av. bet. Potomac and Miami.

HYDE PARK, bet. Salisbury and Bremen av. 12th and 14th.

JACKSON PLACE, 10th and North Market.

LACLEDE PARK, Iowa, av. and Gasconade.

LAFAYETTE PARK, Lafayette av. Park and Mississippi avs.

LINDELL PARK, St. Louis av nr. Glasgow av.

MISSOURI PARK, Olive, St. Charles, 13th and 14th.

RED STOCKING BASE BALL PARK, Compton av. nw. cor. Larned.

ST. LOUIS BASE BALL PARK, ws. Grand av. nr. Sullivan av.

ST. LOUIS PARK, Benton and Hebert, W. 17th and W. 18th.

TOWER GROVE PARK, Grand av. bet. Magnolia av. and Arsenal St. rd.

WASHINGTON SQUARE, Market, 12th and 13th.

This 1875 listing of St. Louis city parks shows the city's first big league base ball parks. The Red Stockings Park is shown on page 8, and the St. Louis Base Ball Park (also called the Grand Avenue Grounds) on page 18. There is no longer a street named Larned. (From *Goulds' Street & Avenue Directory of St. Louis*, courtesy of the St. Louis Public Library.)

This is the first page of the original Articles of Incorporation of the St. Louis Base Ball Association. Formed by a group of St. Louis investors late in 1874, it was St. Louis's first professional base ball association. It organized a National Association team called the Brown Stockings, and used the Grand Avenue Grounds for the home field. The document declares $20,000 as the company's capital stock. (Courtesy of the Missouri Secretary of State Archives.)

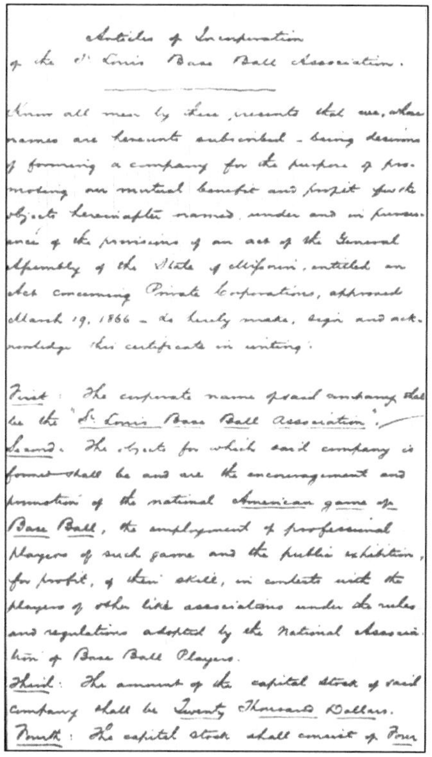

Articles of Incorporation
of the St. Louis Base Ball Association.

Know all men by these presents that we, whose names are hereunto subscribed - being desirous of forming a company for the purpose of promoting our mutual benefit and profit for the objects hereinafter named, under and in pursuance of the provisions of an act of the General Assembly of the State of Missouri, entitled an Act concerning Private Corporations, approved March 19, 1866 - do hereby make, sign and acknowledge this certificate in writing:

First: The corporate name of said company shall be the "St. Louis Base Ball Association";

Second. The objects for which said company is formed shall be and are the encouragement and promotion of the national American game of Base Ball, the employment of professional players of such game and the public exhibition, for profit, of their skill, in contests with the players of other like associations under the rules and regulations adopted by the National Association of Base Ball Players.

Third: The amount of the capital stock of said company shall be Twenty Thousand Dollars.

Fourth: The capital stock shall consist of Four

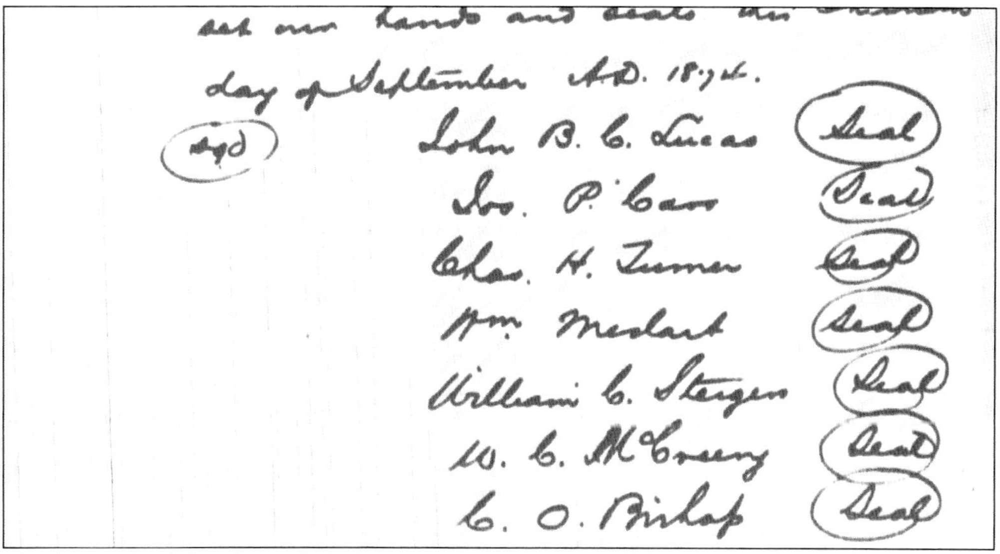

day of September A.D. 1874.

(sgd) John B. C. Lucas (Seal)
Jos. P. Carr (Seal)
Chas. H. Turner (Seal)
Wm. Medart (Seal)
William C. Steigers (Seal)
W. C. McCreery (Seal)
C. O. Bishop (Seal)

The last part of the above document, signed by the association's directors on September 30, 1874, reveals several names closely associated with both St. Louis and St. Louis baseball history. John B.C. Lucas (see picture on page 20) was brother to Henry V. Lucas, a pivotal figure in the Union League of 1884 (see chapter two). Charles H. Turner is mentioned by Jeremiah Fruin in his interview published in 1910. Fruin calls him the little "Red Head" who caught for an amateur club called the Unions. C.O. Bishop (C. Orrick) was a St. Louis judge who drafted the National League's first constitution and players contract. The Brown Stockings joined that league when it formed in 1876. (Courtesy of the Missouri Secretary of State Archives.)

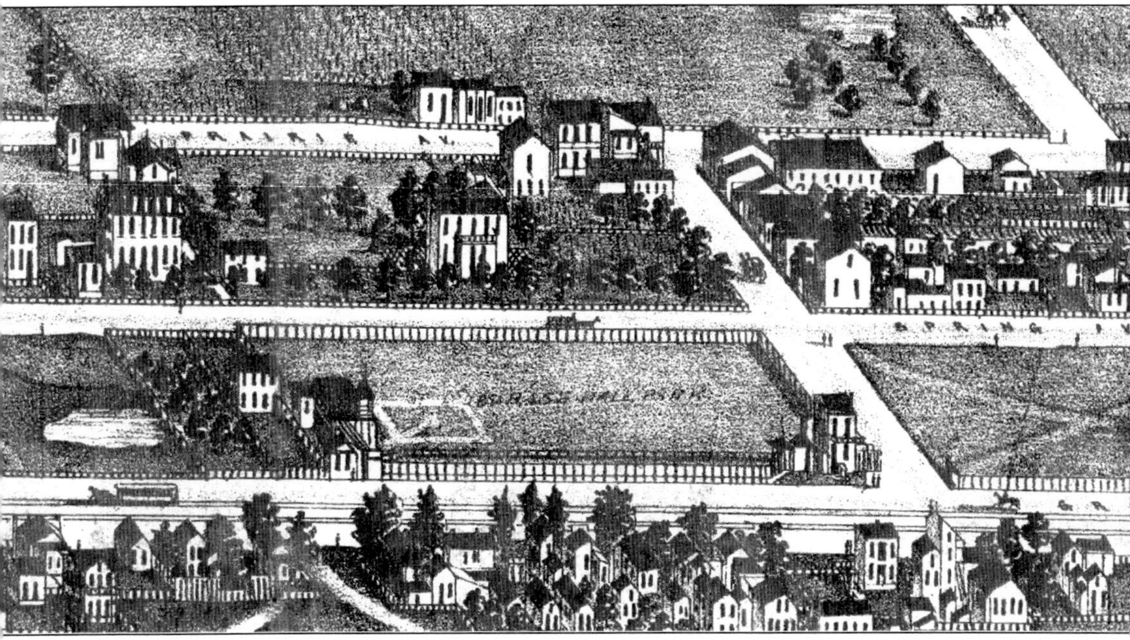

This 1875 pictorial shows the Grand Avenue Grounds before it became Sportsman's Park. A base ball diamond laid out there in the 1860s, the site later served the big leagues longer than any other spot in St. Louis. At the time of this artist's rendering, this area of St. Louis was the city's outskirts. Sullivan is the street intersecting both Spring and Grand. Dodier has yet to be carved into the landscape. Fruin's Empire Club began play there in 1868. The National Association Brown Stockings engaged in their first professional game played with an out-of-town team, the Chicago Nationals, defeating that team 10-0 on May 6, 1875. (From *Pictorial Saint Louis, 1875*, by Camille N. Dry, courtesy of the St. Louis Public Library.)

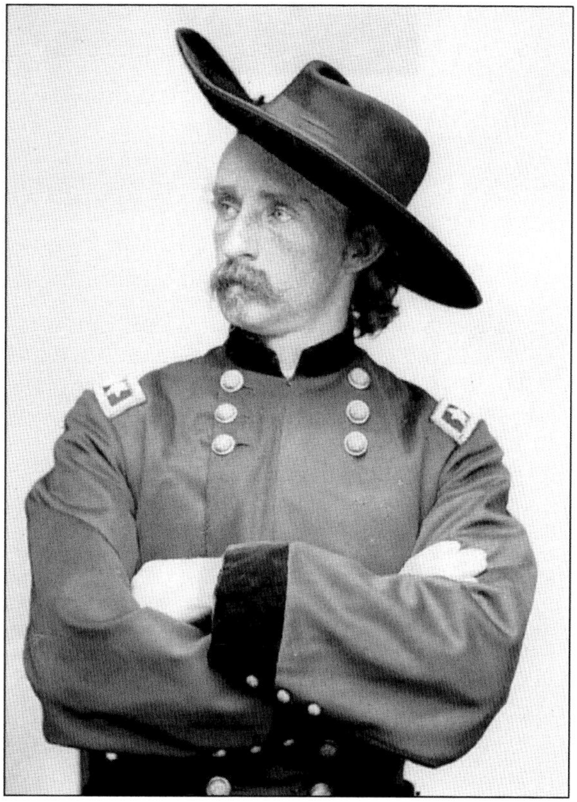

This man led a force of 212 U.S. soldiers in an attack on an encampment of some 2,500 Native-American warriors on June 25, 1876. By the time the news of the massacre of Col. George Armstrong Custer and his troops at the Little Big Horn reached St. Louis, local ball fans thrilled to a first for the then-fledgling National League: At the Grand Avenue Grounds on July 15, Brown Stockings' pitcher George Washington Bradley hurled the league's first no-hitter. Some historians count this as the first major league no-hitter, but Joe Borden of the Philadelphia National Association club chalked one up the previous season. (Courtesy of the Library of Congress, Photo Division.)

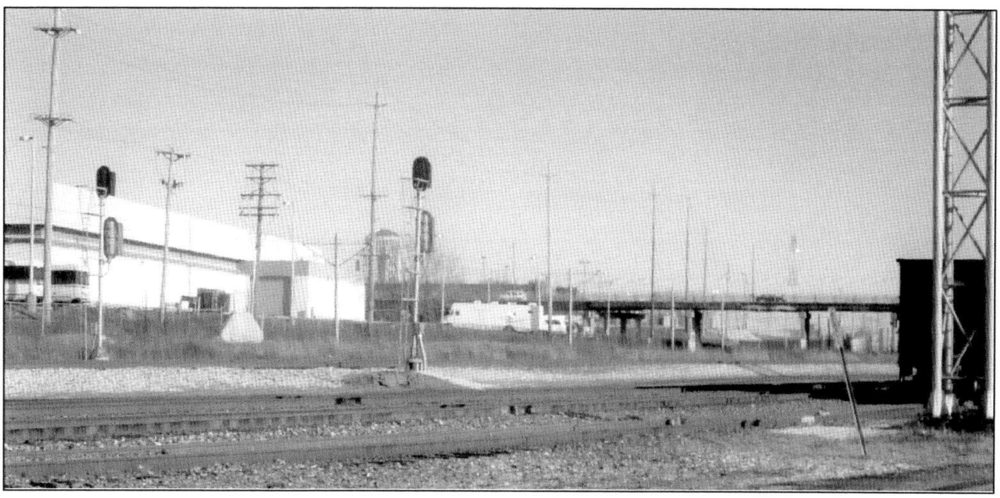

Looking east toward the Compton Avenue overpass in 2004, one can view the area where St. Louis's first fully professional game of base ball took place 129 years ago. To the left of the railroad tracks, the National Association St. Louis Red Stockings and St. Louis Brown Stockings met on the Reds' home turf. Compare this with the 1875 pictorial on page 8, which views the area looking west.

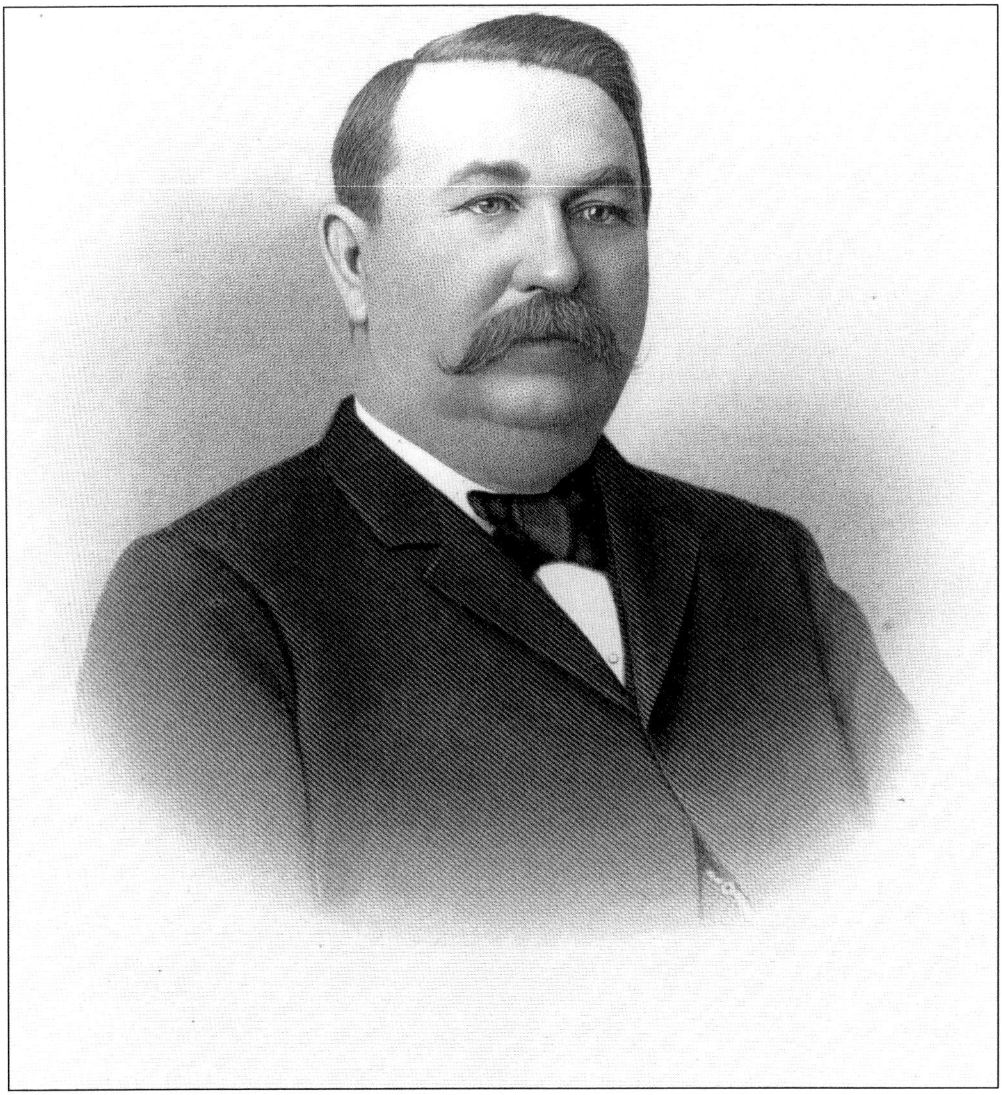

Lucas is a cognomen that frequently surfaces when studying St. Louis history. John B.C. Lucas, shown in this picture, was the grandson of J. Baptiste Charles Lucas, a French lawyer appointed land commissioner and Federal Territory Judge by President Thomas Jefferson. John B.C. enjoyed all aspects of the game of base ball. As you shall soon see, both he and his brother Henry played key roles in the evolving story of the big leagues. (Steel engraving by Williams, 1899. Courtesy of the Missouri Historical Society, St. Louis–Photograph and Print Collection.)

Two

Four Forgotten Big League Baseball Parks

In addition to the Red Stockings Park described in chapter one, four more baseball parks emerged and disappeared in St. Louis before the middle of the twentieth century. In sequential order by the year of each grand opening, they were: Union League Park, 1884–1886; New Sportsman's Park, AKA League Park, Robison Field and Cardinal Field, 1893–1920; Federal League Park, AKA Handlan Park and Steininger Field, 1914–1915; and Stars Park, 1922–1931.

The first came about with the formation of the renegade Union League of 1884. In opposition to the reserve rule, a group of businessmen organized the new group. Arguing that the regulation constituted slavery, they persuaded players from the existing leagues to sign with the Unions. Henry V. Lucas, brother to John B. C. Lucas, sided with the players, and was a primary figure in the formation of the new league and its St. Louis club, the Maroons. During the baseball war that ensued, the team was referred to as the Unions, or "Onions" by its detractors. Located at the southeast corner of Jefferson and Cass, it was closer to downtown St. Louis than any previously built big league park.

Named for the original Sportsman's Park at Grand and Sullivan, New Sportsman's Park was erected at Vendeventer and Natural Bridge Road, across from the Fairgrounds Park. The St. Louis Brown Stockings National League club of 1893 described in this chapter moved there from old Sportsman's Park in the spring of that year. At first accommodating 15,000 fans, it expanded by 5,000 before the team, by then called the Cardinals, played its last game there on June 6, 1920. Supported by several different owners during those years, it was where the Knot Hole Gang free passes were first used.

In 1914, a major league club called the Terriers began play at a spanking new stadium at the northeast corner of Grand and Laclede. An entry in the short-lived Federal League formed that year, the Terriers played there both years of its existence. Their stadium was built on private property called Handlan Park, so many fans continued to call it that. Others called it Federal League Park, and some called it Steininger Field, for Edward Steininger, the club's president. The league folded at the end of the 1915, and the ballpark soon followed suit. Today, the only remaining ballpark built for a Federal League club is Weeghman Park in Chicago—now called Wrigley Field.

Just north of the site of old Red Stockings Park on Compton, owners of the St. Louis Negro National League Stars built a wooden ballpark, called Stars Park, in 1922. Situated on the southeast corner of Compton and North Market, it was located on land now occupied by Harris-Stowe State College. Playing in the park that seated 10,000 fans, the Stars captured the NNL flag in 1928 with the talent of players like James "Cool Papa" Bell. They played there until they disbanded in 1931, when the Depression afflicted most everyone in this country.

Each of these parks opened with grand expectations, the local officials making pompous speeches, and the fans filled with excitement. Yet, relatively few fans of today have any knowledge of their existence.

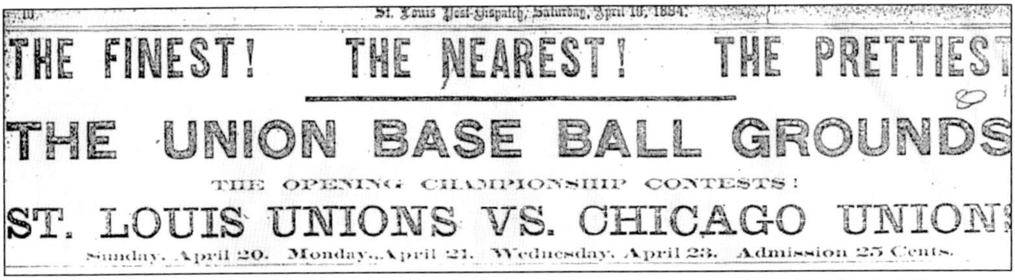

This newspaper ad touts the new Union Park in an announcement of its April 20, 1884 grand opening. Only a 30 minute ride (by horse-drawn conveyance) from downtown, it was indeed the nearest. It may well have also been the finest and the prettiest. Henry V. Lucas, the team's owner, spared little expense. The painted white wooden grandstands stood at the northwest corner of the lot. Two wings with opera chairs and a long promenade allowed additional seating. The St. Louis Union Maroons sported white uniforms with maroon caps and stockings, and played on a diamond surrounded by blue grass and clover. The St. Louis team defeated their Chicago adversaries that day, 7-2, in six innings, rain preventing the full nine. (From the *St. Louis Post-Dispatch*, courtesy of the St. Louis Public Library.)

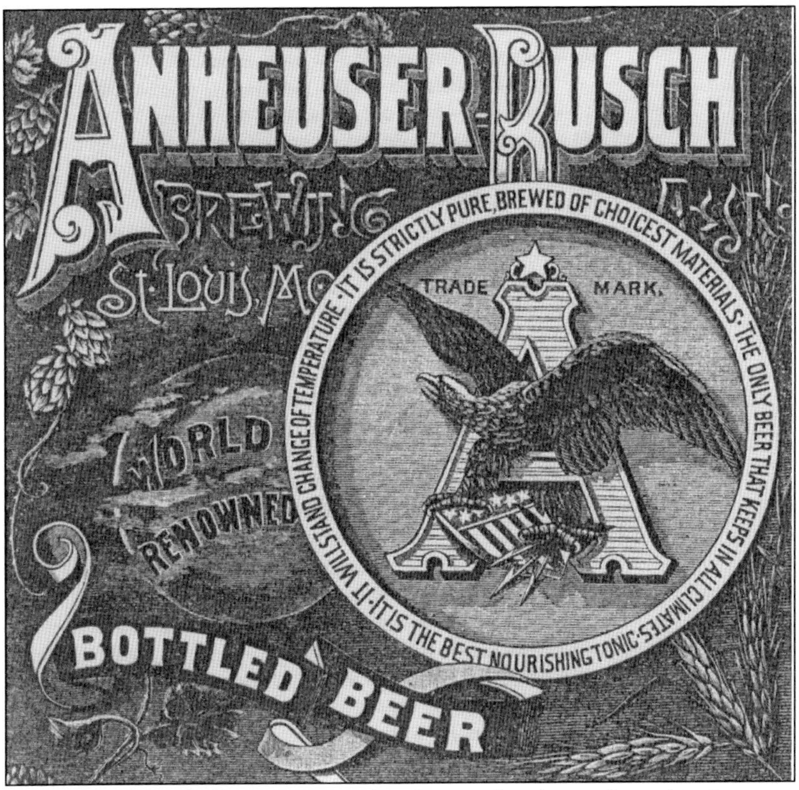

The St. Louis beer and baseball connection already manifest (as explainedin the next chapter), other major investors in the St. Louis Union team of 1884 included local beer baron Adolphus Busch. At that time, the Brown Stockings down at Sportsman's Park belonged to the American Association that formed in 1881 (not to be confused with the American League of the next century). The older National League prohibited both Sunday baseball and the selling of liquor during its games then. Like the AA, the new Union League permitted both. This ad from the 1890s could be mistaken for its contemporary counterpart.

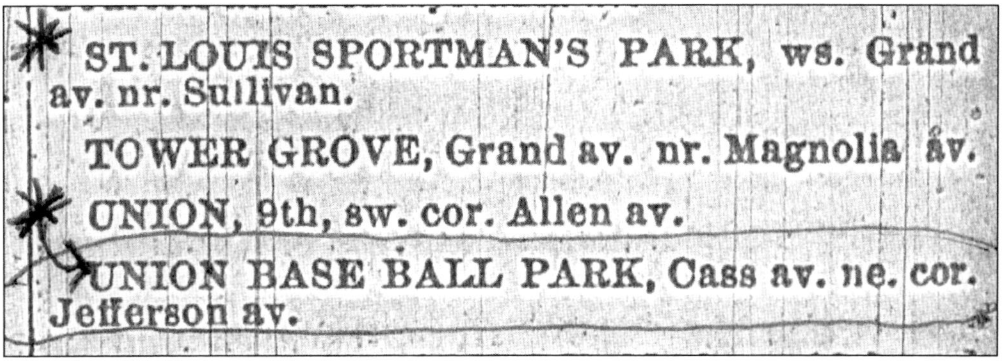

ST. LOUIS SPORTMAN'S PARK, ws. Grand av. nr. Sullivan.
TOWER GROVE, Grand av. nr. Magnolia av.
UNION, 9th, sw. cor. Allen av.
UNION BASE BALL PARK, Cass av. ne. cor. Jefferson av.

The park listings in the *1880 St. Louis City Directory* is one of the few remaining vestiges of the St. Louis Union League Park. Sometimes called Lucas Park, after Henry V. Lucas, the St. Louis club's owner and the league's main instigator, it served the majors for only three years. The 1884 Maroons had the Union League's best players, winning 97 of the 118 games they played that season. That alone discouraged the other contenders. That coupled with competition from the two other leagues of the time, the American Association and the National League, forced the Union group to fold after only one year. The Maroons then acquired a National League franchise, and continued to play ball at Jefferson and Cass for the following two years. (From *Goulds' Street & Avenue Directory of St. Louis*, courtesy of the St. Louis Public Library.)

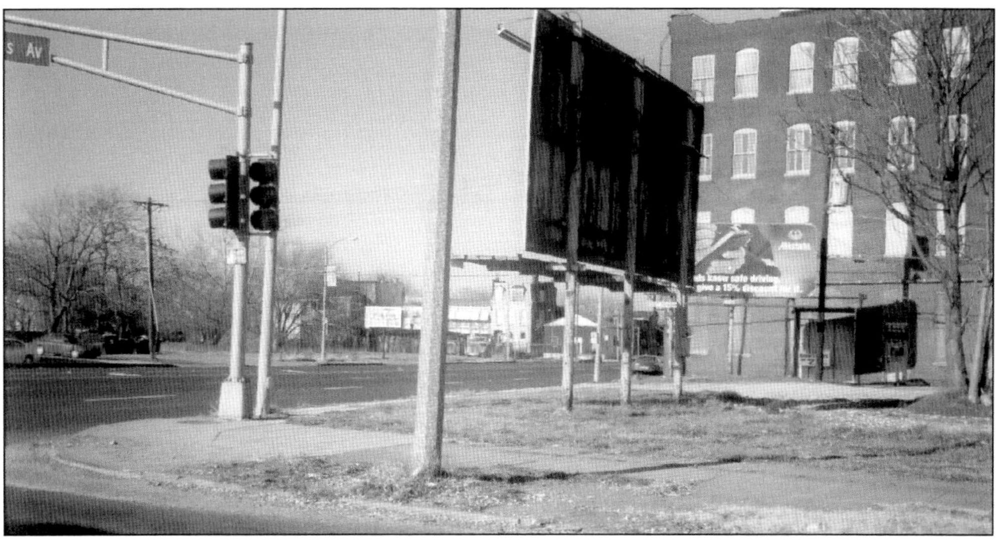

This is the corner where, according to one reporter, the Maroons with their "silk stockings and lambs wool sweaters" marched onto the field to the music of a brass band. A generous owner, Henry V. Lucas provided amenities like billiard tables in the reception room of the player clubhouse. Plus, he supplied financial assistance to the league's other clubs. Consequently, the Union League venture seriously depleted his personal wealth. The Maroons were sold to an Indianapolis concern following the season of 1886. There they became the National League Hoosiers.

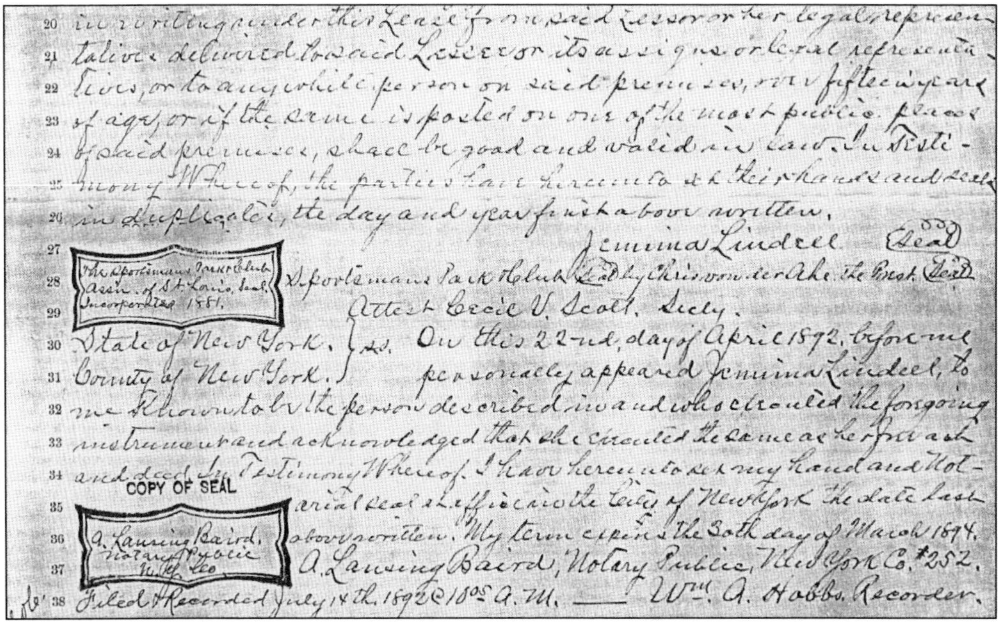

in writing under this Lease from said Lessor or her legal representatives delivered to said Lessee or its assigns or legal representatives, or to any white person on said premises, over fifteen years of age, or if the same is posted on one of the most public places of said premises, shall be good and valid in law. In Testimony Whereof, the parties have hereunto set their hands and seals in Duplicate, the day and year first above written.

Jemima Lindell (Seal)

The Sportsman's Park & Club Assn. of St. Louis, Incorporated 1881. Sportsman's Park Club by Chris von der Ahe, the Prest. (Seal)

Attest Cecil V. Scott, Secty.

State of New York, } ss. On this 22nd day of April 1892, before me
County of New York.} personally appeared Jemima Lindell, to me known to be the person described in and who executed the foregoing instrument and acknowledged that she executed the same as her free act and deed. In Testimony Whereof, I have hereunto set my hand and Notarial seal at office in the City of New York the date last above written. My term expires the 30th day of March 1894.

COPY OF SEAL

A. Lansing Baird, Notary Public N.Y. Co.

A. Lansing Baird, Notary Public, New York Co. #252.

Filed & Recorded July 14th, 1892 @ 10.05 A.M. —— Wm. A. Hobbs, Recorder.

The American Association and the National League merged in 1891, retaining the older league's name. Two years later, Brown Stocking President Chris Von der Ahe moved his club further north to a newly built park. Located across Natural Bridge Road from old Fairgrounds Park, the site occupied the estate of St. Louis real estate broker, Jesse G. Lindell. This 1892 document bearing Lindell and Von der Ahe's signatures is a 15-year lease agreement of $1,500 per year for eight years, and $2,000 per annum for the remaining seven. Von der Ahe lost his interest in the club long before it expired. (Courtesy of St. Louis Recorder of Deeds, City Hall.)

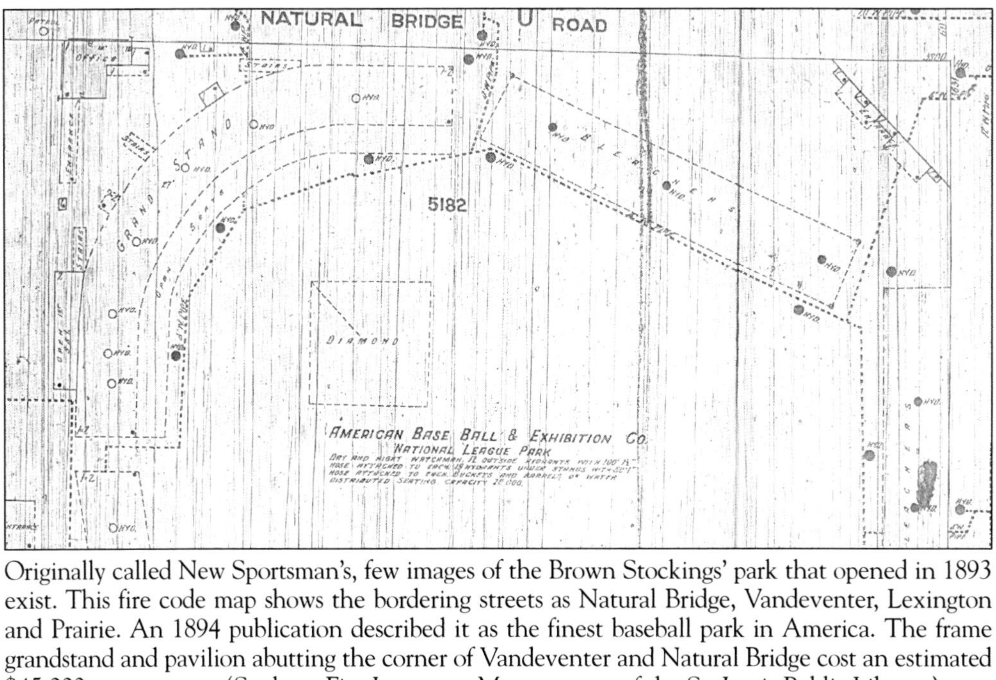

Originally called New Sportsman's, few images of the Brown Stockings' park that opened in 1893 exist. This fire code map shows the bordering streets as Natural Bridge, Vandeventer, Lexington and Prairie. An 1894 publication described it as the finest baseball park in America. The frame grandstand and pavilion abutting the corner of Vandeventer and Natural Bridge cost an estimated $45,000 to construct. (Sanborn Fire Insurance Map courtesy of the St. Louis Public Library.)

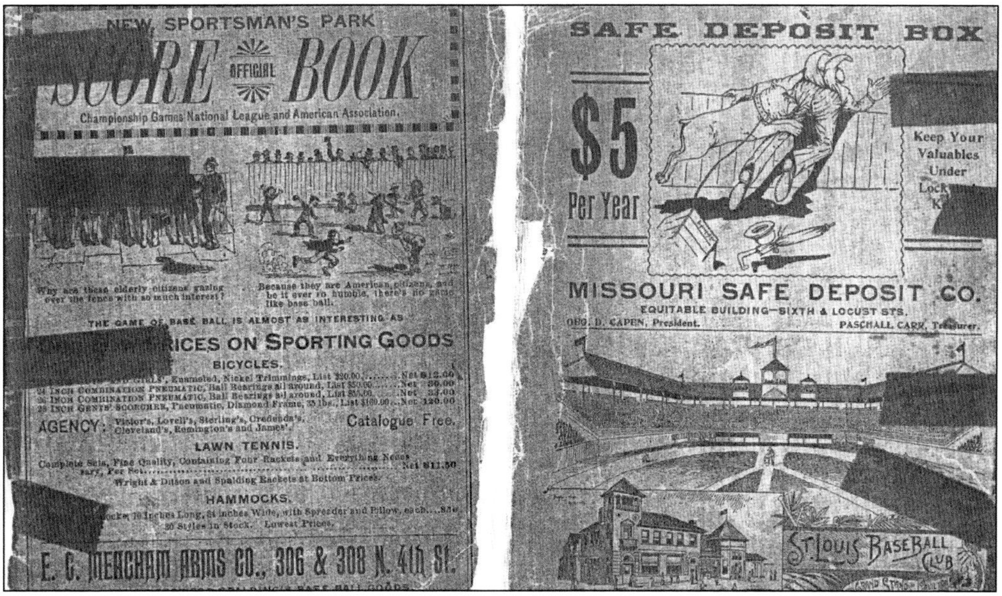

A scorebook sold at New Sportsman's Park includes a rare image of the facility. Inside the multi-paged book, an account of the April 27, 1893 grand opening purports that copies of the day's local newspapers and the *Sporting News* were buried beneath home plate. The *St. Louis Globe-Democrat* reported a planned ceremonial parade leading from downtown to the park. Among the participants would be a coach pulled by four of Adolphus Busch's finest black steeds, Gus Busch at the reins. The driver, August Busch, would be the father of August "Gussie" Busch Jr., who years later headed both Anheuser-Busch and the Cardinals. (Courtesy of the Missouri Historical Society, St. Louis.)

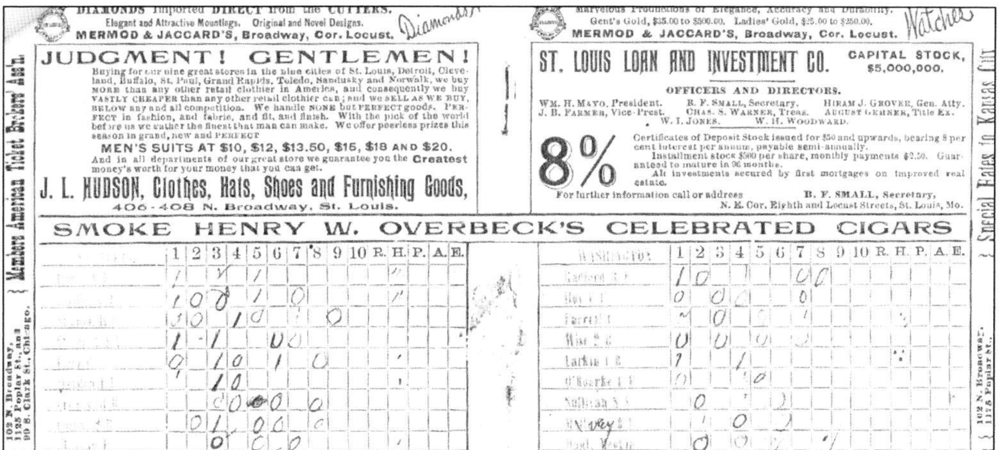

The scorekeeping section of the inside of the above-pictured book demonstrates the unchanging nature of baseball. It also reflects the changing nature of the cost of living. Ten dollars for a man's suit! (Courtesy of the Missouri Historical Society, St. Louis.)

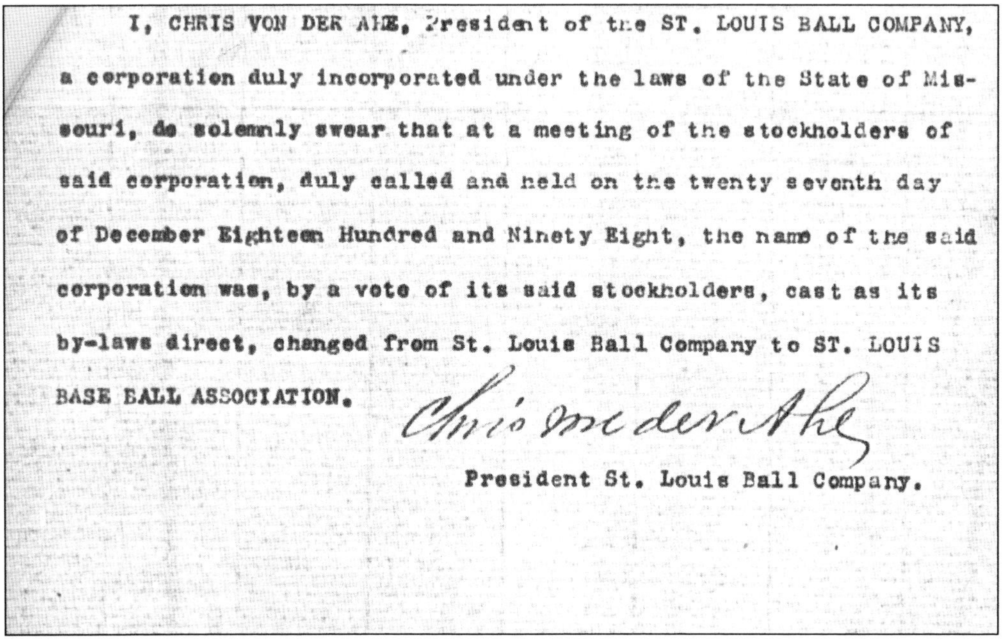
I, CHRIS VON DER AHE, President of the ST. LOUIS BALL COMPANY, a corporation duly incorporated under the laws of the State of Missouri, do solemnly swear that at a meeting of the stockholders of said corporation, duly called and held on the twenty seventh day of December Eighteen Hundred and Ninety Eight, the name of the said corporation was, by a vote of its said stockholders, cast as its by-laws direct, changed from St. Louis Ball Company to ST. LOUIS BASE BALL ASSOCIATION.

Chris von der Ahe

President St. Louis Ball Company.

The Brown Stockings never earned a pennant at the new park, and their gregarious owner Chris Von der Ahe tried various promotions to raise money. Drawing harsh criticism for bringing gamblers into the park by installing a horse race track around the playing field, he also added a thrill ride called the shoot-the-chutes in the outfield. But in 1898, a fire that started in the grandstands resulted in injured spectators and a number of lawsuits. Immersed in debt, Von der Ahe finally lost his baseball concern. This legal document dated December 27, 1898, shows his attempt to evade that debt by changing the corporate name. The ploy failed. The club was sold at a public auction and soon became the property of two Cleveland brothers. (Courtesy of the Missouri Secretary of State Archives.)

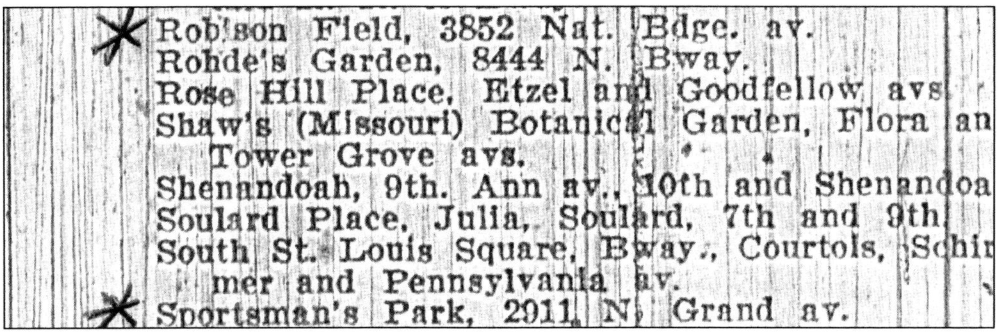
Robison Field, 3852 Nat. Bdge. av.
Rohde's Garden, 8444 N. Bway.
Rose Hill Place, Etzel and Goodfellow avs
Shaw's (Missouri) Botanical Garden, Flora an
Tower Grove avs.
Shenandoah, 9th. Ann av., 10th and Shenandoa
Soulard Place, Julia, Soulard, 7th and 9th
South St. Louis Square, Bway., Courtois, Schir
mer and Pennsylvania av.
Sportsman's Park, 2911 N. Grand av.

Frank De Haas and Matthew Robison, owners of the Cleveland NL club, the Spiders, obtained ownership of the Brown Stockings in 1899. Switching the members of their two teams, the St. Louis franchise benefited by getting the better players, including now-legendary Cy Young. Making several improvements to the St. Louis park, the Robison's also changed the team uniform color from brown to red. Called the Perfectos for a while, the team soon got the name Cardinals due to the scarlet color of its players' stockings. This early twentieth century park listing shows old Sportsman's Park again hosting a big league club, the new American League Browns. The Browns began play there in 1902. By then named after the Cardinals' owners, the park on Natural Bridge was called Robison Field. (From Goulds' *Street & Avenue Directory of St. Louis*, courtesy of the St. Louis Public Library.)

The Robisons purchased their ballpark's property for $60,000 when the lease ran out. After Frank died, Stanley modernized it with steel and concrete, and increased the seating capacity to at least 20,000. His passing in 1911 left his niece Helene Robison Britton (see above photo), Frank's daughter, owner of his baseball holdings. The first woman to own a major league baseball club, she took an active role in her position, and retained ownership of the Cardinals and the park until 1917. She then sold it to a group of investors for $350,000. After that the park was called Cardinal Field. (Courtesy of *The Sporting News*.)

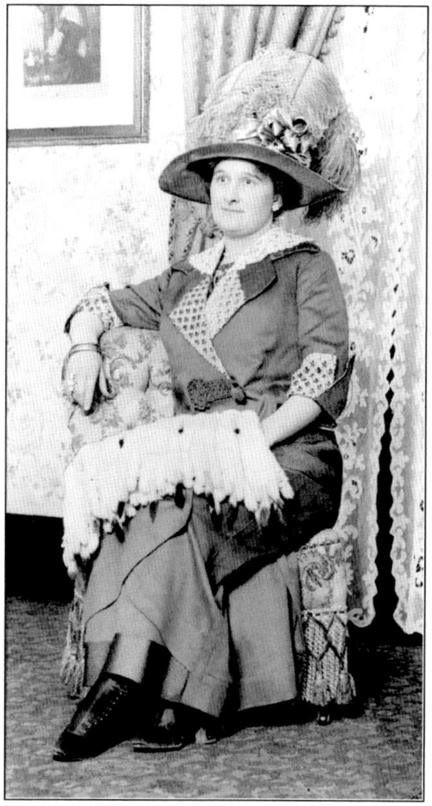

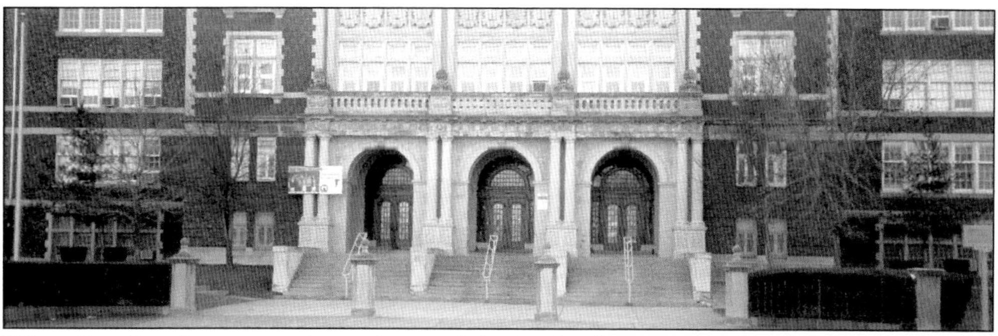

When Sam Breadon acquired presidency of the Cardinal organization in 1920, one of his first moves included moving the club to another park. He arranged to share old Sportsman's Park with the AL Browns. On June 6 of that year, the Cardinals played their last game at Cardinal Field, the place once called the most beautiful baseball park in America. Not long after that, Beaumont High School was built there. A stately structure, as shown in this recently captured image, it continues to serve the city today.

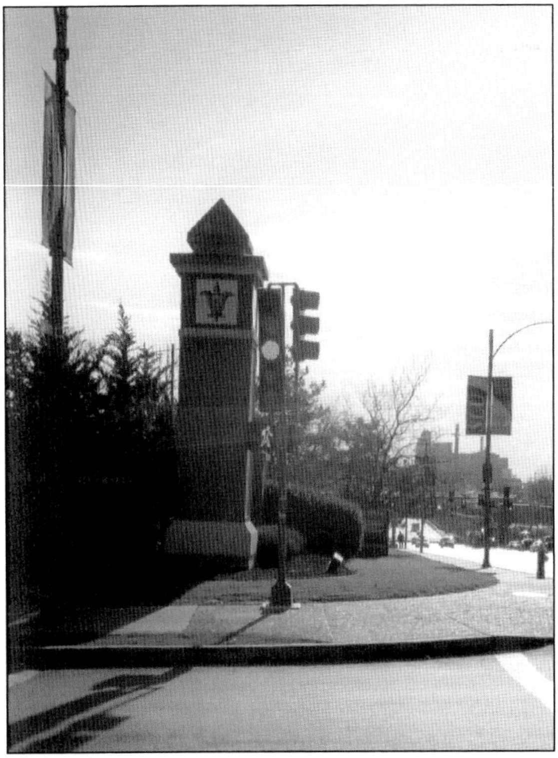

This current view of the southeast corner of Grand and Laclede belies its divergent history. In St. Louis's early days, Wesleyan Cemetery occupied the space here. The cemetery later moved and then the grounds came under the ownership of Alexander H. Handlan, head of an internationally known St. Louis railway supply house. According to Handlan's grandson, Edward, Alexander sold gravel taken from the property, later charging locals to use it as a dumping grounds—an early landfill. Eventually, he fashioned it into a private park aptly named Handlan's. In 1914, when St. Louis already had two major league clubs, a third resulted from the formation of yet another pro baseball league, the Federal League. The owners of the St. Louis franchise choose Handlan's as the site for their baseball park.

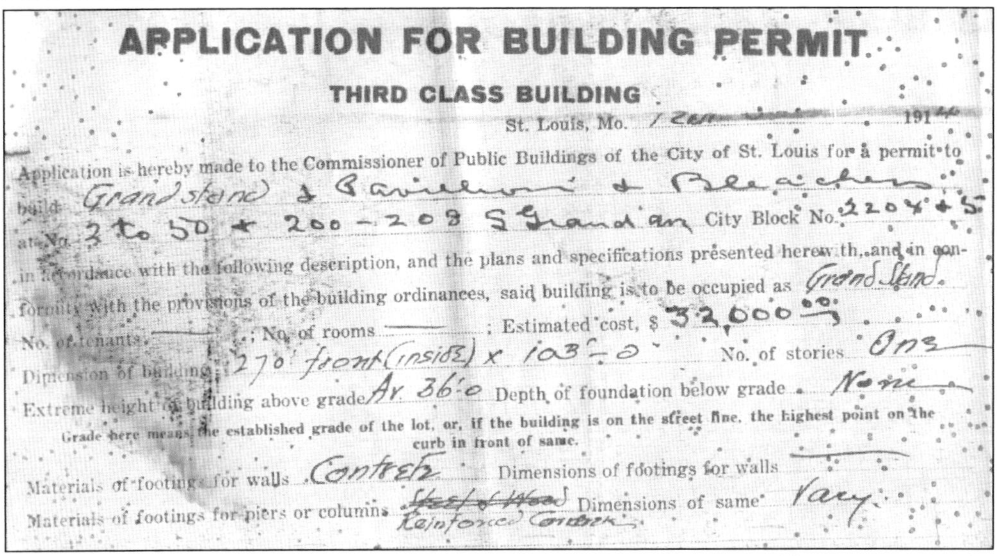

APPLICATION FOR BUILDING PERMIT

THIRD CLASS BUILDING

St. Louis, Mo. 1914

Application is hereby made to the Commissioner of Public Buildings of the City of St. Louis for a permit to build Grandstand & Pavilion & Bleachers at No. 3 to 50 + 200-208 S Grand av City Block No. 2204 + 5 in accordance with the following description, and the plans and specifications presented herewith, and in conformity with the provisions of the building ordinances, said building is to be occupied as Grand Stand.

No. of tenants ——— ; No. of rooms ——— ; Estimated cost, $ 32,000.00

Dimension of building 270' front (inside) x 103'-0" No. of stories One

Extreme height of building above grade Av. 36'0 Depth of foundation below grade None

Grade here means the established grade of the lot, or, if the building is on the street line, the highest point on the curb in front of same.

Materials of footings for walls Concrete Dimensions of footings for walls ———

Materials of footings for piers or columns ~~Steel & Wood~~ Reinforced Concrete Dimensions of same Vary.

Because of St. Louis' by-then strict fire code, this application for a building permit for the Federal League Park grandstands was originally rejected. Note that Steel & Wood for footings for piers and columns is replaced with Reinforced Concrete. Edward A. Steininger, president of the St. Louis Federals, arranged a three-year lease on the property for $10,000 per year with a purchase option of $250,000 at any time. But the league dissolved before the end of the lease. The grounds remained under the Handlan's ownership until 1961, when it passed to St. Louis University. In the meantime, some Negro League teams played there, and for a time the Royal American Circus used the grounds. (Courtesy of the St. Louis Recorder of Deeds, City Hall.)

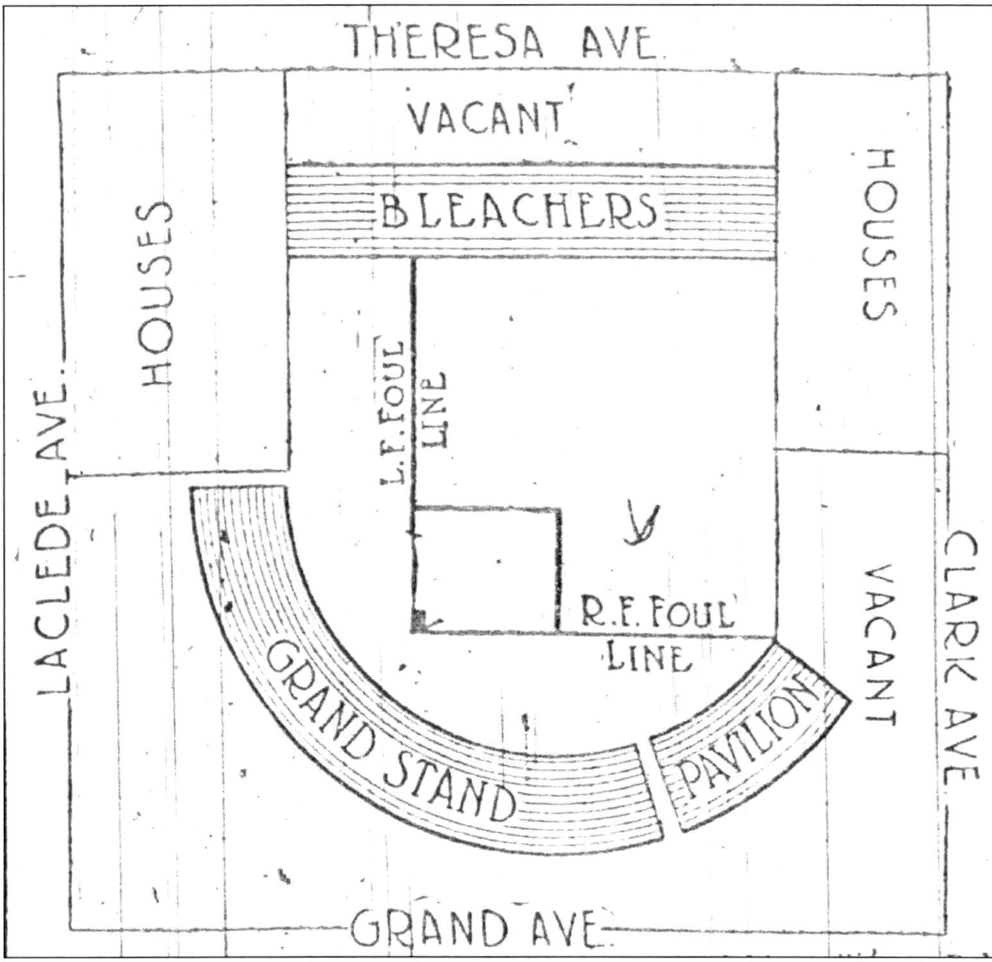

This outline of the Federal League Park, often called Handlan's Park or Steininger Field, appeared in the *St. Louis Daily Globe-Democrat* on January 30, 1914. The plan, along with other blueprints in existence, reveal fenced-off houses sharing the lot along both Laclede and Clark. A single deck wooden grandstand on the southeast corner of Laclede and Grand curved toward the pavilion situated near the corner of Grand and Clark. Bleachers stretched behind center field between the barricaded houses. (From the *St. Louis Daily Globe-Democrat*, courtesy of the St. Louis Public Library.)

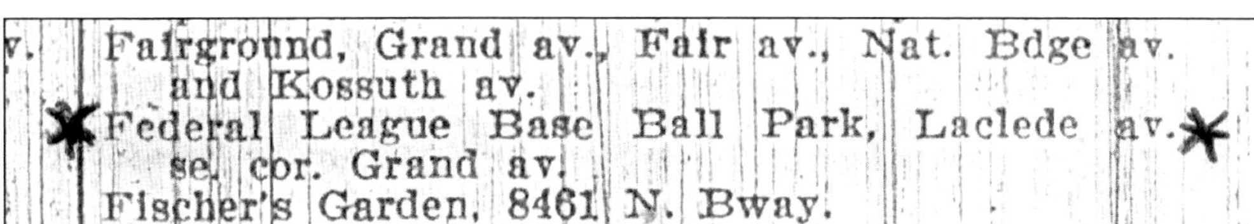

Fairground, Grand av., Fair av., Nat. Bdge av. and Kossuth av.
* Federal League Base Ball Park, Laclede av. se. cor. Grand av. *
Fischer's Garden, 8461 N. Bway.

In 1914, the first year of the Federal League's brief life, the St. Louis Terriers finished last in their league. Displaying considerable improvement the following year, the team nearly captured first, losing by one game to the Chicago Whales. After that 1915 season, the Federal League collapsed. But for two glorious years, St. Louis baseball fans frequented three major league parks: Handlan, Robison and Sportsman's. (From *Goulds' Street & Avenue Directory of St. Louis*, courtesy of the St. Louis Public Library.)

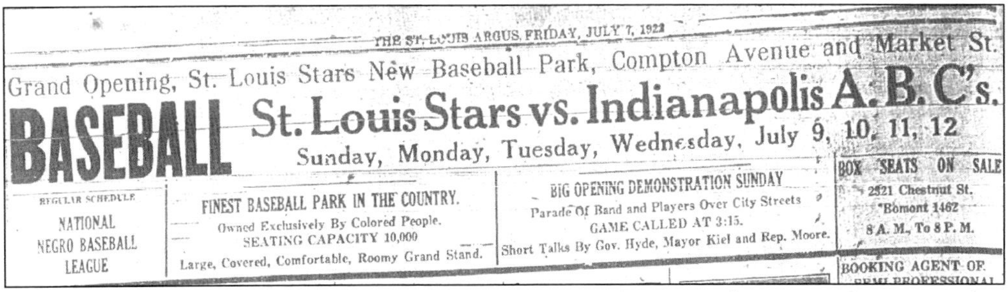

THE ST. LOUIS ARGUS, FRIDAY, JULY 7, 1922

Grand Opening, St. Louis Stars New Baseball Park, Compton Avenue and Market St.

BASEBALL St. Louis Stars vs. Indianapolis A. B. C's.

Sunday, Monday, Tuesday, Wednesday, July 9, 10, 11, 12

REGULAR SCHEDULE NATIONAL NEGRO BASEBALL LEAGUE

FINEST BASEBALL PARK IN THE COUNTRY.
Owned Exclusively By Colored People.
SEATING CAPACITY 10,000
Large, Covered, Comfortable, Roomy Grand Stand.

BIG OPENING DEMONSTRATION SUNDAY
Parade Of Band and Players Over City Streets
GAME CALLED AT 3:15.
Short Talks By Gov. Hyde, Mayor Kiel and Rep. Moore.

BOX SEATS ON SALE
2521 Chestnut St.
Bomont 1462
8 A. M. To 8 P. M.

BOOKING AGENT OF

The professional St. Louis Giants Baseball Club, organized in 1910, became a charter member of the Negro National League, established in 1920. The Giants played at a park on North Broadway until new ownership changed the club name to Stars, and built a park named for the club at Compton and North Market Streets in 1922. These news headlines state the seating capacity as 10,000 with a large covered comfortable, roomy grandstand. The grand opening ceremony featured Missouri Governor Hyde and Mayor Keil. (From the July 7, 1922 *St. Louis Argus* of the St. Louis Public Library.)

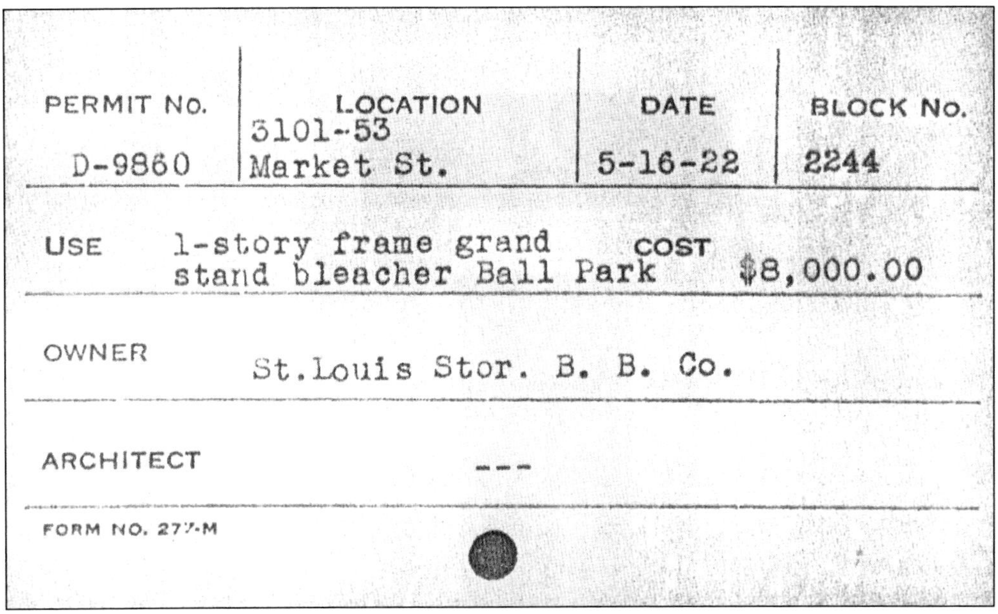

PERMIT No.	LOCATION	DATE	BLOCK No.
D-9860	3101-53 Market St.	5-16-22	2244

USE 1-story frame grand stand bleacher Ball Park COST $8,000.00

OWNER St.Louis Stor. B. B. Co.

ARCHITECT ---

FORM NO. 27?-M

This May 16, 1922 building permit gives the exact location of the Stars Park (incorrectly typed as Stor). It occupied land running a full block on the north side of Market, east of Compton. The grandstand was built at the corner of Compton and Market, and bleachers ran along Cardinal. Authors of *The Negro Leagues Book* write that a trolley car barn was located in left field about 250 feet away. Sources from that period bear this out: The *St. Louis Argus* described the park as just south of the Laclede Car Barn, and a 1920–1930 Sanborn Fire Insurance map shows a Public Service Car Barn & Repair Shop just beyond Laclede, the next street parallel to and north of Market. (Courtesy of St. Louis City Hall Central File.)

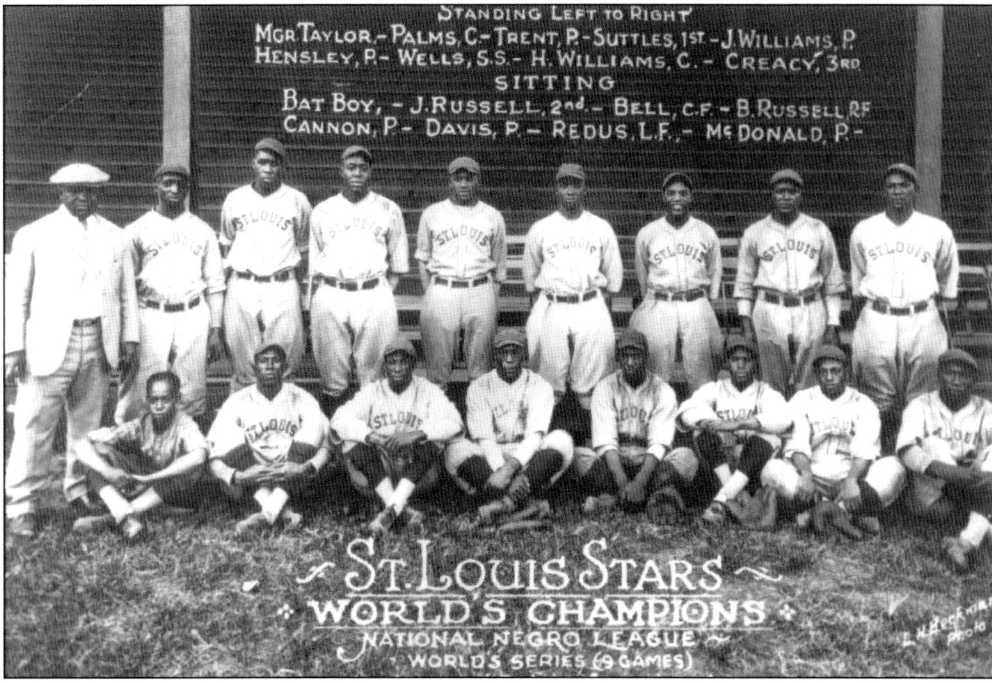

Here the World Champion St. Louis Negro National League Stars of 1928 pose for a group photo, most likely taken at Stars Park. Years later, in 1974, the player sitting in the front row third from the left, James "Cool Papa" Bell, gained national recognition when inducted in Cooperstown's National Baseball Hall of Fame. Another star, George "Mule" Suttles, stands in the back row fourth from the left. Local St. Louis historian, Normal "Tweed" Webb once wrote that Suttles was a long ball hitter, and constantly hit the ball against the car barn at old Stars Park. (Courtesy of the Negro Leagues Baseball Museum, Kansas City, MO.)

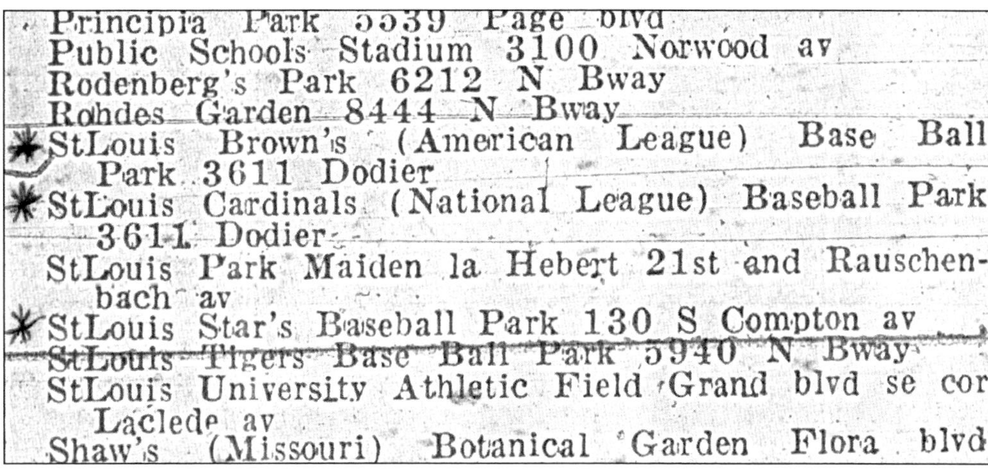

Principia Park 5539 Page blvd
Public Schools Stadium 3100 Norwood av
Rodenberg's Park 6212 N Bway
Rohdes Garden 8444 N Bway
*StLouis Brown's (American League) Base Ball Park 3611 Dodier
*StLouis Cardinals (National League) Baseball Park 3611 Dodier
StLouis Park Maiden la Hebert 21st and Rauschenbach av
*StLouis Star's Baseball Park 130 S Compton av
StLouis Tigers Base Ball Park 5940 N Bway
StLouis University Athletic Field Grand blvd se cor Laclede av
Shaw's (Missouri) Botanical Garden Flora blvd

The *1920s St. Louis City Directory* lists big league baseball parks by the names of the teams. It also lists Sportsman's Park alphabetically. Star's Park is listed by the Compton Avenue location. It is the same corner as the Market Street address printed on the above permit. Today Harris-Stowe State College occupies that corner where the Stars played baseball from 1922 until early in 1931. (From *Goulds' Street & Avenue Directory of St. Louis*, Courtesy of the St. Louis Public Library.).

Year	Park Name	Location	Team Name	League
1875	Red Stockings	Compton/Gratiot W of Compton	Red Stockings	National Association
1884	Union	Jefferson & Cass NE corner	Maroons	Union League
1885	"	"	"	National League
1886	"	"	"	"
1893–1898	New Sportsman's	Vandeventor& Natural Bridge	Brown Stockings	National League
1899	League Park	"	Perfectos	"
1900–1917	Robison Field	"	Cardinals	"
1918–1920	Cardinal Field	"	"	"
1914–1915	Federal League AKA: Handlan Park Steininger Field	Grand & Laclede SE Corner	Terriers	Federal League
1922–1931	Stars Park	Compton & North Market	Stars	Negro National League

THREE

Sportman's Park
A Century of Baseball

The ballpark called the Grand Avenue Grounds (see page 18) laid on the property in north St. Louis now bounded by Grand, Dodier, Spring and Sullivan. Today, it is home to the Herbert Hoover Boys and Girls Club. Ownership of the real estate can be traced back to Charles Lucas, one of J. Baptiste Charles Lucas's sons (see page 20). Charles was killed in 1817 in a famous duel with Senator Thomas Hart Benton—great-uncle to the famous Missouri artist. Eventually a man named John Dunn gained possession of the land, and leased it to Mr. August Solari. Solari lived there, and formed a base ball diamond at the corner of Grand and Sullivan near his house. That was in 1866, and that was just the beginning of a century of baseball.

In 1867 local ball fans witnessed the first game held in St. Louis between a local group and an out-of-town team. A Washington D. C. club trounced their St. Louis opponents by a score of 113 to 26. But that failed to dampen the city's growing ardor for base ball. Then in 1875, St. Louis's first professional team, the Brown Stockings of the National Association used the Grand Avenue diamond for their home grounds. The following year the team became a charter member of the still-existing National League. Hosted at the Grand Avenue Grounds, the first National League game held in St. Louis took place on May 5, 1876. The Brown Stocking defeated the Chicago White Stockings (predecessors of the Cubs) by a then-unusually low score of 1-0.

The Brown Stockings played well the following season, but scandal forced the club's withdrawal from the league in 1878. A number of another city's players who signed to play with the Browns that season were involved in a game-fixing scheme. Though no longer affiliated with the NL, a Brown Stockings team continued to compete at the Grand Avenue park for the next four years. During this period, German immigrant Chris Von der Ahe formed a corporation called Sportsman's Park and Club to manage the ballpark. An ambitious entrepreneur who owned a saloon and boarding house near the site, Von der Ahe brewed his own beer. He realized that baseball games served as a good draw for his product. So, in 1882 he organized a new Brown Stockings team to compete in a newly organized major league, the American Association. Unlike the NL, the AA did not ban Sunday games and the sale of liquor.

Playing at what was by then called Sportsman's Park, the 1880s Brown Stockings did much to infuse the blossoming city with baseball fever. Capturing four consecutive AA pennants and one World title, Von der Ahe's club provided St. Louis with a decade of outstanding baseball. Finally, after being adopted by the National League, the team moved to another park in 1893. Still used for baseball and other sports, old Sportsman's remained void of big league play until 1902 when the new American League's Browns moved in.

The National League Cardinals became joint tenants with the Browns in 1920. Eventually, the name of the park on Grand changed from Sportsman's to Busch Stadium. That was in 1954 when Anheuser-Busch owned both the Cardinals and the park, and the Browns began their first season in Baltimore as the Orioles. During those many years leading up to the Cardinals' 1966 move downtown, scores of baseball fans built incalculable precious memories of the National Game at that old Grand Avenue Grounds. The following pages allow a glimpse into some of the remarkable, engaging major league baseball events that occurred there.

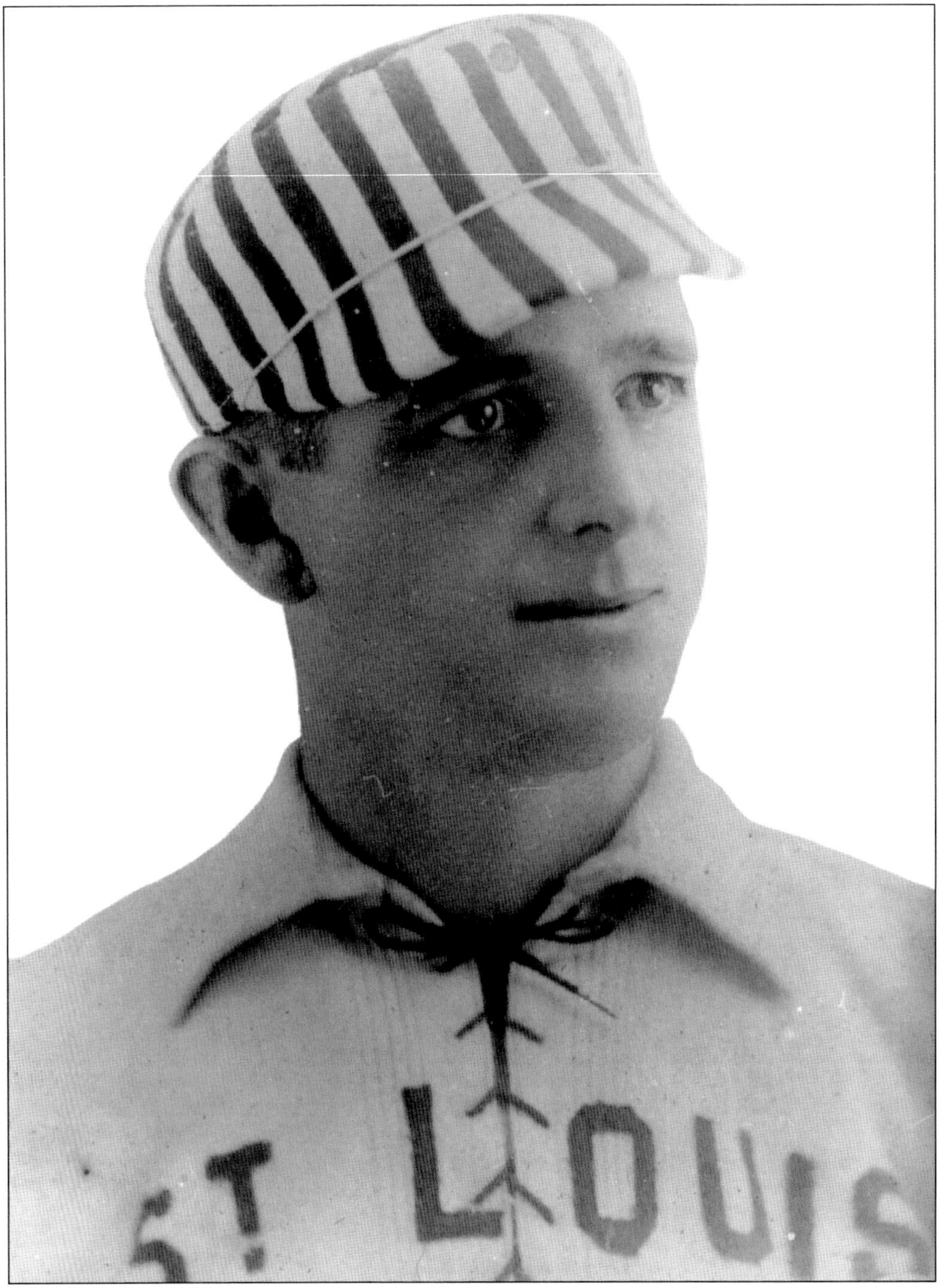

Charles Comiskey came to Von der Ahe's 1881 Brown Stockings from an Iowa baseball club called the Rabbits. An outstanding player with managerial skills, Comiskey soon took on the role of manager-first baseman. Baseball historians claim him as the first to play that position off the bag. Under his leadership, the Brown Stockings captured four league pennants in a row—1885, '86, '87, and '88. In 1886, they went on to defeat the NL Chicago White Stockings, four games to two, claiming St. Louis' first World Series victory.

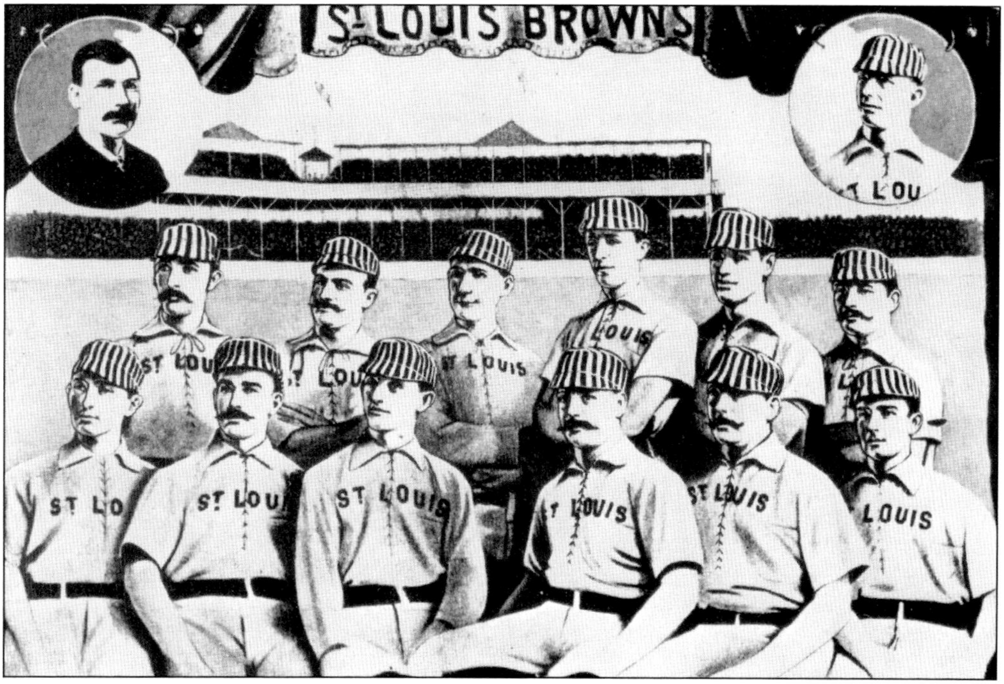

This postcard image of the 1885 Brown Stockings shows, in the top inset, from left to right, der Poss President Chris Von der Ahe (his German ancestry-derived handle) and Charles Comiskey. Old Sportsman's Park's grandstand is seen in the background.

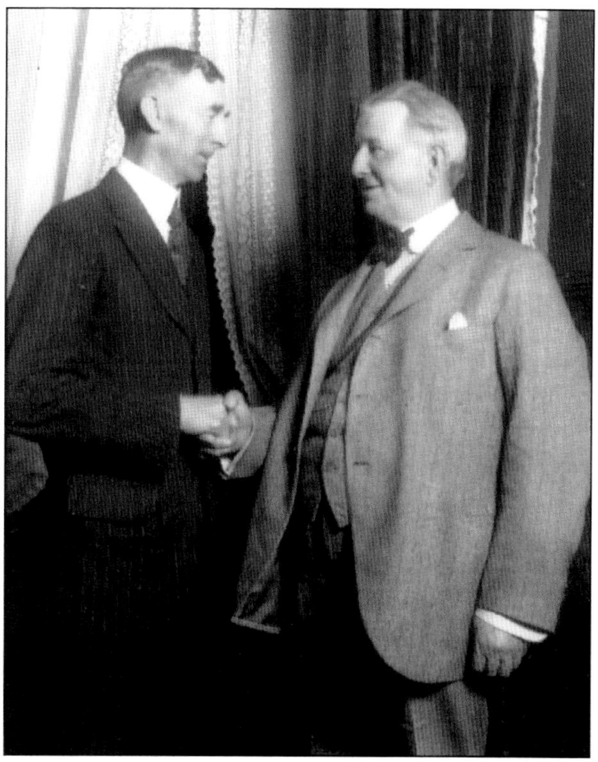

Fast-forwarding, a portlier Comiskey shakes hands with fellow baseball executive Cornelius Alexander "Connie" Mack. In 1890 Commy (Comiskey's nickname) joined Connie, then the NL Washington club's catcher, in jumping to the rebel Brotherhood League of that year. Mack caught for the Buffalo club, and Comiskey was the Chicago team's first sacker. St. Louis had no entry in the Brotherhood. As with the Unions of 1884, the new group intent on breaking the reserve rule dissolved after its inaugural season. Briefly returning to the Brown Stockings, Comiskey eventually gained ownership of the American League White Sox from 1901 to 1931. Mack ended up manager of the Philadelphia Athletics for a record setting half-century (1901–1950) and president of the same club from 1937 to 1954.

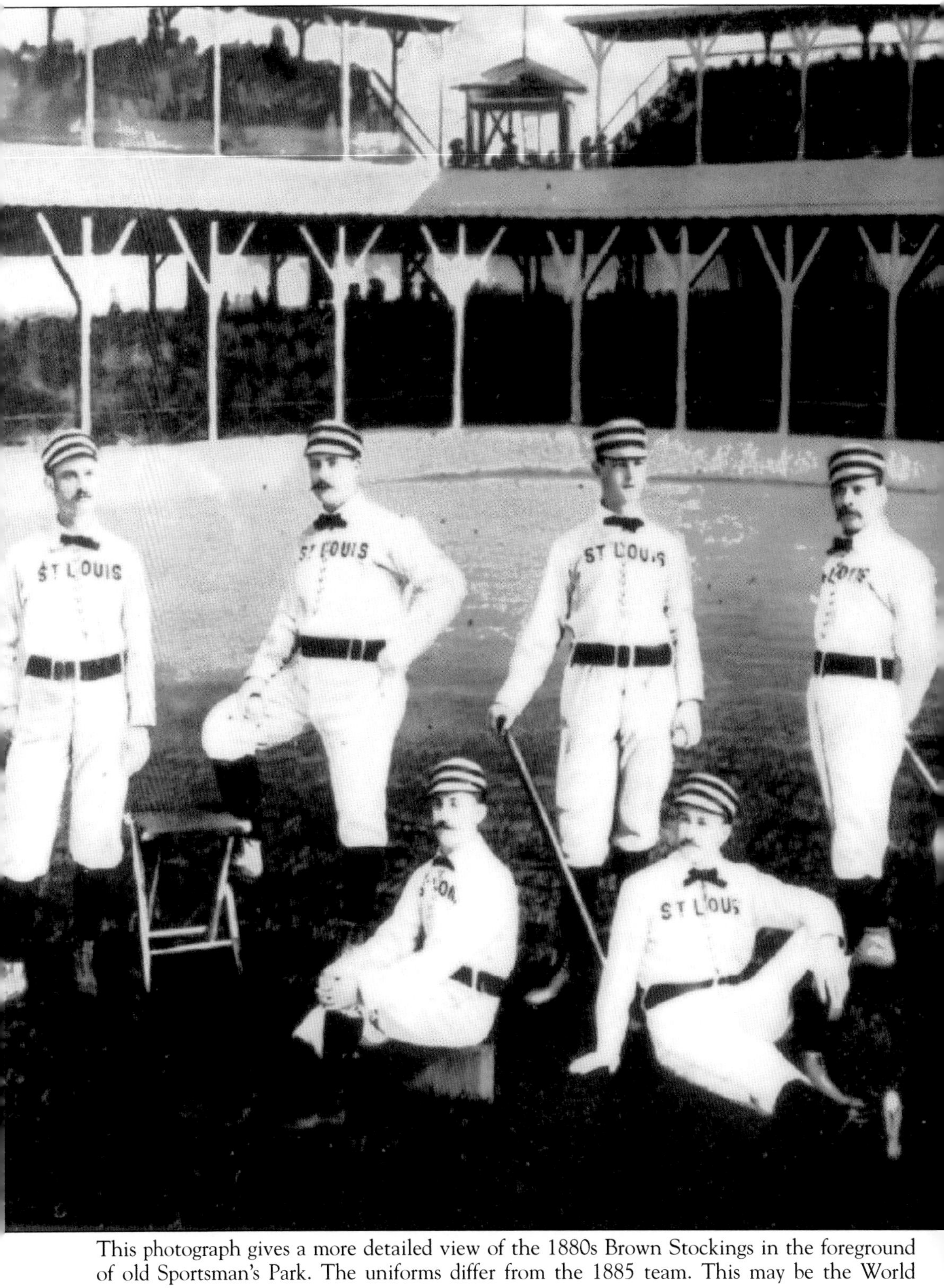

This photograph gives a more detailed view of the 1880s Brown Stockings in the foreground of old Sportsman's Park. The uniforms differ from the 1885 team. This may be the World

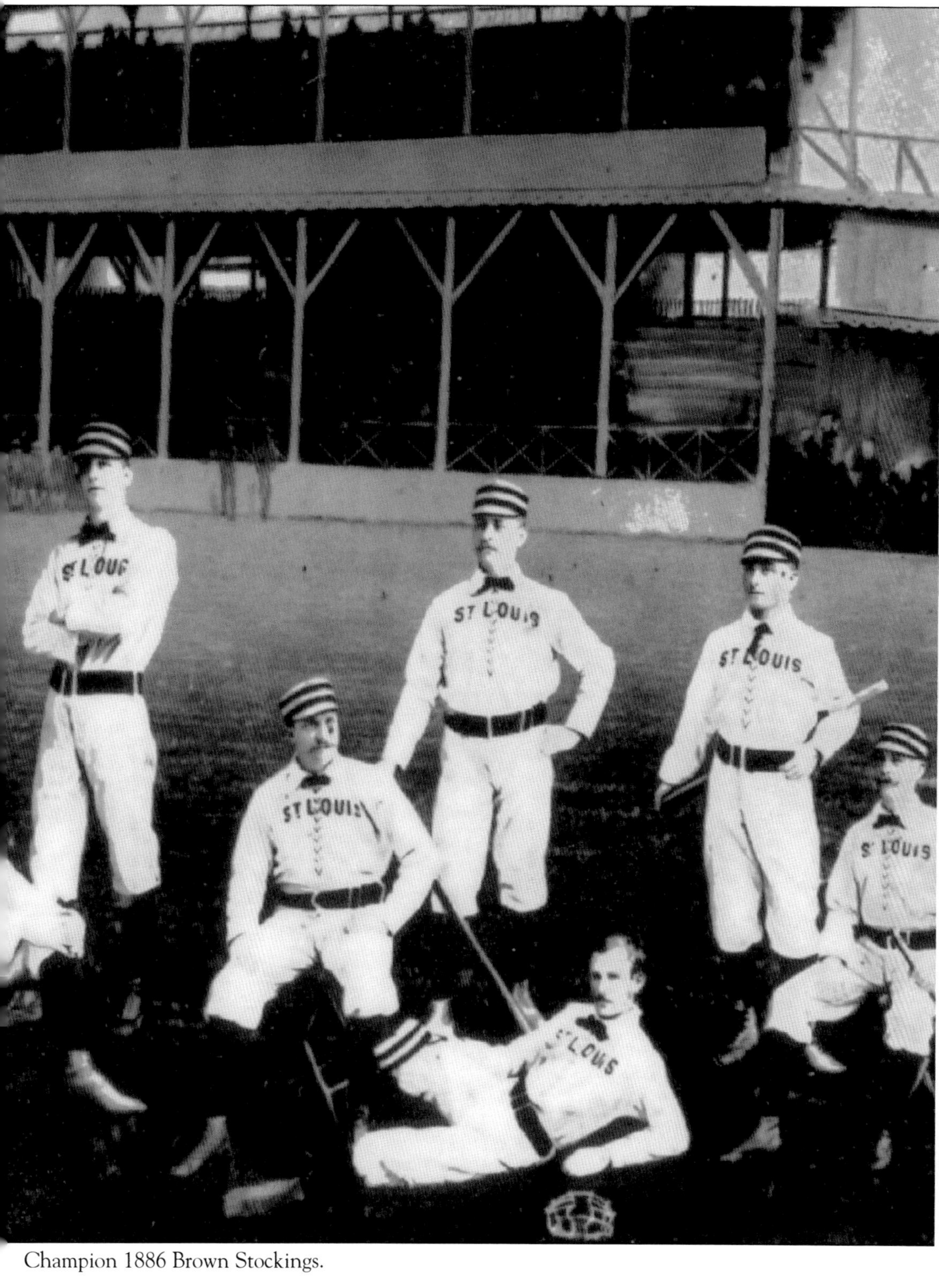

Champion 1886 Brown Stockings.

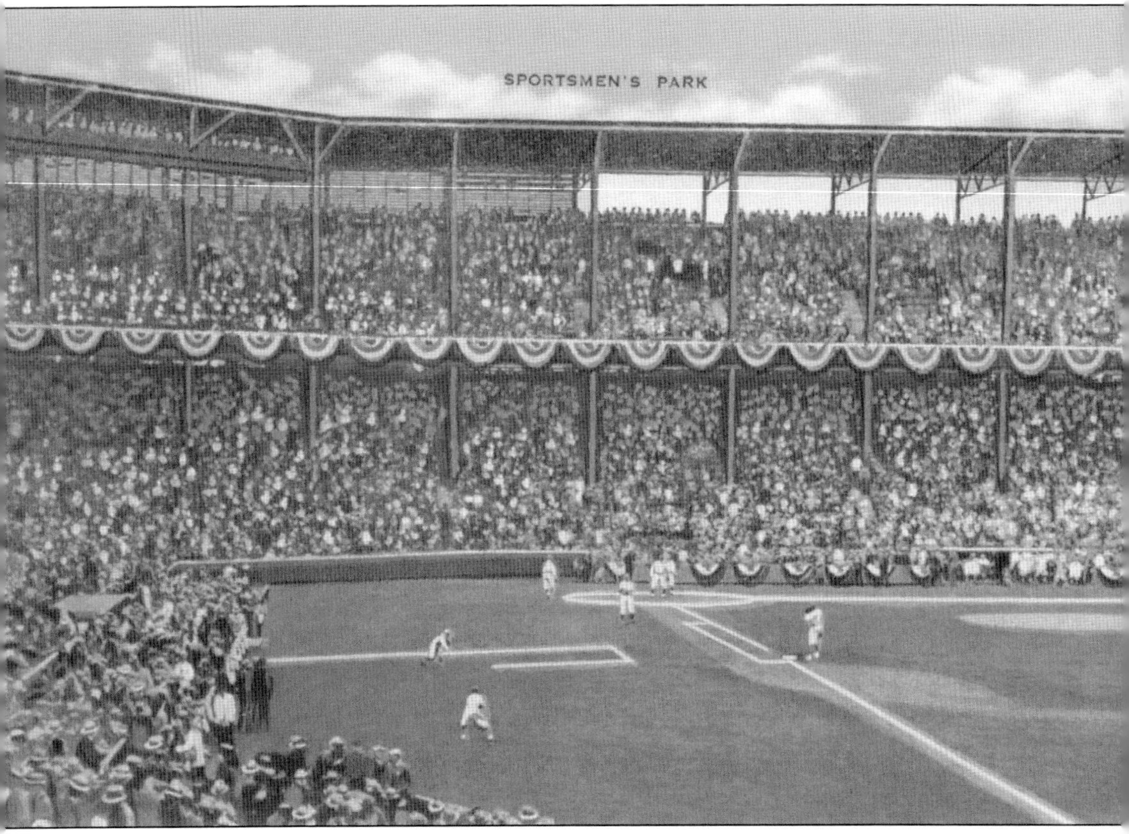

A twentieth century postcard, this image depicts Sportsman's Park before lights. A time when men's straw hats dotted the stands like dandelions in summer, beginning in 1902, the American League Browns played there through the teens, while the NL Cardinals competed down at Robison Field at Natural Bridge and Vandeventer. Though the American League Browns ended their first season in St. Louis only one spot out for first place, their performance was less than stellar for some time after that. In 1911 they finished dead last with only 45 wins to 107 losses. The Brown's dismal performance led to the expression describing St. Louis—"first in booze, first in shoes, and last in the American League." (Courtesy of Fred Longshaw Postcards, Des Peres, Missouri.)

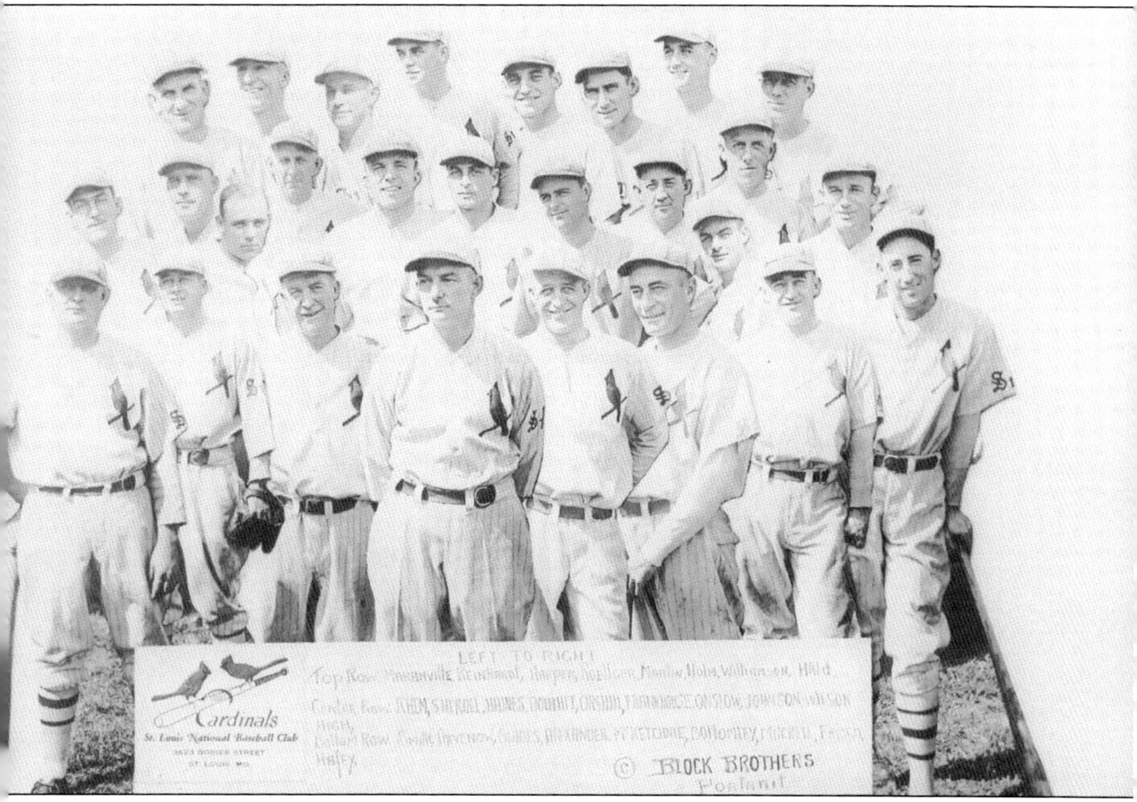

After the Cardinals moved into Sportsman's Park in 1920, one could see a major league game there almost any day during the baseball season. American League fans rooted for the Brownies. And National League fans were ecstatic when the Cardinals brought home the city's first World Series championship in forty years, defeating the 1926 New York Yankees in the best of seven. The '28 Cardinals, pictured in this postcard, again met the Yankees in the big event, but lost in four games straight. (Courtesy of Fred Longshaw Postcards, Des Peres, Missouri.)

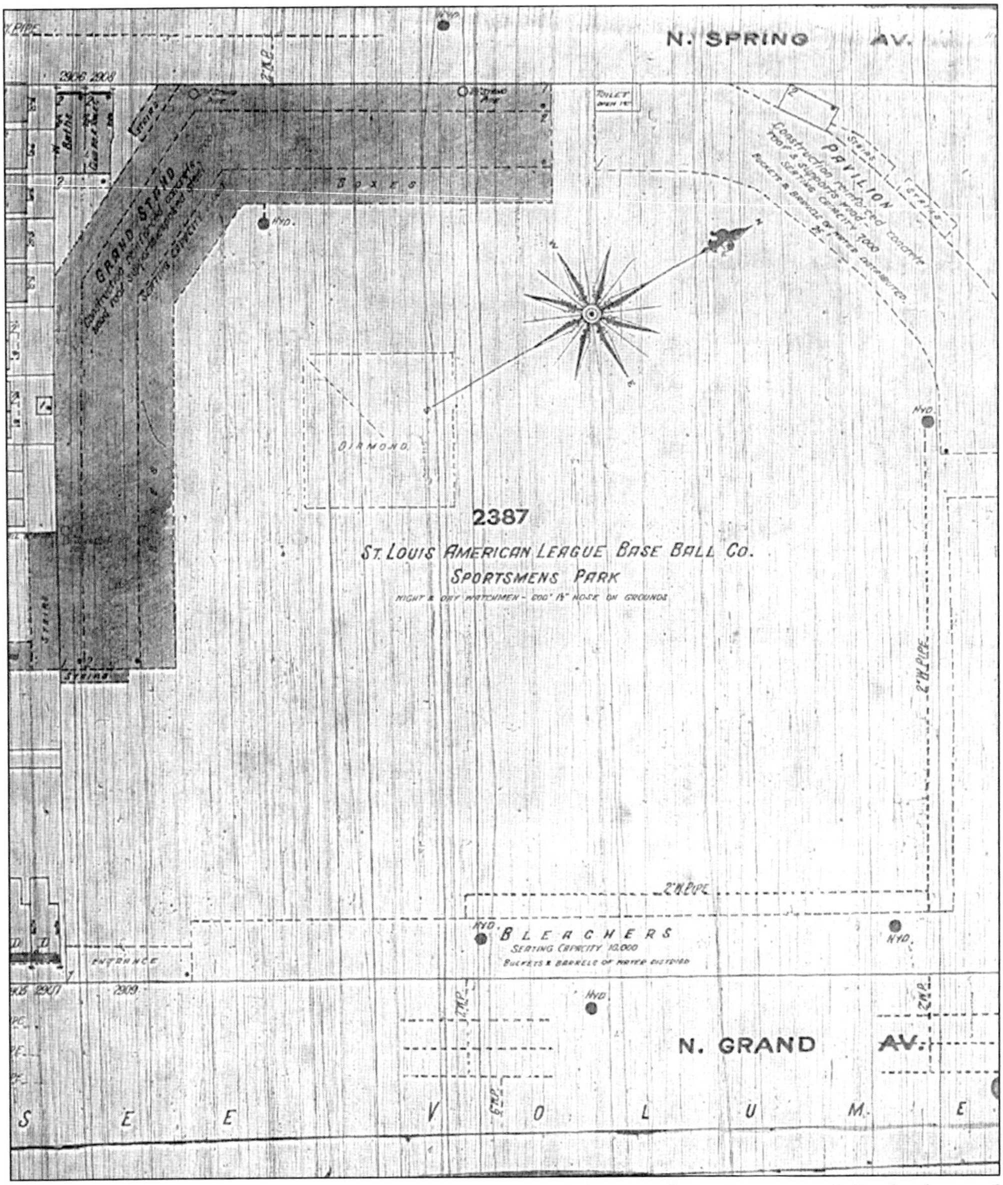

The configuration of the diamond and placement of the stands at Sportsman's Park changed over time. When Browns President Robert L. Hedges built a new grandstand in 1909, the diamond and the grandstand were repositioned to Dodier and Spring, the southwest corner of the lot. This fire insurance map depicts the basic layout of that period. (Sanborn Fire Insurance Map, courtesy of the St. Louis Public Library.)

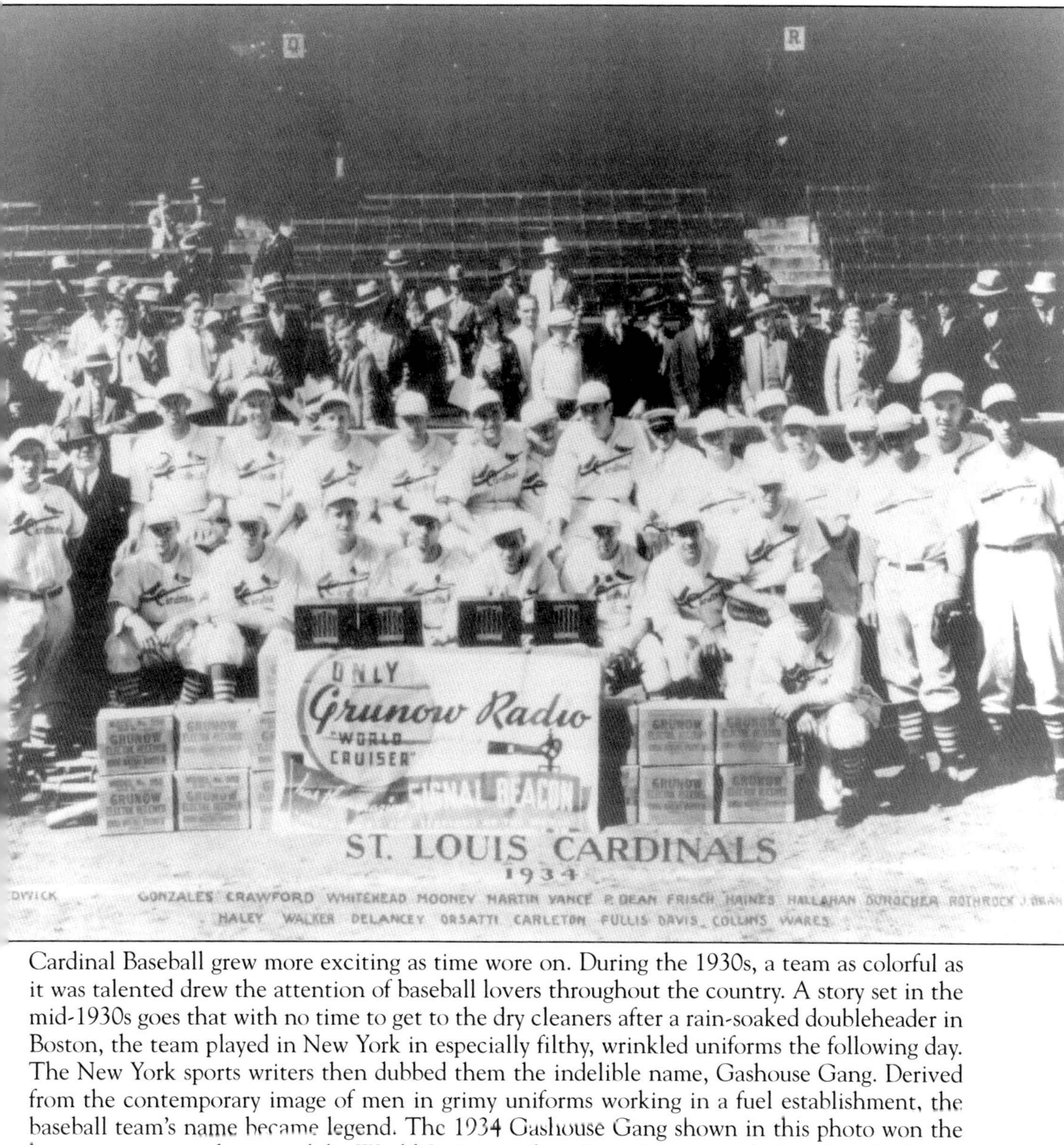

Cardinal Baseball grew more exciting as time wore on. During the 1930s, a team as colorful as it was talented drew the attention of baseball lovers throughout the country. A story set in the mid-1930s goes that with no time to get to the dry cleaners after a rain-soaked doubleheader in Boston, the team played in New York in especially filthy, wrinkled uniforms the following day. The New York sports writers then dubbed them the indelible name, Gashouse Gang. Derived from the contemporary image of men in grimy uniforms working in a fuel establishment, the baseball team's name became legend. The 1934 Gashouse Gang shown in this photo won the league pennant and captured the World Series cup from Detroit at a time before playoffs altered the concept of the big event. Back then, the team with the best NL record met the team with the best AL record. A curious note about the name Grunow in this photo: William Grunow, who co-founded the company that sold the Majestic radio, marketed radios under his own name after 1930. And, 1934 was the year that the FCC, which regulates broadcasting, was created. Most likely meant as an ad for Grunow Radio, this shot was taken at Sportsman's Park.

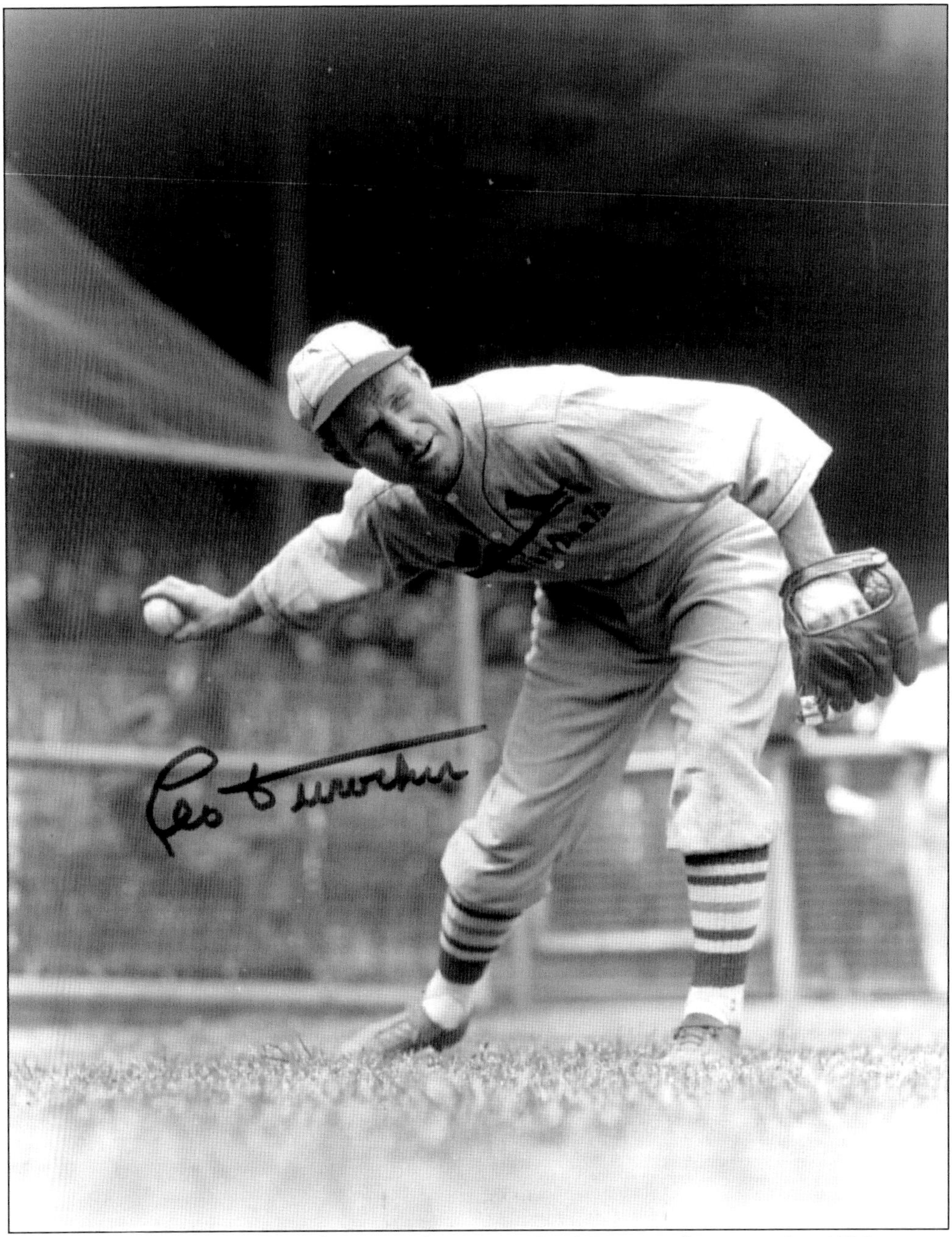

Former sports editor of the *Chicago Daily News*, Lloyd Lewis reflects on the 1930s in an introduction to a book titled The Gashouse Gang: "A lot of us . . . wrote about those Dean-Durocher-Frisch-Medwick-Martin-Ripper Collins Gashousers every chance we got." With the exception of Collins, they all later gained acceptance to baseball's Hall of Fame in Cooperstown. Leo "The Lip" Durocher, seen in this autographed photo, played short for the Cardinals (1933–1937). He went on to earn his plaque in Cooperstown as manager for Brooklyn, New York, Chicago, and finally Houston in 1973.

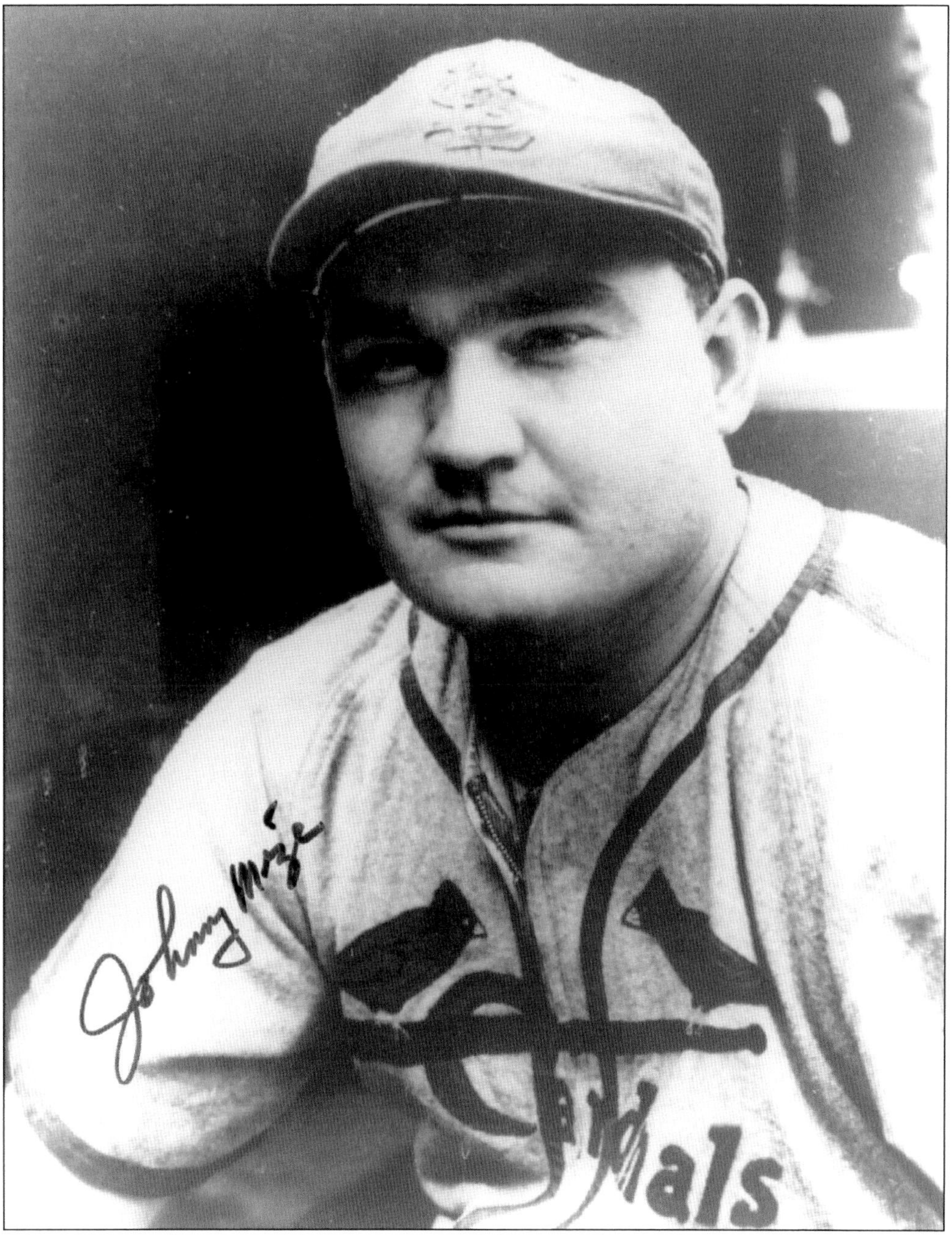

Johnny Mize, "The Big Cat" from Georgia, made his major league debut with the Cardinals in 1936. This power hitting first baseman tallied his career high batting average of .349 in '39, and walloped 43 homers the following year—setting a St. Louis record at the time. Closing out his playing career in New York, first with the Giants, and then the Yankees, he is among the many great players now enshrined at Cooperstown who added incredible memories of baseball at old Sportsman's Park.

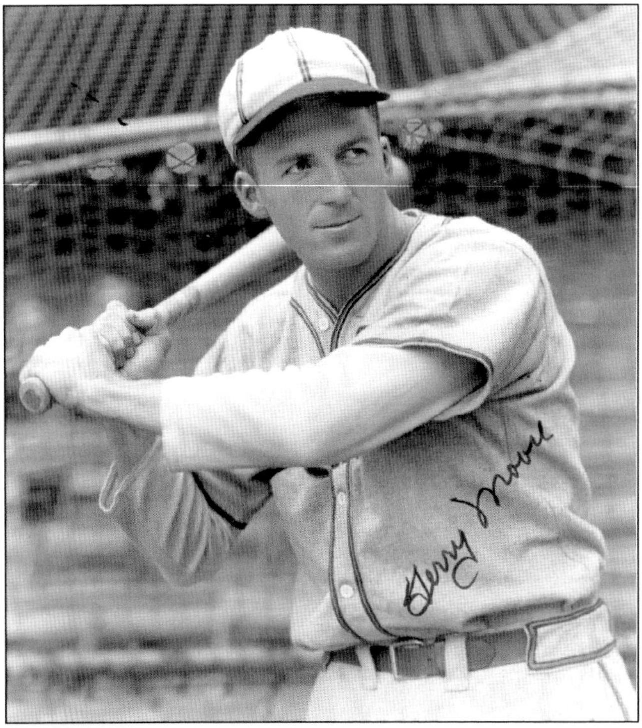

Joining the Gashouse Gang in 1935, outfielder Terry Moore played with the Cardinals through '42. Talented and popular, he played in four consecutive All Star games (1939–1942), spending the next three war years in the military. World War II affected St. Louis baseball as well as the other big league cities of the times. Moore wasn't the only ballplayer turned soldier. He returned to the Mound City to finish out his playing career in 1948.

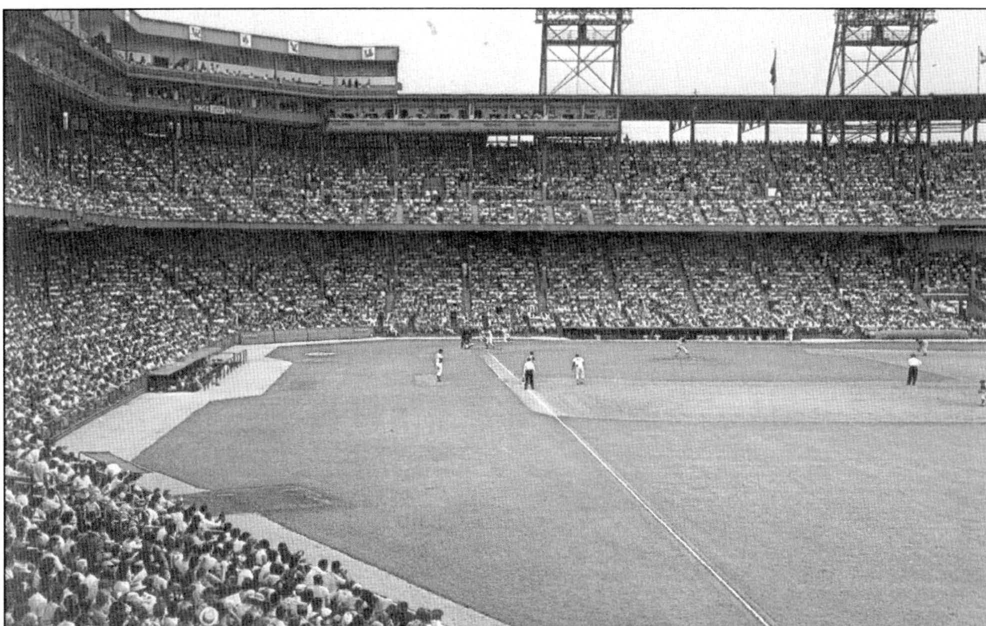

Old Sportsman's Park changed over time. Bringing the seating capacity to over 34,000, Browns owner Phil Ball expanded the grandstand and turned the right field bleachers into a pavilion after the 1925 season. Time wore on, and the Browns and Cardinals shared the expense of modernizing the park with lights. On May 24, 1940, the Browns hosted St. Louis's first night game in the stadium. This postcard photo shows two of the light towers recognizable to fans of the next quarter century. (Courtesy of Fred Longshaw Postcards, Des Peres, Missouri.)

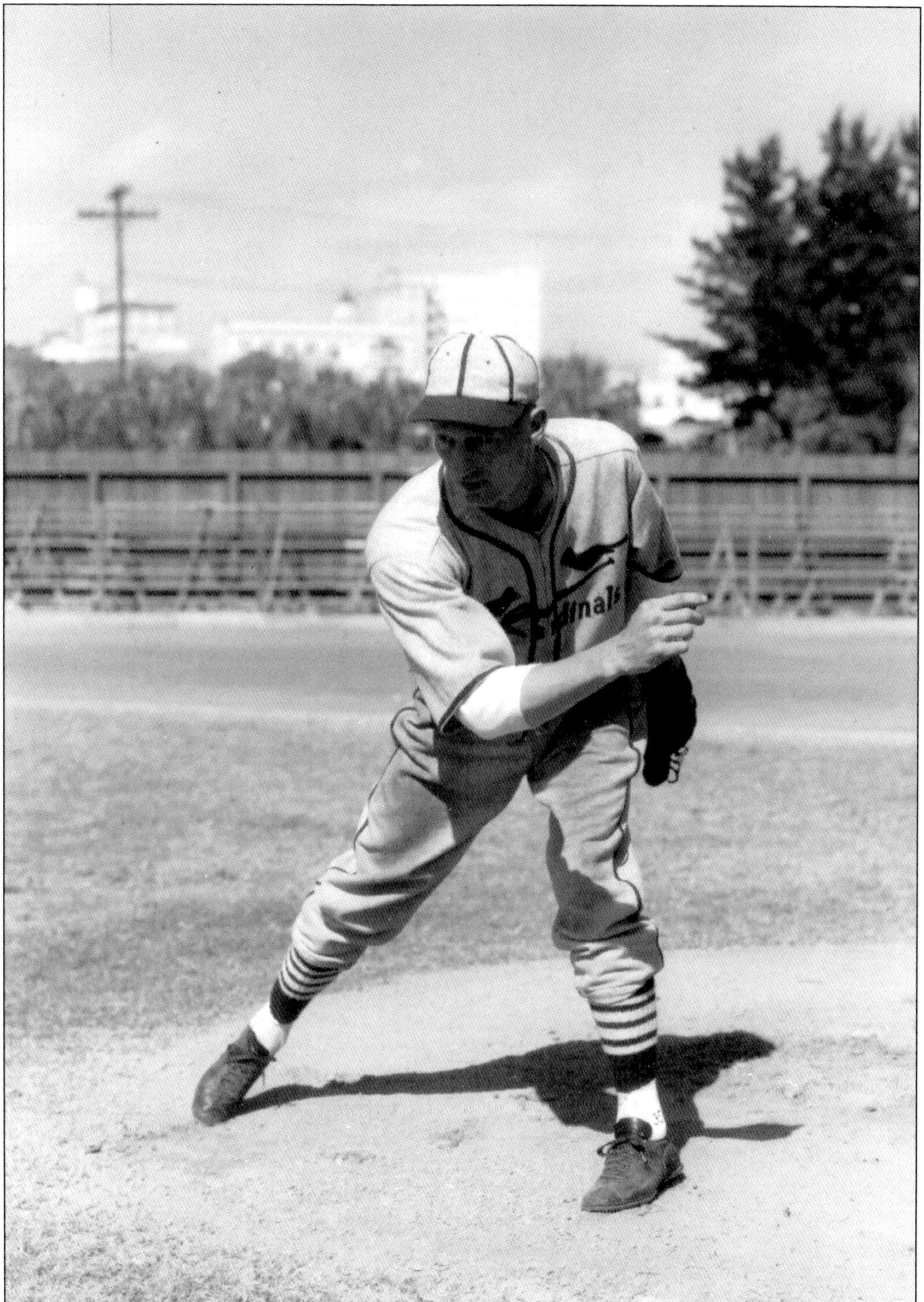

Good pitching, ever an essential to building a winning team, the Cardinals gained with this player, Lon Warneke, in a swap with Chicago for Rip Collins in 1937. Dubbed the Arkansas Hummingbird, Warneke gave St. Louis five good seasons before returning to the Cubs during the '42 season. He later became a National League umpire from 1949 to 1955.

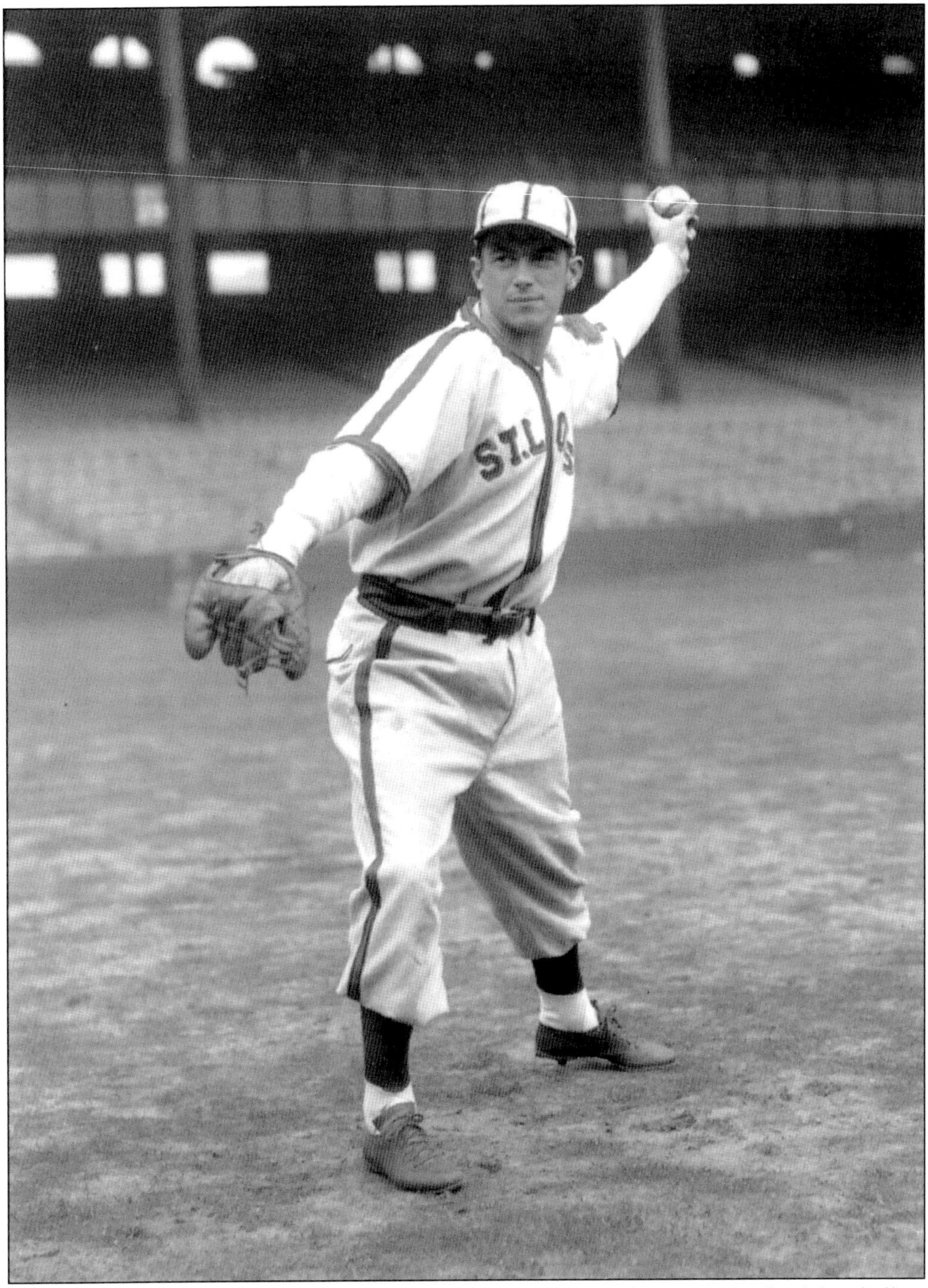

While St. Louis ball fans witnessed some spectacular National League Cardinal baseball at Sportsman's Park during the 1930s, the city's American League team hovered in and near last place. But good players like Wally Judnich, shown in this photo taken during spring training, helped to boost them into third at the end of the 1942 season.

Pitcher Vern Kennedy won 21 games for the Chicago White Sox in 1936, and came to play for the Browns during the '39 season. But the best he ever achieved for the St. Louis club was 12 wins and 17 losses the following year. After he moved on to pitch for Cleveland, the hapless Brownies captured their first and only American League pennant in 1944. That year Sportsman's Park hosted the only all-St. Louis World Series ever—the Cardinals defeated the Browns, four games to two.

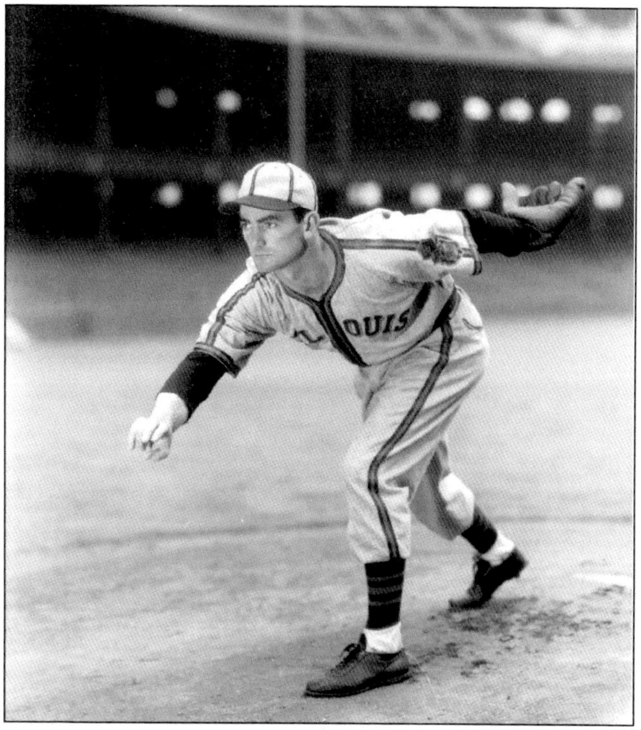

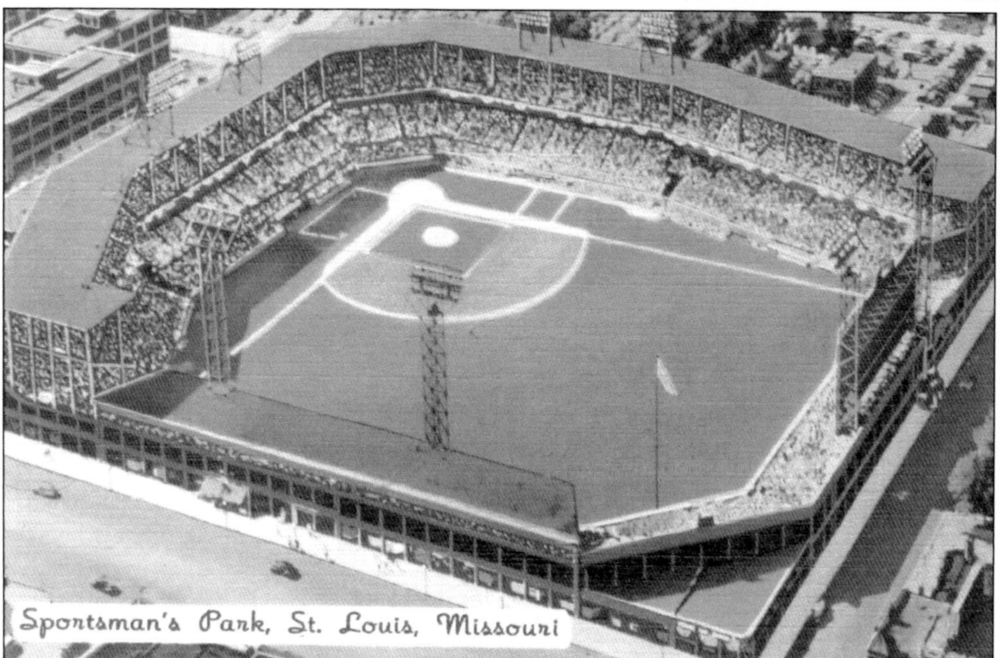

This postcard overview of old Sportsman's Park shows it as most fans still around remember it. At the left on Dodier is the Carter Carburetor building. Still there at this writing, it is no longer in use. Grand Avenue runs along the bottom of the image, Sullivan runs parallel to Dodier, and Spring is the street at the top of the image, parallel to Grand. John Dunn, mentioned earlier, once owned the property. He lived at 3007 Spring, across from the park.

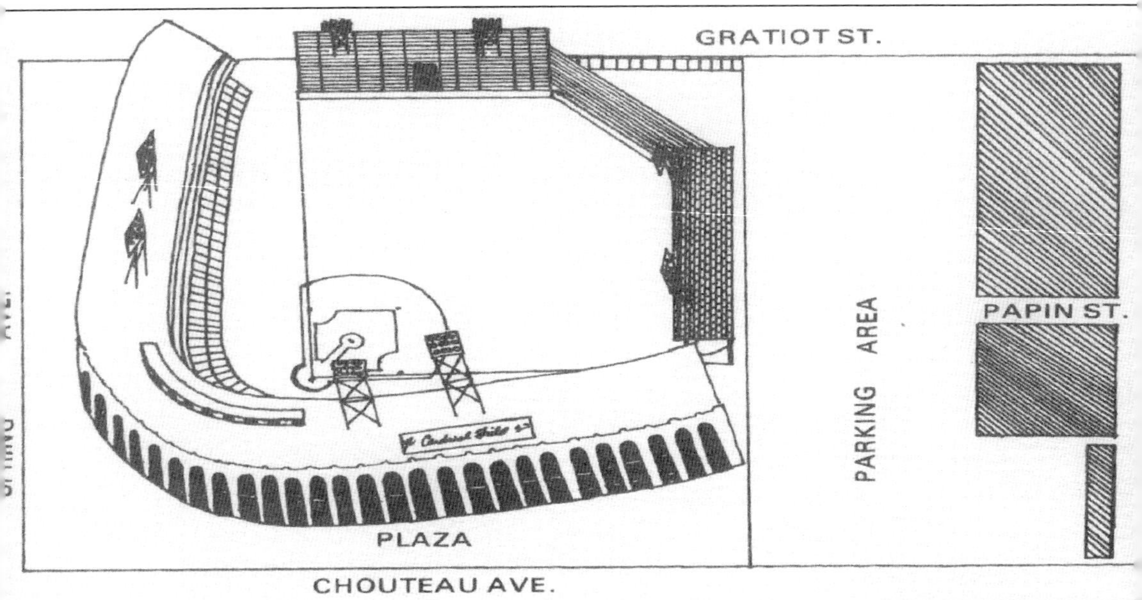

This plan for a new Cardinal stadium never reached fruition. Sam Breaden, the club's president, revealed this scheme for a 40,000-seat ballpark on November 11, 1944. Notably, the plot of land just west of Grand on Chouteau, is but a few blocks west of the site of Red Stockings Park described in chapter two. Chouteau is the first street parallel to the railroad tracks that bordered that historical site.

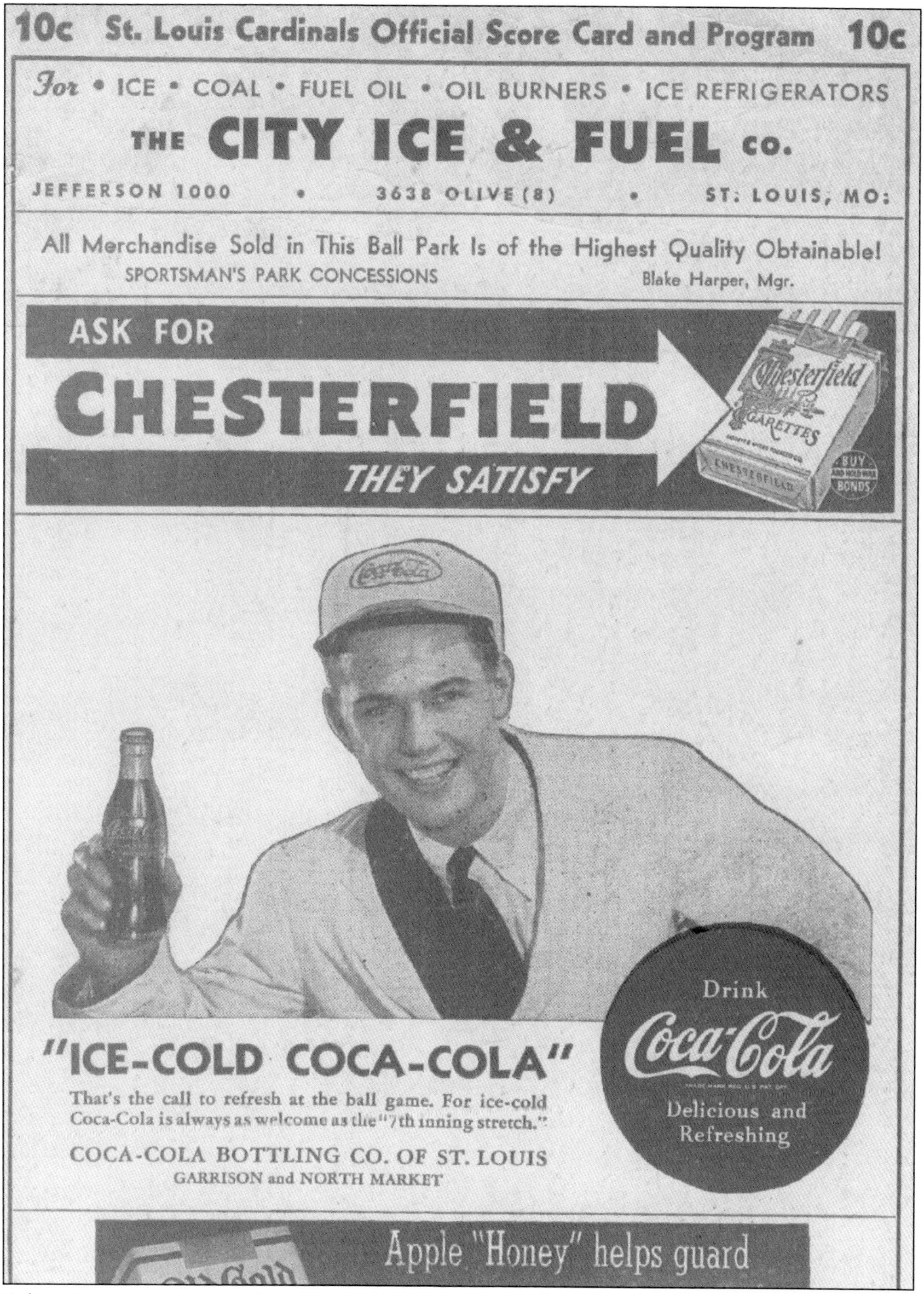

Advertisements consume the cover of this keepsake Cardinal scorecard's cover. Hand dated July 22, 1945, its purchase price of ten cents reflects the cost of such items at that time. By 2003, a scorecard at Busch Stadium cost $2.50. Notice the location of the plant in the Coca Cola ad. In 1916 the Trolley League Base Ball Park was listed at Garrison and North Market. And, later the NNL Stars Park (described in Chapter Two) was built in the same general area.

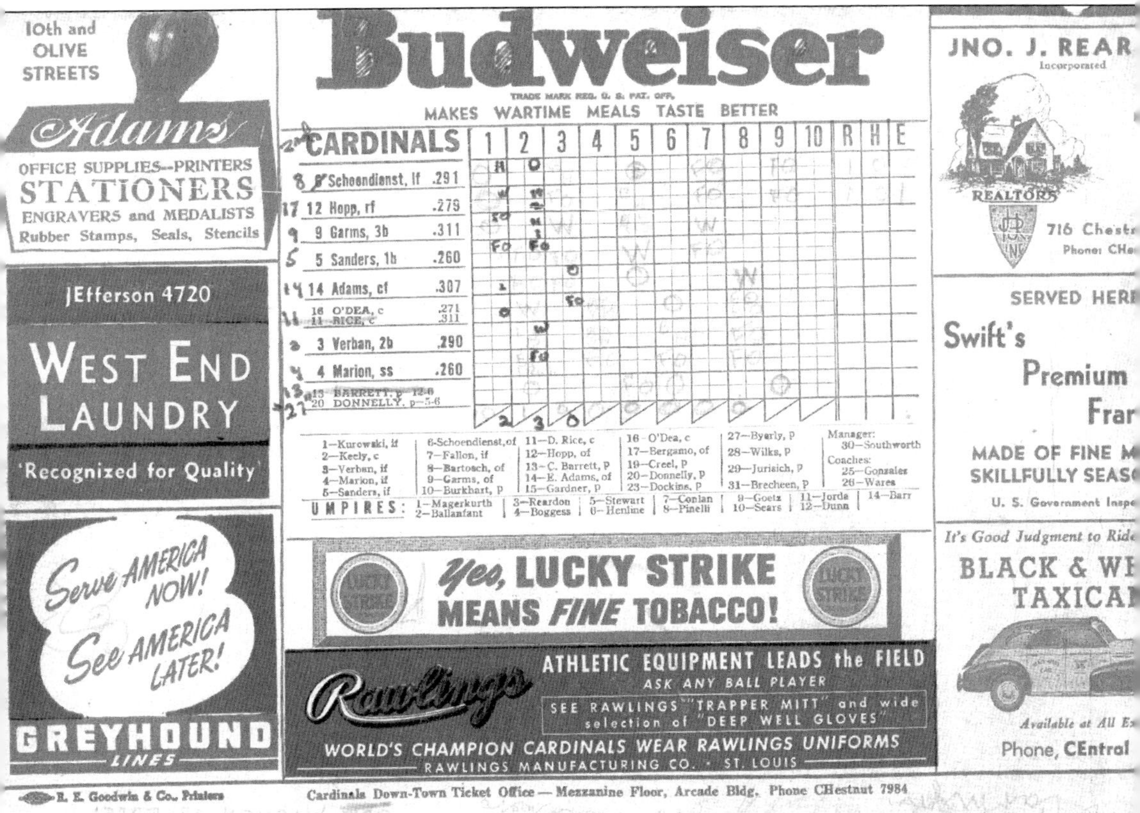

The scoring section of the scorecard on the previous page reveals the Cardinal lineup in a game with the Brooklyn Dodgers. The first St. Louis pitcher on the day's schedule, Charles "Red" Barrett, won 21 games for the Cards that year. That proved to be his best season, as after a disappointing '46 season, he went on to Boston, and retired three years later. But, as a promising contender at the beginning of the '46 season, his spring training photo graced the cover of the April 1 *Time* magazine that year. The magazine cost ten cents, the same as a Cardinal score card.

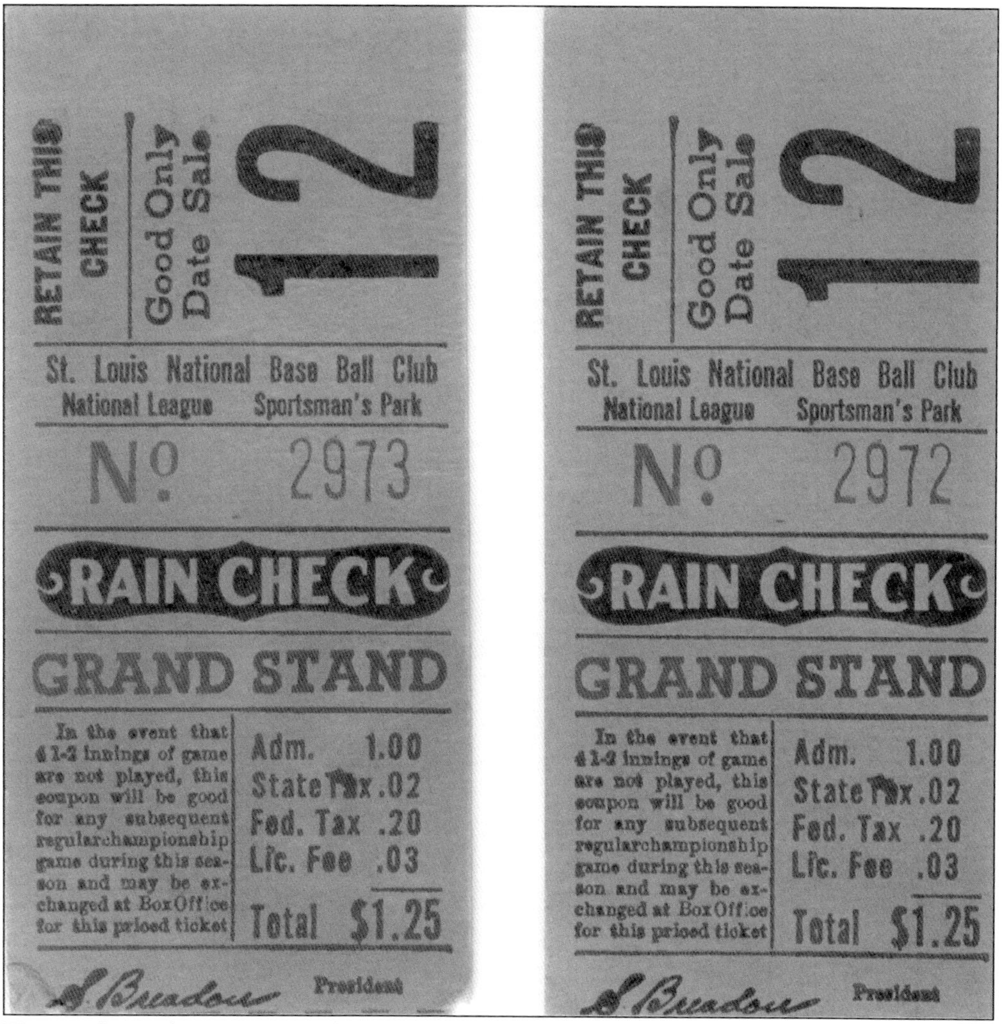

These ticket stubs accompany the scorecard shown on the previous two pages. The two people who used them later married, and the scorecard and rain checks became precious family keepsakes. As with legions of other baseball fans, such items remain invaluable mementos of the time and place of a shared experience. The time was the summer of 1945. The place was St. Louis's old Sportsman's Park at Grand and Dodier. The price of a single admission to the grand stand was $1.25.

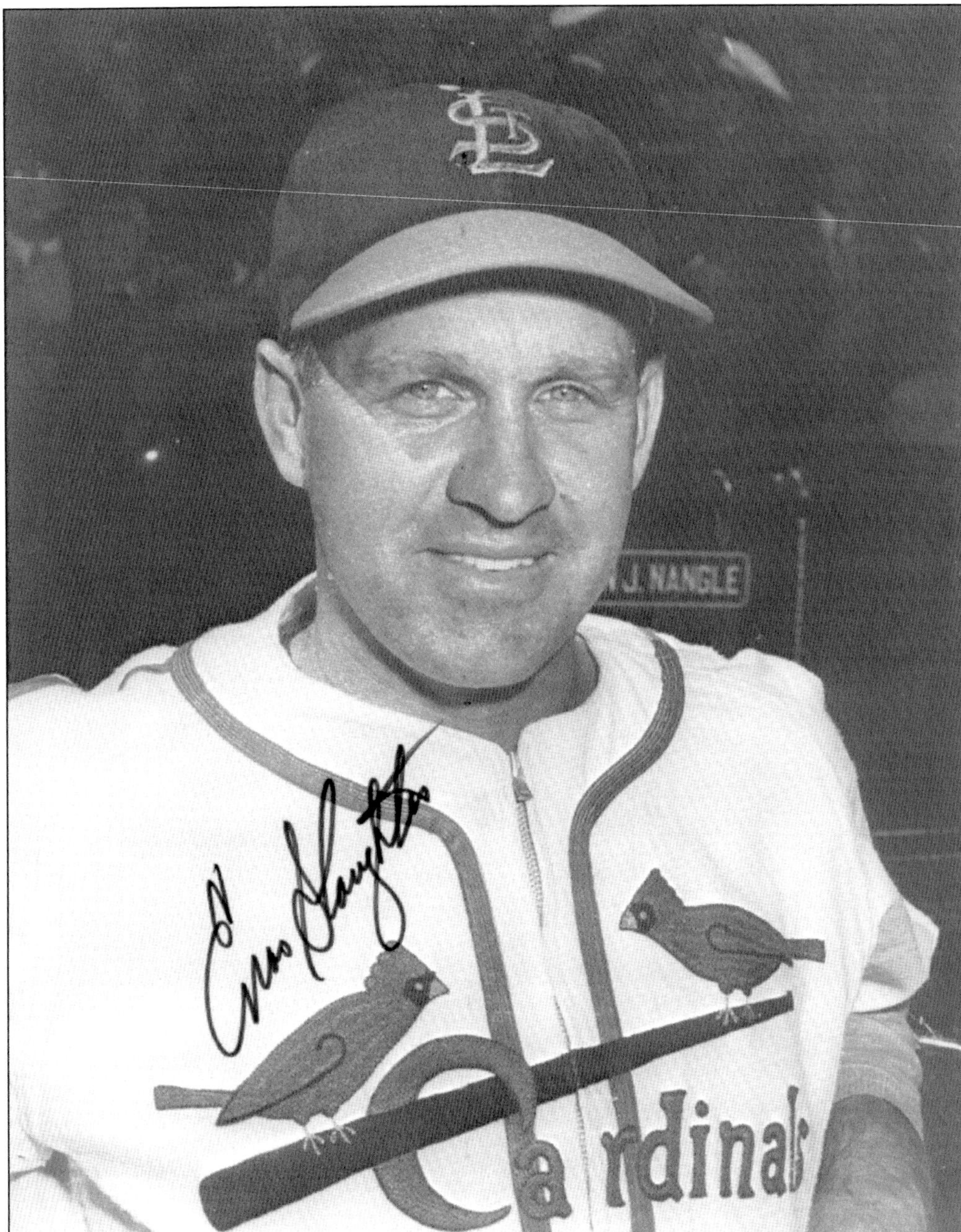

Inducted into the Hall of Fame in 1985, outfielder Enos Slaughter supplied Cardinal fans with 13 stellar years of baseball (1938–1953). Playing in ten All Star games during that time, he imprinted his name in the annals of outstanding World Series play on October 15, 1946. With the score tied 3-3 in the bottom of the eighth inning of the seventh game of the series played between the Cardinals and the Boston Red Sox, Slaughter made his famous mad dash. On first when Cardinal Harry Walker doubled (though some believe it should have been ruled a single) Slaughter caught everyone off guard by racing from first to home, scoring the winning run of the World Series. That happened at Sportsman's Park, where baseball became a St. Louis way of life.

Native St. Louisan Erma Bergmann, a right handed pitcher for the All American Girls Professional Baseball League (AAGPBL), witnessed Slaughter's famous mad dash home in person. Though she never played baseball at Sportsman's Park, she studied big league style there for years, beginning in her youth as a member of the Knot Hole Gang. Then, after playing her first season as a professional, Erma managed to get standing room tickets to the seventh game of the 1946 World Series. A retired police officer nearly 60 years later, she still vividly recalled gasping at Slaughter's famous dash home. Photographed in uniform in 1947, she stands outside the Dayton Hotel in Kenosha, Wisconsin.

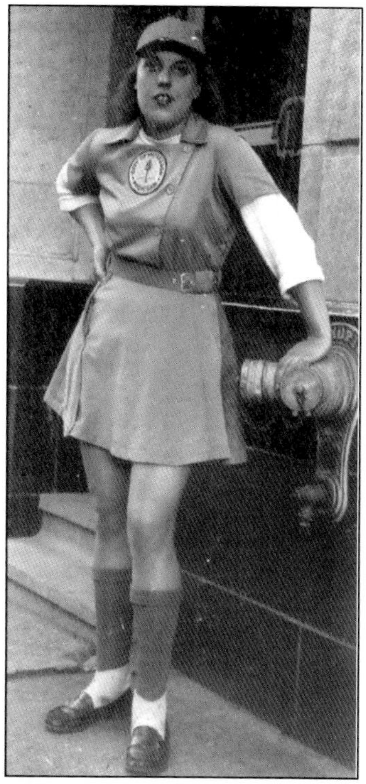

23

A-A GPBL

ERMA BERGMAN

pitcher

Born:6/18/24
St. Louis, MO
Height:5'7"
Weight:155
Batted: Right
Threw: Right

PITCHING RECORD

YEAR	TEAM	G	IP	R	ER	ERA	BB	SO	HB	WP	W	L	PCT
1946	Muskegon	35	263	119	60	2.05	94	62	16	3	15	16	.484
1947	Muskegon	27	207	74	40	1.74	71	47	6	3	11	10	.524
1948	Springfield	32	236	127	80	3.05	85	77	16	3	9	19	.321
1949	Racine	32	225	80	52	2.08	71	42	5	1	11	14	.440
1950	Racine	29	208	108	62	2.68	68	51	9	2	11	14	.440
1951	Battle Creek	27	200	119	87	3.92	73	59	7	5	7	18	.280
Total		**182**	**1339**	**627**	**381**	**2.56**	**462**	**338**	**59**	**17**	**64**	**91**	**.413**

In her rookie year with her parents & brothers watching, "Bergie" hit the game winning and only home run of her career, beating Peoria 2-1. Her sidearm pitching helped Muskegon win the pennant in 1947. In that same year, she pitched a no-hitter against Grand Rapids,

Bergmann's stats during her career with the AAGPBL reveal a remarkable combined earned run average of 2.56. The reverse side of her collectors card reads that her side arm pitching helped Muskegon win the league pennant the same year she posed for the above photo. Note that her last name is spelled incorrectly with only one "n."

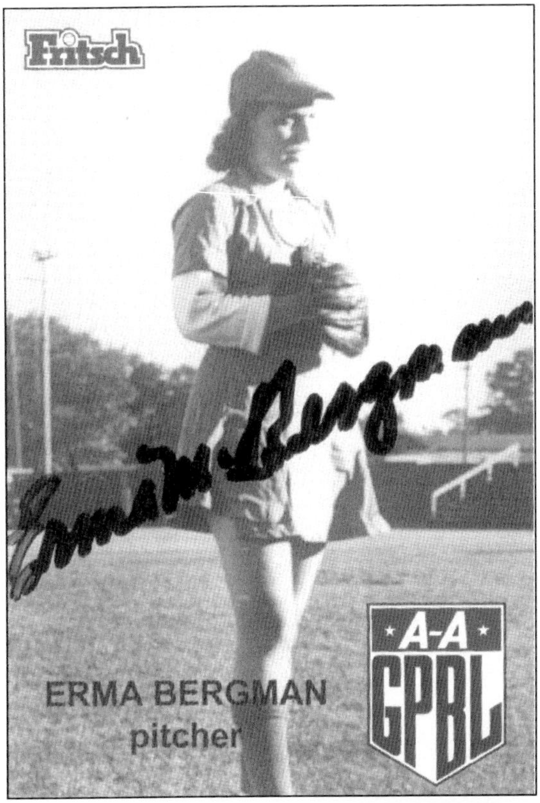

Erma Bergmann (correct spelling) prepares to pitch, as seen in this photo side of the card shown at the bottom of page 53. After leaving the AAGPBL, Bergmann signed with the Chicago Professional Baseball League, pitching on two different teams during the three seasons to follow. Finally, after hanging up her glove and returning to St. Louis, she soon found a job that required a different kind of uniform. Among the first women to become commissioned police officers in St. Louis, she adapted her pitching expertise to achieve a rating as expert on the pistol range. Staying with her new team, the St. Louis Metropolitan Police Department, for 25 years, she proved the versatility of baseball talent.

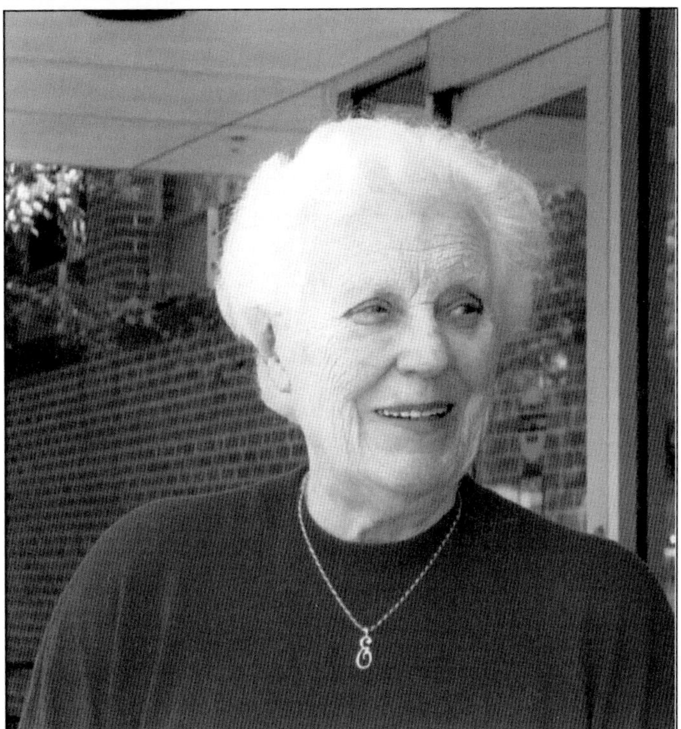

Retiring from the police department in 1981, Erma Bergmann continued to enjoy following the home team, the St. Louis Cardinals. During the summer of 2003, shortly before she posed for this snapshot, she was honored at Busch Stadium with other retired members of the AAGPBL. In June that year, she threw the ceremonial first pitch at the VBBA Perfectos' season opener held at Lafayette Park (see info on the VBBA on page 13).

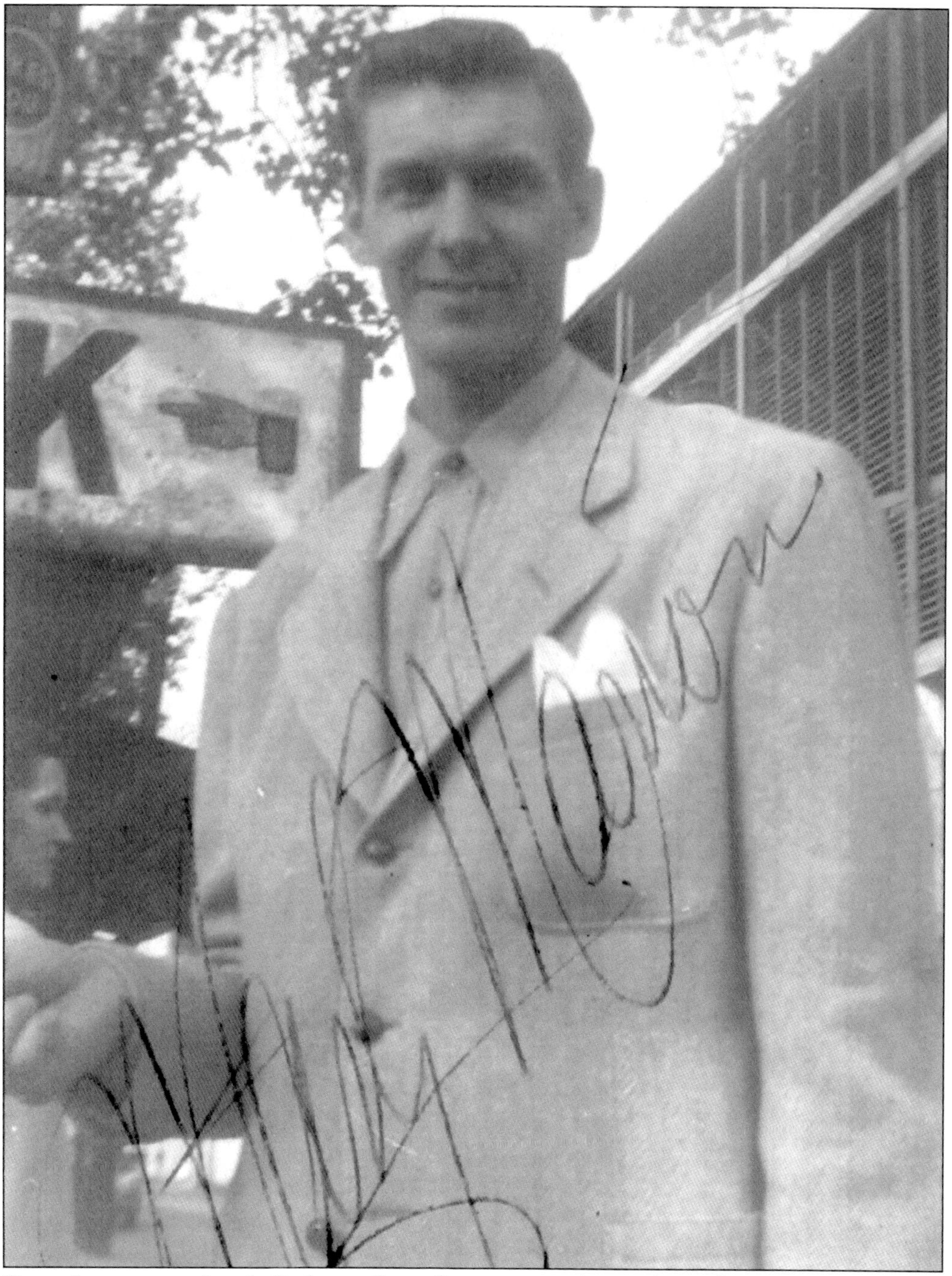

One of many great baseball players Erma Bergmann and countless other St. Louis fans saw play the game at old Sportsman's Park, Marty Marion predated awesome Ozzie Smith by some 40 years. Playing in St. Louis throughout his career—the Cardinals (1940–1950) and the Browns (1952–1953)—the tall thin shortstop called "Slats" is considered one of the greatest fielding shortstops ever. A fan snapped this photo of him in street clothes. The date hand written on the back is April 27, 1946. His name is seen on the lineup of the 1945 scorecard shown on pages 49 and 50.

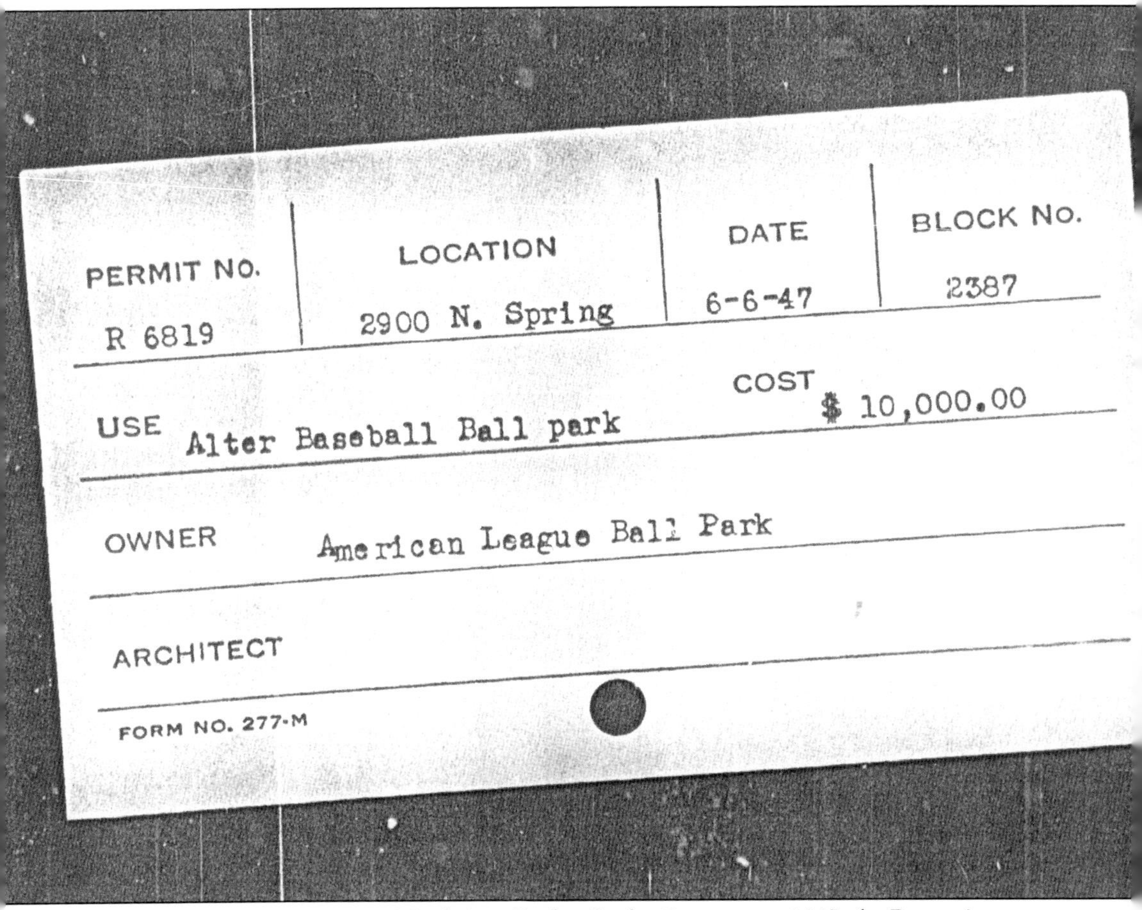
PERMIT NO. R 6819
LOCATION 2900 N. Spring
DATE 6-6-47
BLOCK No. 2387
USE Alter Baseball Ball park
COST $ 10,000.00
OWNER American League Ball Park
ARCHITECT
FORM NO. 277-M

After purchasing Sportsman's Park from Dodier Realty Company in 1947, the Browns' owners spent over $100,000 for park improvements. This building permit, dated June 6 of that year, represents at least one-tenth of those enhancements. (Courtesy of St. Louis City Hall Central File.)

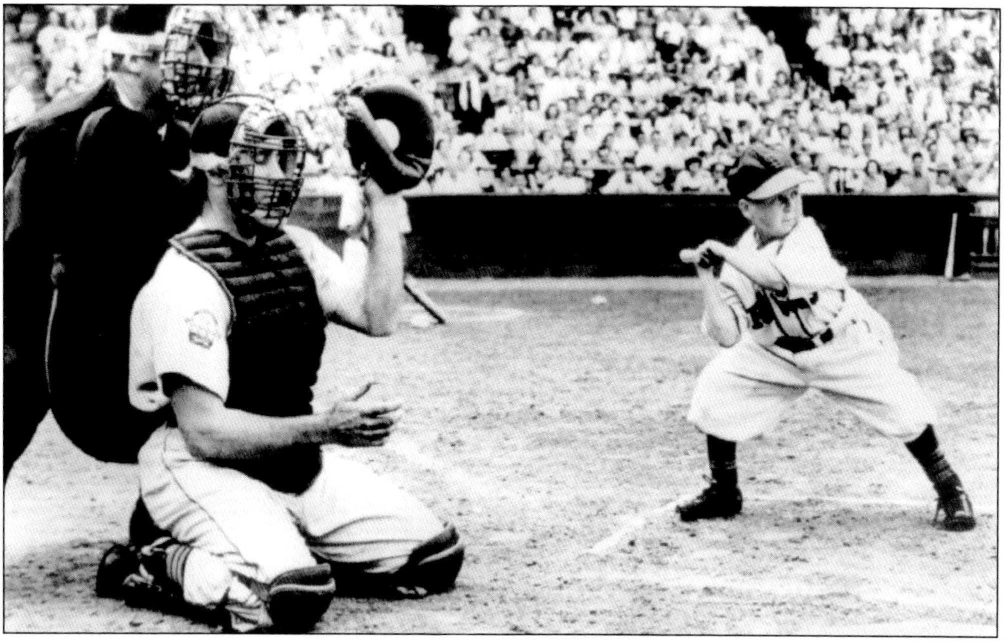

By the middle of the 1951 season, the Browns got a new owner, Bill Veeck. He concocted all sorts of promotions to draw patrons to see the Browns, who by then had resumed their losing ways. Probably the most notorious of Veeck's schemes involved the little person seen here at Sportsman's Park. Three-foot seven-inch tall, 26 year-old Eddie Gaedel popped out of a cake between games of a Browns-Tigers double-header. Dressed in a Browns uniform, Gaedel was announced as an authentic Brownie. He then shocked the crowd of 18,000-plus when he batted for rookie outfielder Frank Saucier, who replaced Browns regular center fielder, Jim Delsing, in the second game. After taking four pitches in a row, all over his head, Gaedel infuriated the umpire and the opposing manager by trotting down to first. Fast runner Delsing then replaced Gaedel.

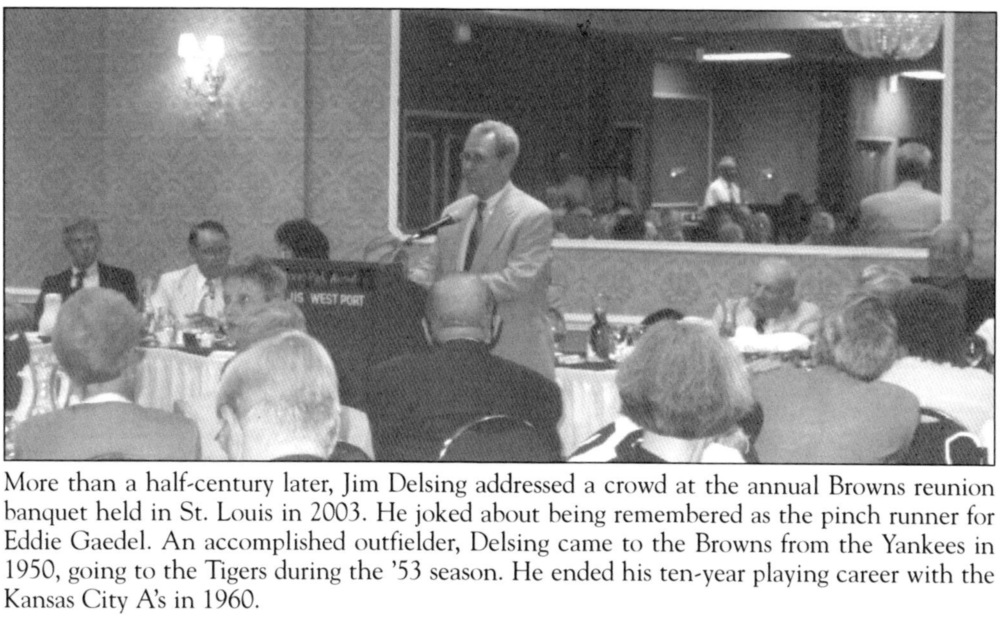

More than a half-century later, Jim Delsing addressed a crowd at the annual Browns reunion banquet held in St. Louis in 2003. He joked about being remembered as the pinch runner for Eddie Gaedel. An accomplished outfielder, Delsing came to the Browns from the Yankees in 1950, going to the Tigers during the '53 season. He ended his ten-year playing career with the Kansas City A's in 1960.

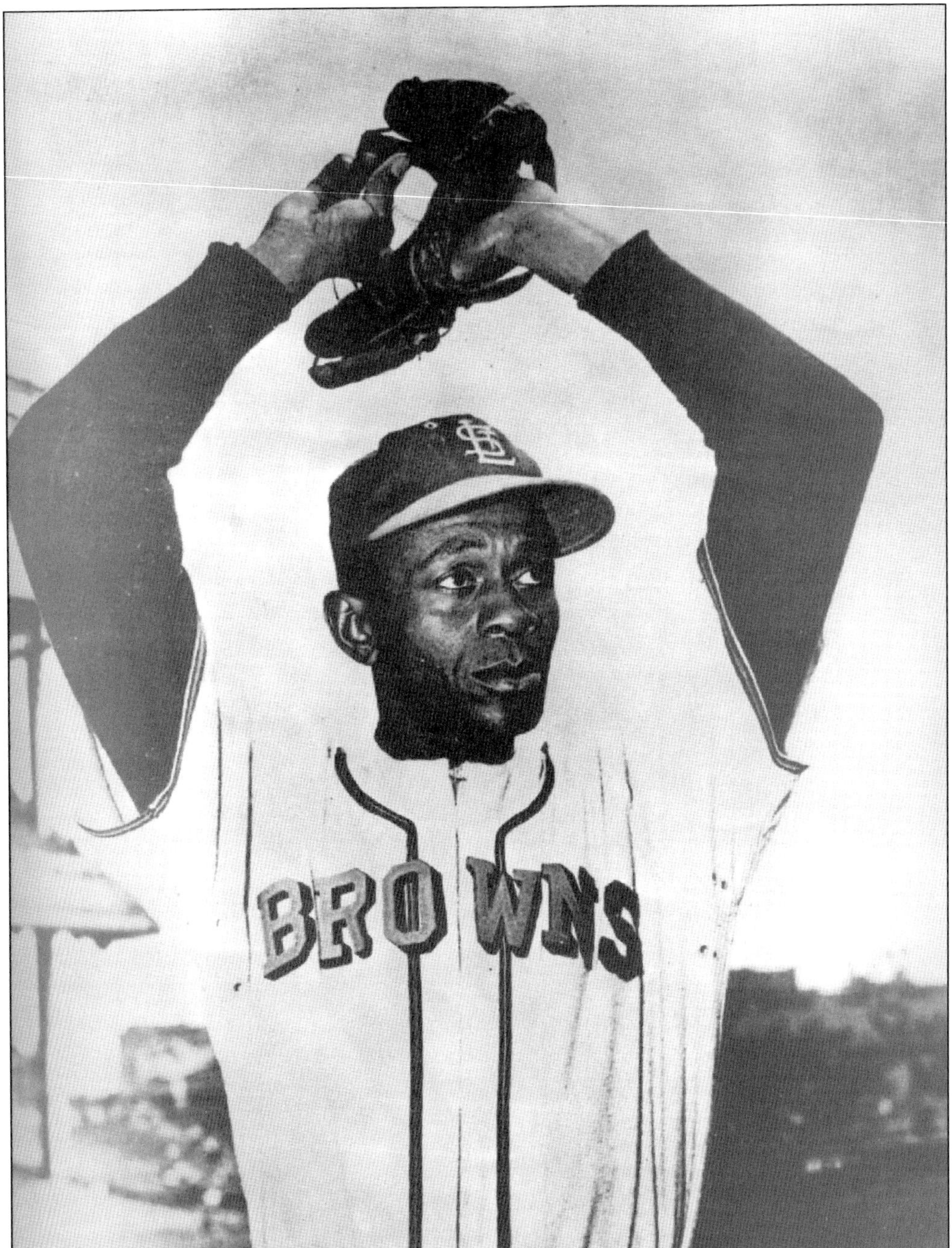

Robert LeRoy (Satchel) Paige pitched for a number of Negro League teams, including the newly formed Negro American League St. Louis Stars of 1937 (the NNL Stars disbanded after 1931). Then, after Jackie Robinson broke major league baseball's color line in 1947, the gates opened for talented players like Paige. Signing with Cleveland the following year, Satchel later pitched for the St. Louis Browns (1951–1953). The site of many Negro League games before that group disappeared in the mid-1950s, Sportsman's Park by then hosted games integrated on the field as well as in the stands.

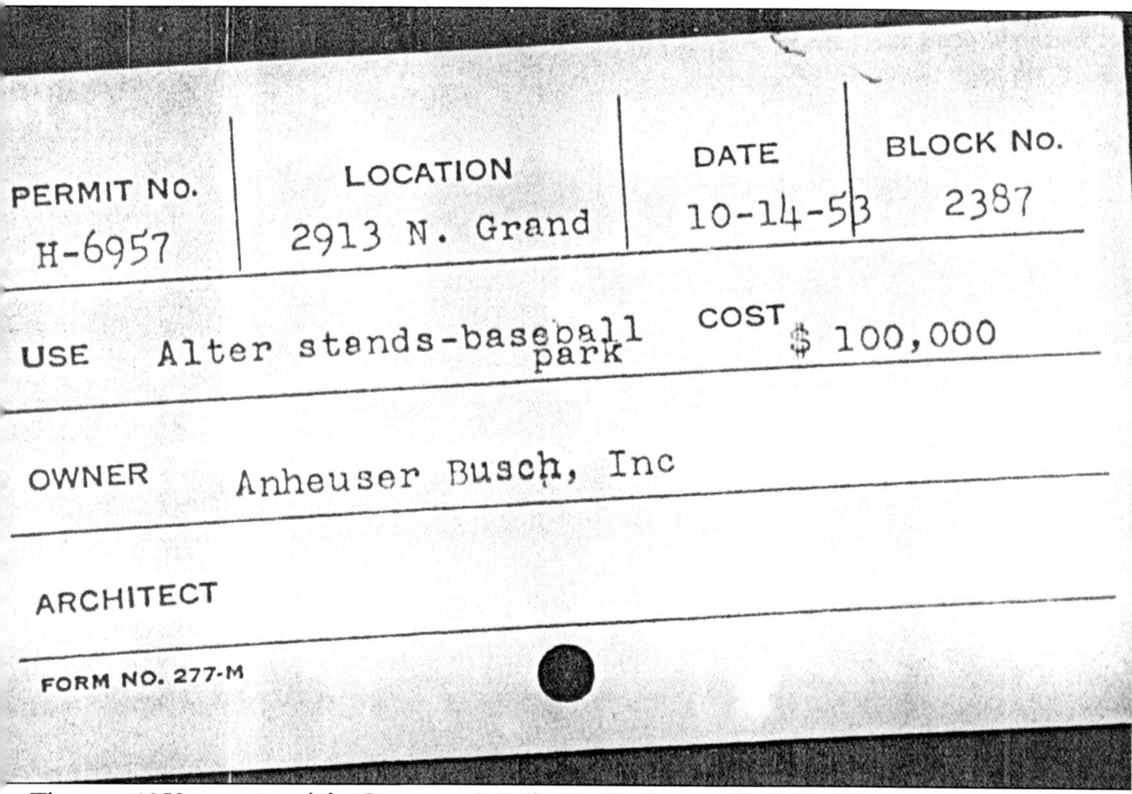
PERMIT NO. H-6957

LOCATION 2913 N. Grand

DATE 10-14-53

BLOCK NO. 2387

USE Alter stands-baseball park

COST $ 100,000

OWNER Anheuser Busch, Inc

ARCHITECT

FORM NO. 277-M

The year 1953 was pivotal for Sportsman's Park. Cardinal owner Fred Saigh's conviction on tax evasion led to a sale of the Cardinals to local beer king, Anheuser-Busch, Inc. Selling Sportsman's Park to the new Cards owner, Bill Veeck sold the Browns to Baltimore when the season ended. Renamed Busch Stadium for the new owner, the park benefited by some needed renovations. Much of the work was done during the off season, this building permit documents the estimated cost of stand alterations. (Courtesy of the St. Louis City Hall Central File.)

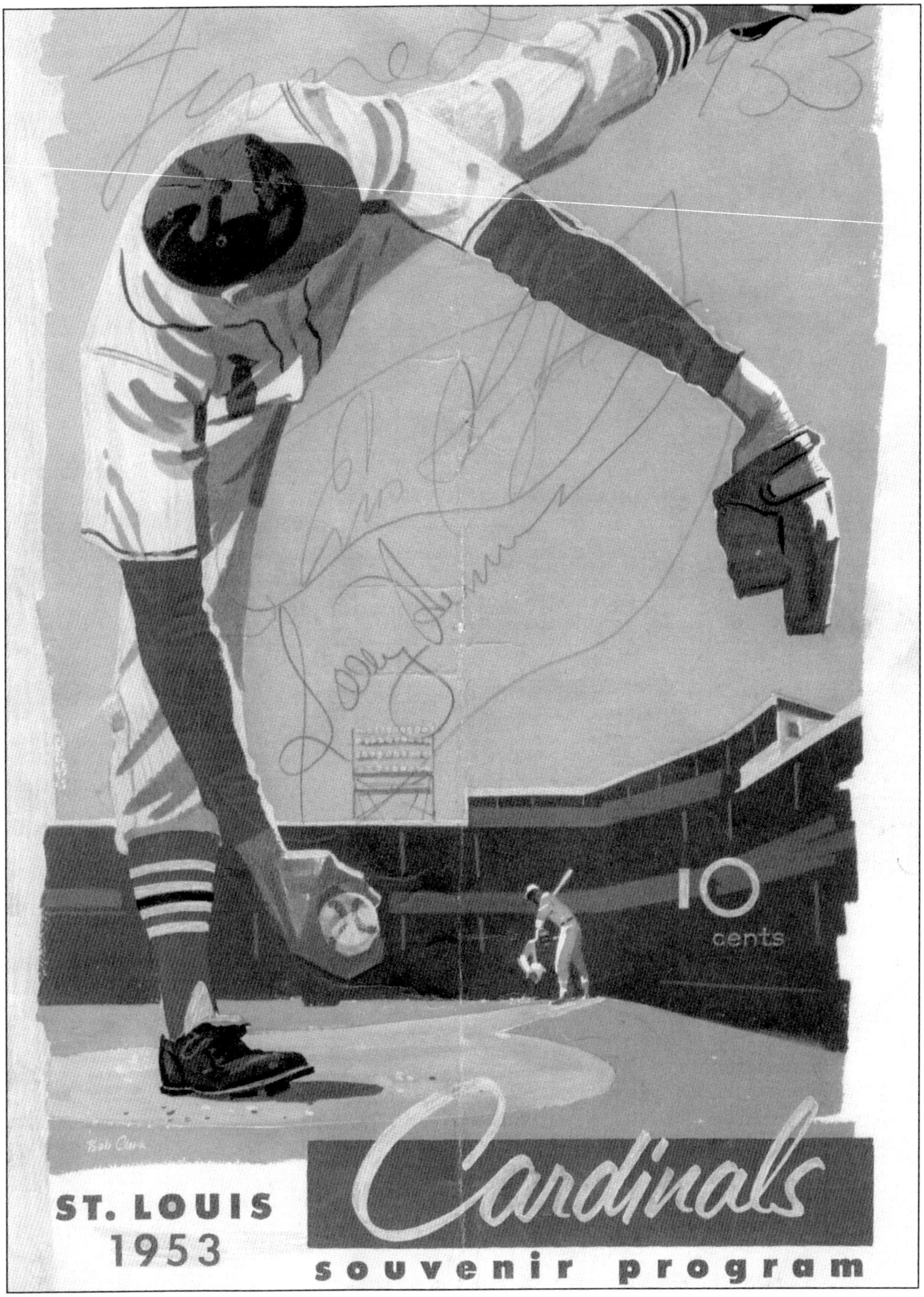

This 1953 Cardinal program looks considerably different than the '45 version seen on page 49, but the price is still a dime. Looking closely, one can see penciled autographs of Enos Slaughter (see photo on page 52) and Solly Hemus. Infielder Hemus played with the Cards from 1949 to 1956 before going to the Phillies. He returned to the Cards in 1959 to end his career at Sportsman's Park.

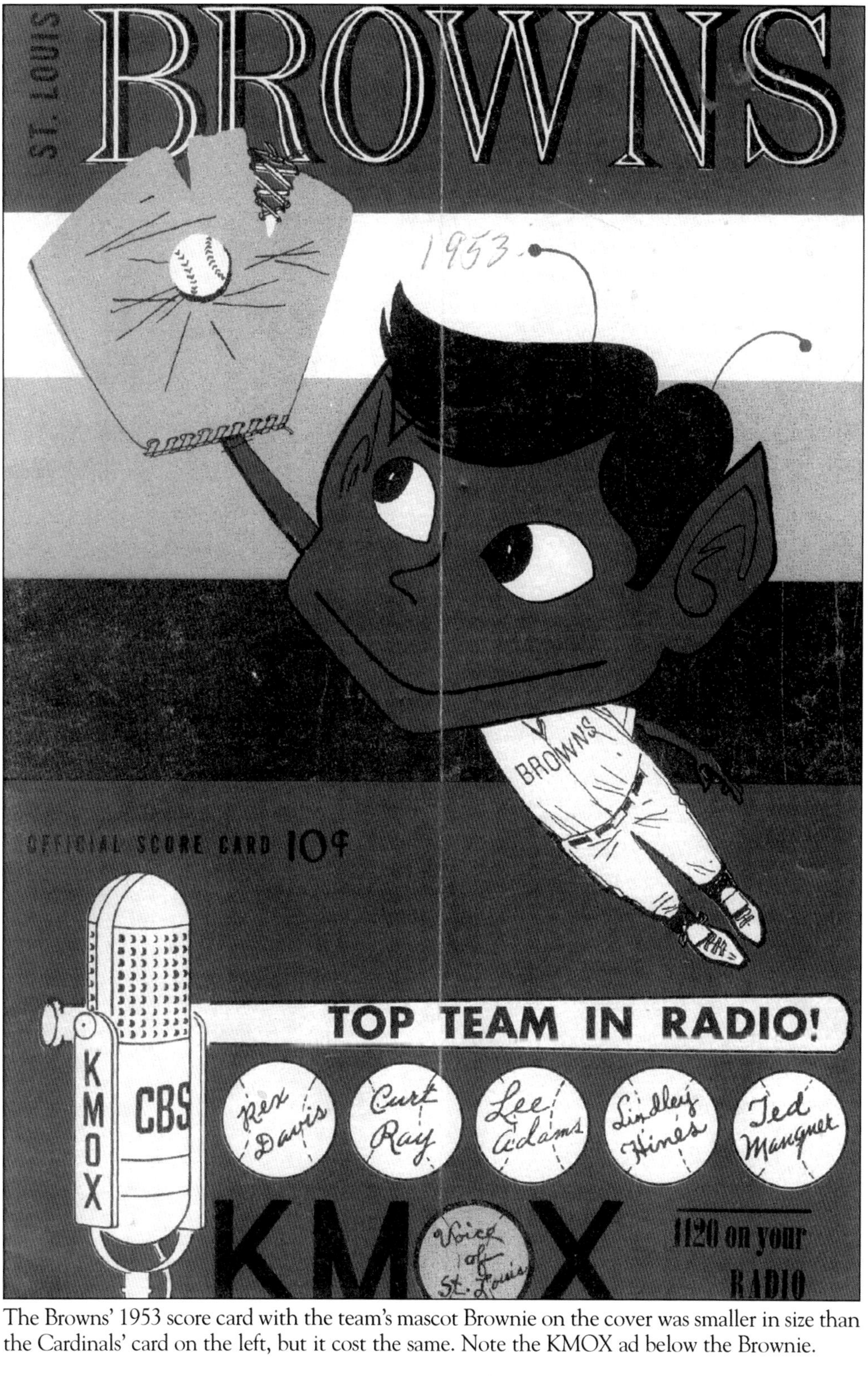

The Browns' 1953 score card with the team's mascot Brownie on the cover was smaller in size than the Cardinals' card on the left, but it cost the same. Note the KMOX ad below the Brownie.

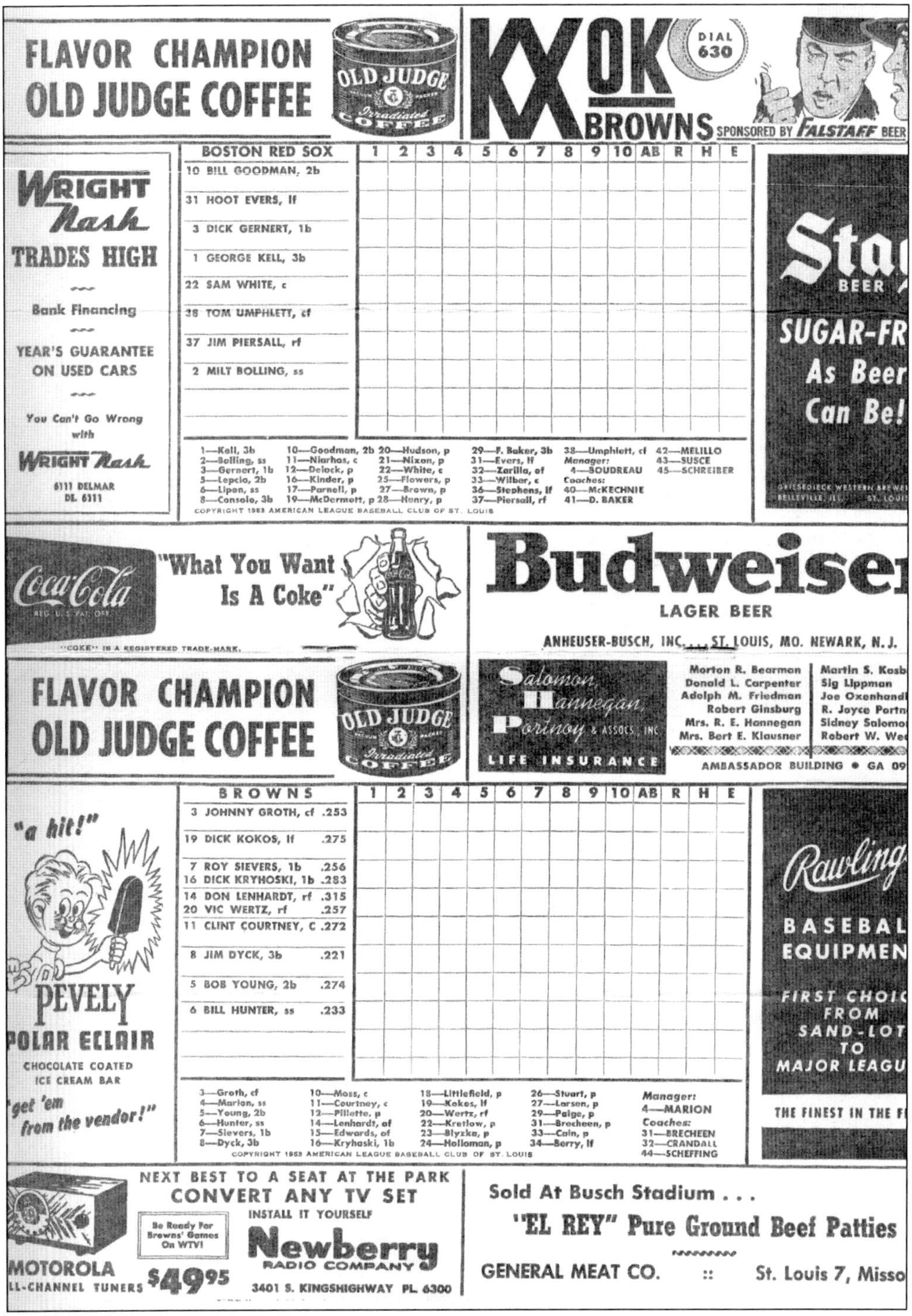

With KMOX advertised on the cover of this 1953 score card, KXOK touts the Browns games inside (see top right). Television in its infancy at the time, radio was still king. Note the Newberry Radio ad (bottom left).

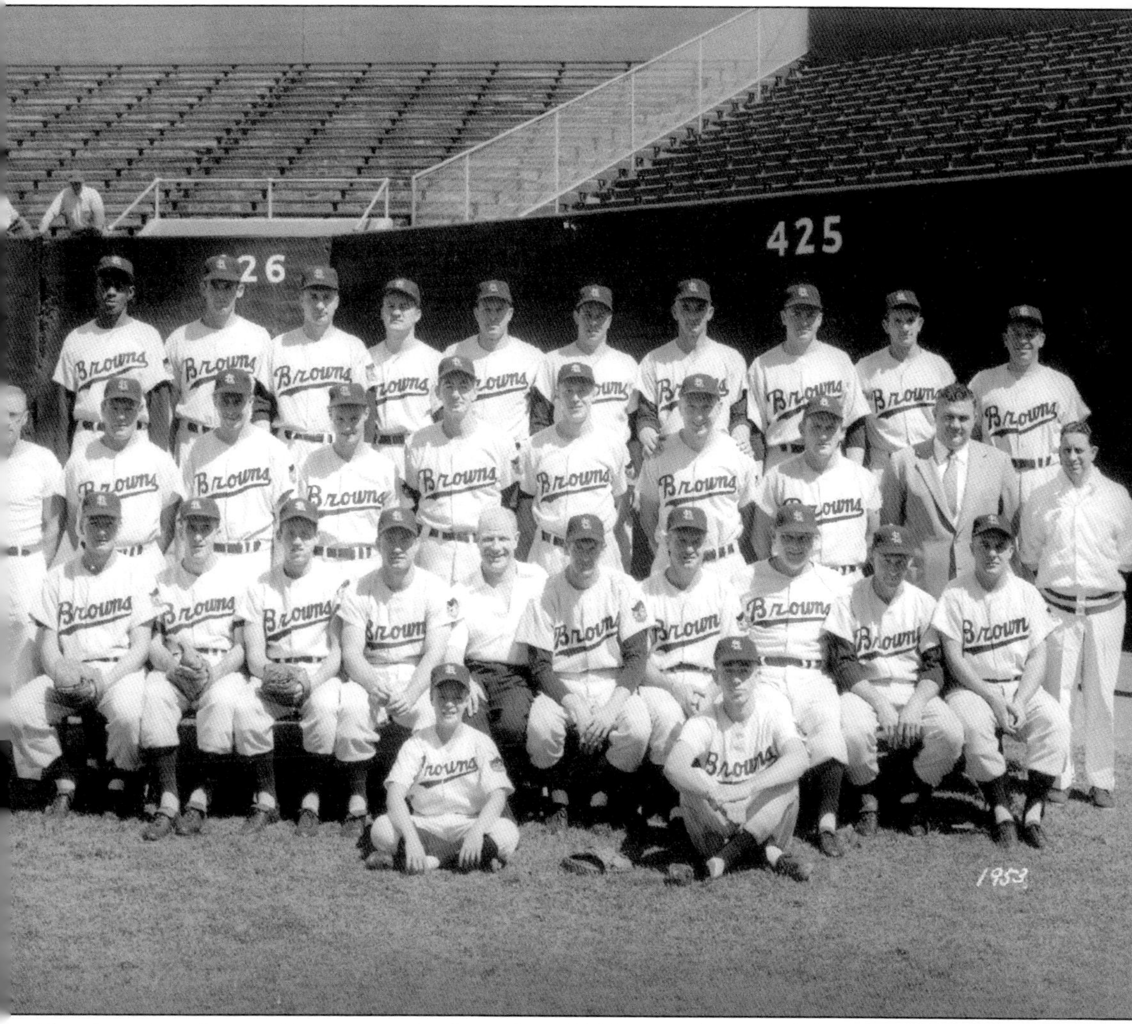

The American League Browns, posing here for a 1953 team photo, left St. Louis to become the 1954 Baltimore Orioles. Proving that the cherished memories of true baseball fans only grow stronger, a Browns' Fan Club formed over 30 years later. During the season of the fiftieth anniversary of the Browns' departure, the fan club hosted a reunion banquet in St. Louis. The event, scheduled to coincide with the weekend of a scheduled Cards-Orioles series, brought a number of former Brownies to town. (Courtesy of of Allied Photo, St. Louis.)

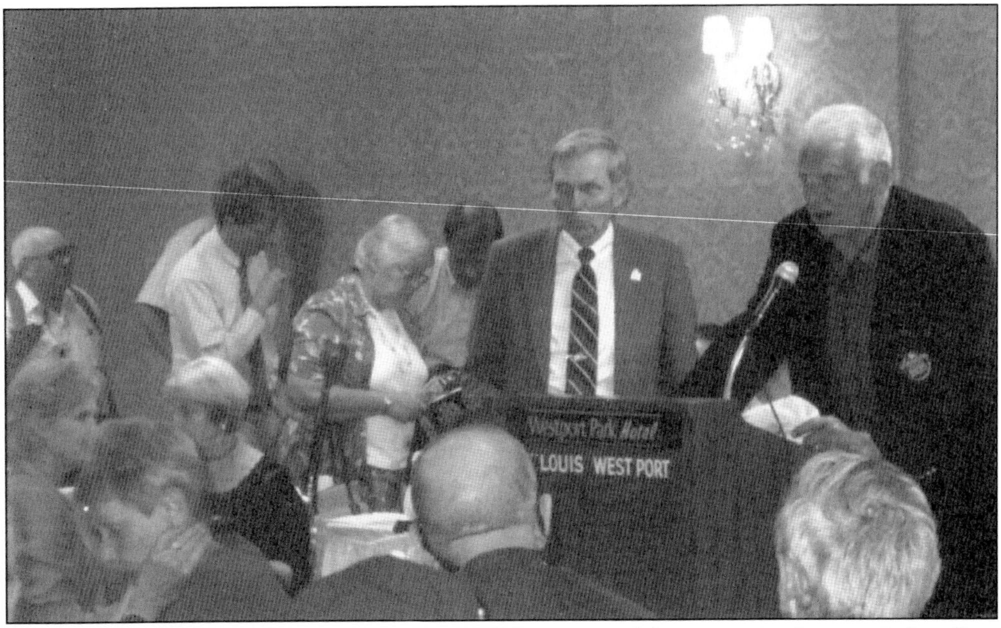

Attending the St. Louis Browns reunion in 2003, renowned former major league pitcher Don Larsen spoke to the assembly. In this photo he is standing to the right of fan club President Fred Heger. Beginning his big league career with the '53 Browns, Larsen later made history on October 8, 1956, by hurling the first, and thus far only, World Series perfect game. As a New York Yankee then, he shut down the Brooklyn Dodgers in game five of the big event.

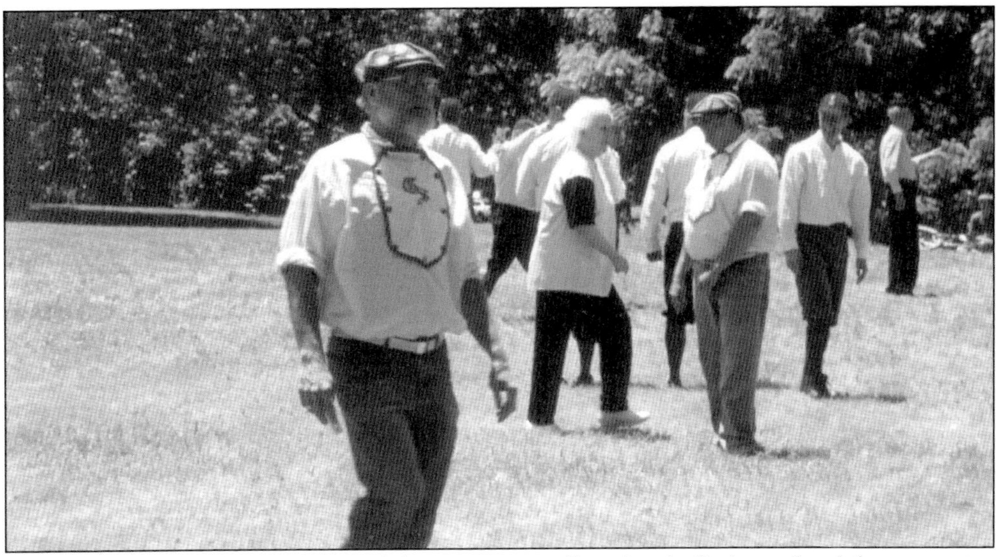

Although Eddie Gaedel (see page 57) was never really a baseball player, he did get a major league at bat. At the time, a rumor circulated that Bill Veeck considered using Erma Bergmann (see pages 53-54) to pitch in the same game that featured Gaedel. But Gaedel's name is listed in the Baseball Encyclopedia right along with all major league players of the past. A better than fair pitcher and all-around baseball player, Erma never got the chance. However, she did throw out the first pitch at a VBBA St. Louis Perfectos game in June of 2003. Seen in this photo moments later, she exits the field followed by team members' admiring smiles.

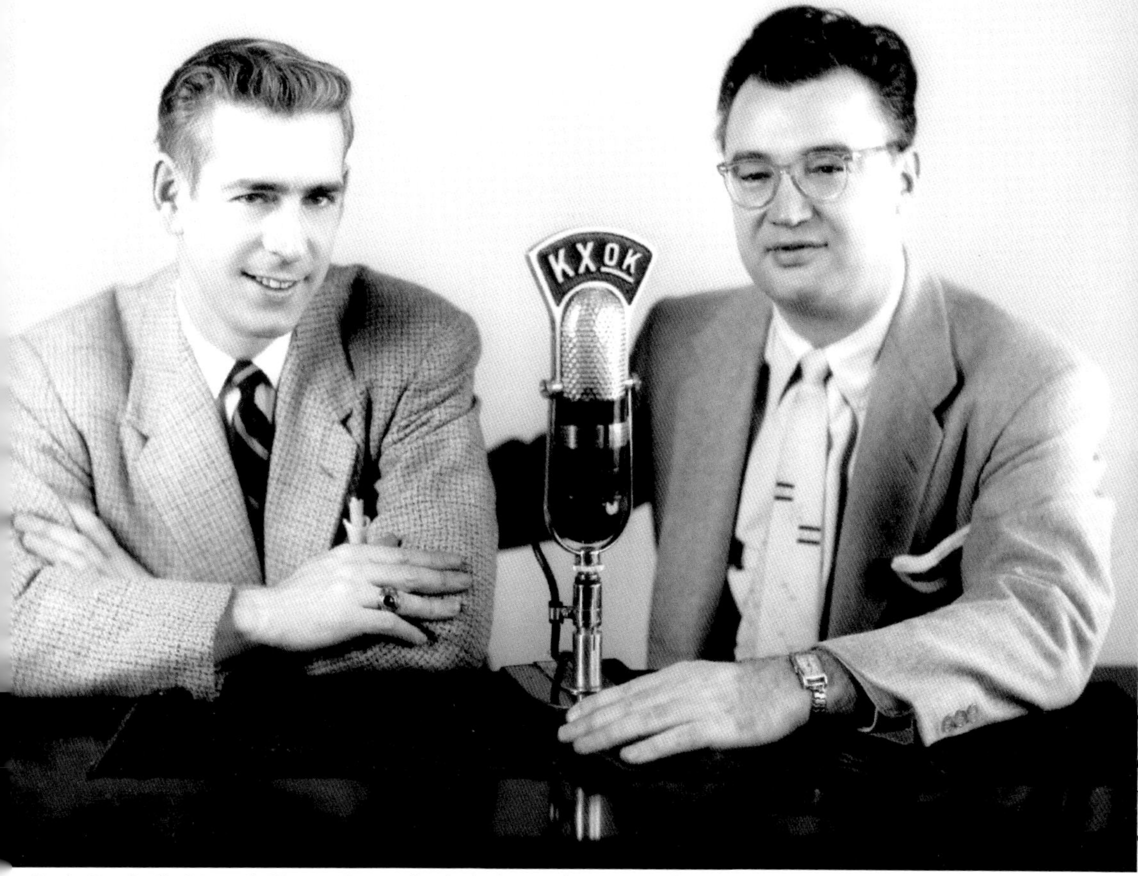

Jack Buck (left) and Harry Caray (right) share the microphone in this1954 photo. A short time later, they began broadcasting from KMOX. Other voices, including France Laux and retired ballplayers Dizzy Dean and Joe Garagiola, brought St. Louis big league baseball over the airwaves. Yet the names of these two young men, both destined for permanent recognition in Cooperstown, remain those most often associated with baseball broadcasting in St. Louis and Chicago. Caray began announcing for the Cardinals in 1945, and Buck joined him nine years later. Leaving St. Louis after 1969, and announcing for Oakland and then the White Sox, Caray spent the remainder of his career doing play-by-play for the Chicago Cubs (1982–1997). Buck, except for a brief detour at ABC in 1960, continued on to be the eminent voice of the Cardinals through 2001. (Courtesy of Allied Photo, St. Louis.)

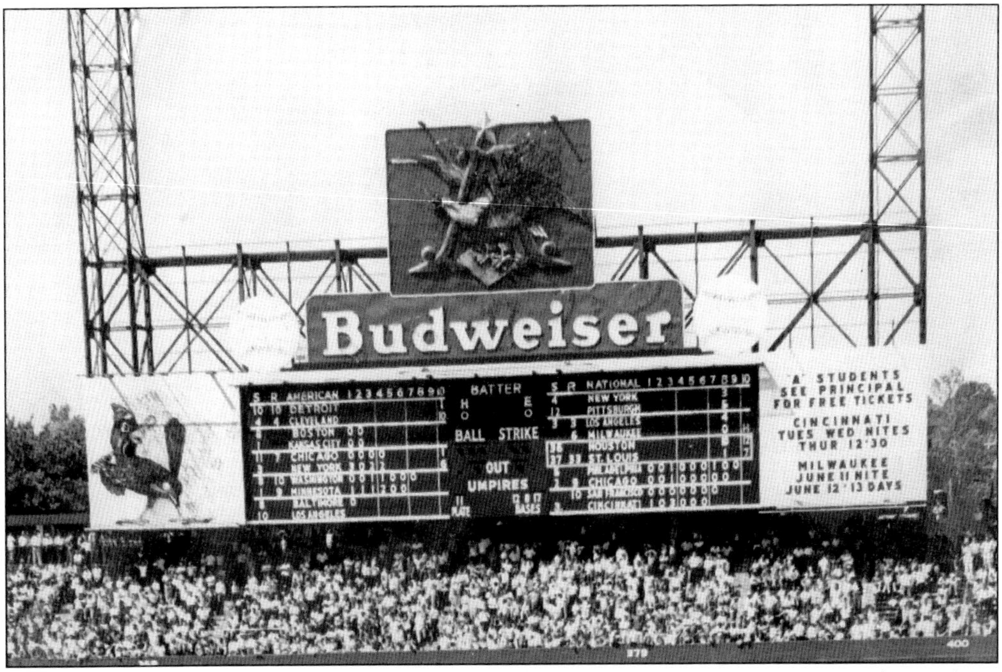

When the 1954 season started, fans were awed by the impressive renovations to the stadium made by new owner Anheuser-Busch. In addition to structural and cosmetic enhancements, the now-familiar flying A and eagle Budweiser sign above the scoreboard made its debut. The other ads gone from the outfield walls, it was to be the only advertising sign in the park. This photo, shot in the mid-1950s by a high school student between games of a double-header, shows the dominance of the famed letter and bird.

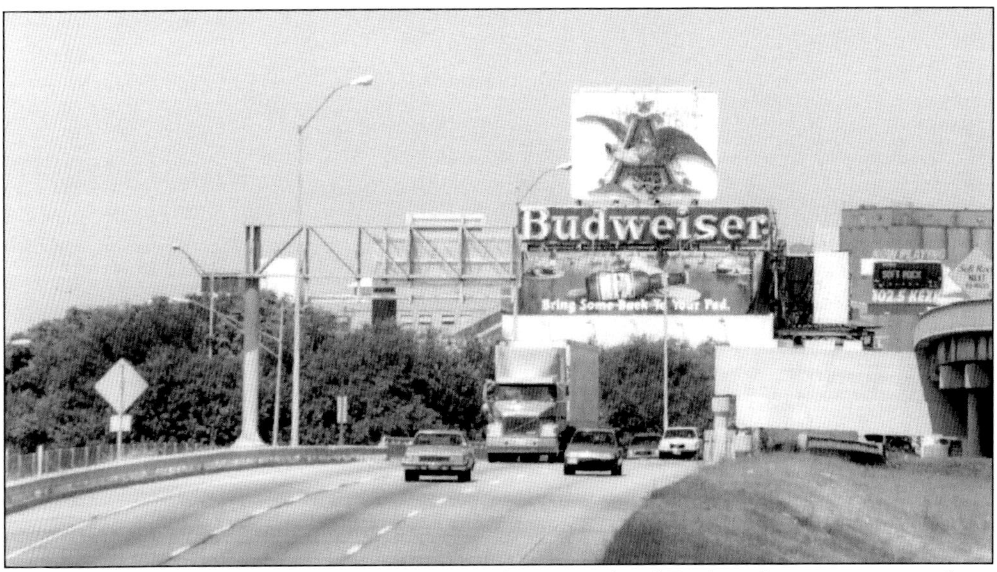

Years after the major leagues abandoned the park at Grand and Dodier, this sign went up along west bound Highway 40 near downtown St. Louis. Still there at this writing, it gave rise to an urban legend that it was the same sign that once lit up above the Cardinals scoreboard at old Sportsman's Park.

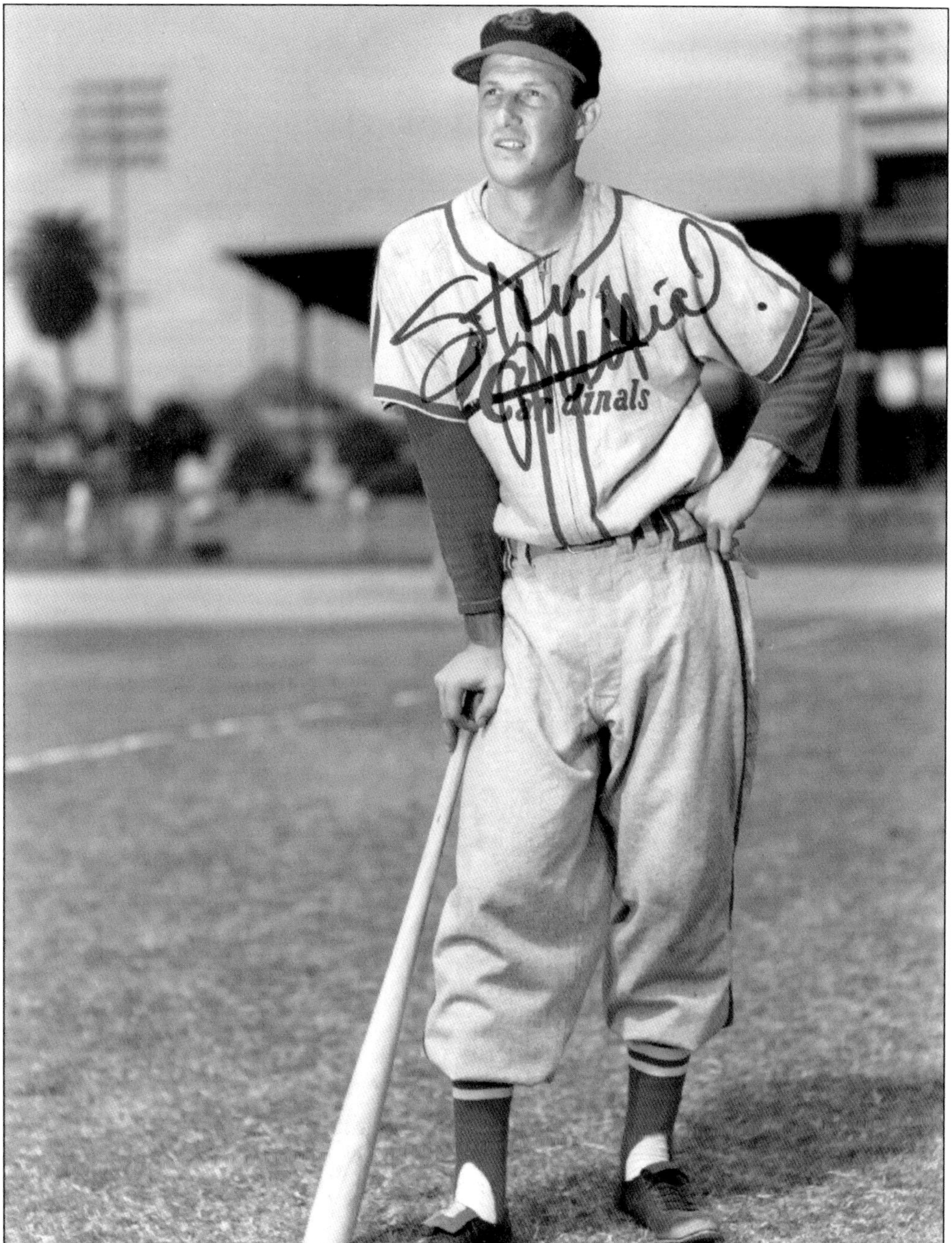

Already a star by the mid-50s, now Hall-of-Famer Stan "The Man" Musial became a Cardinal icon. Spending his entire professional playing career with the Cardinals (1940–1963), his unorthodox batting stance later gained the recognition of generations of fans who grew up too late to see him play. His larger-then-life statue became a landmark and meeting place next to the downtown stadium erected after his retirement.

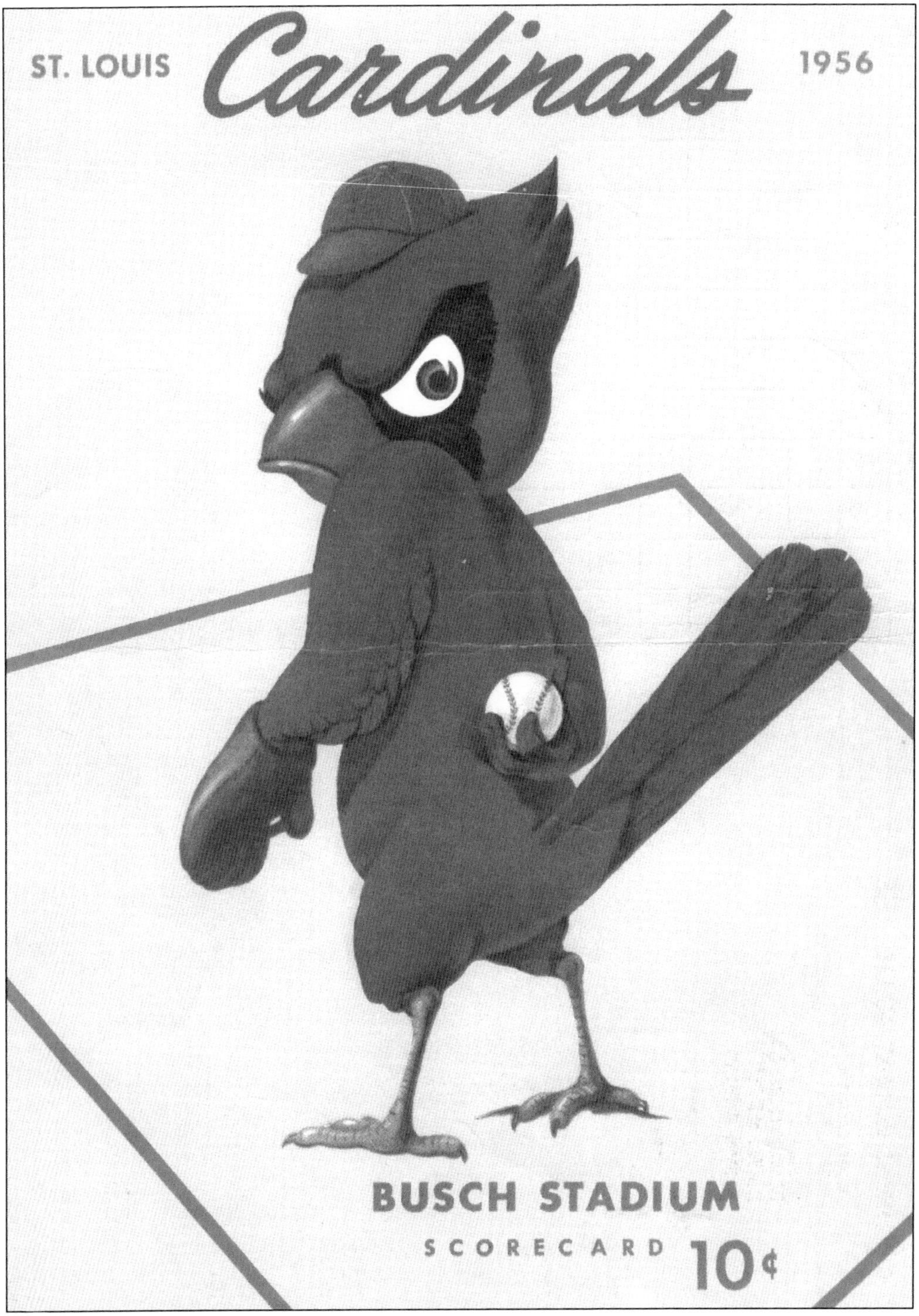

This angry red bird on the 1956 Cardinals scorecard cover resembles the rendering for the 2003 card. However, this bird is a pitcher, and his modern counterpart is an abnormally broad shouldered batter wearing more of a grin than a snarl. And, inflation changed the purchase price, then ten cents, to $2.50 by 2003.

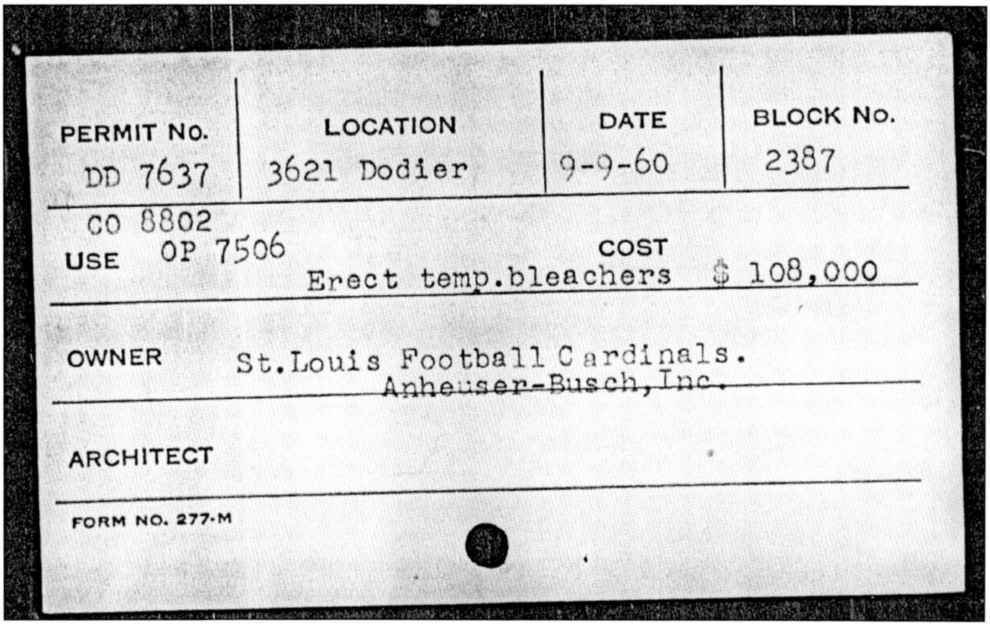

PERMIT No.	LOCATION	DATE	BLOCK No.
DD 7637	3621 Dodier	9-9-60	2387

CO 8802
USE OP 7506 COST
Erect temp.bleachers $ 108,000

OWNER St.Louis Football Cardinals.
~~Anheuser-Busch, Inc.~~

ARCHITECT

FORM NO. 277-M

An acquisition from the windy city, the Chicago Cardinals football team moved to St. Louis in 1961. Busch Stadium, still called Sportsman's Park by many, became the arena for professional football as well as baseball. Following the baseball season that year, the club erected temporary bleachers in right field, the end zones in left field and the first base line. This building permit gives the cost of the bleachers erected before the October 2nd home opener of the NFL St. Louis Cardinals. (Courtesy of St. Louis City Hall Central File.)

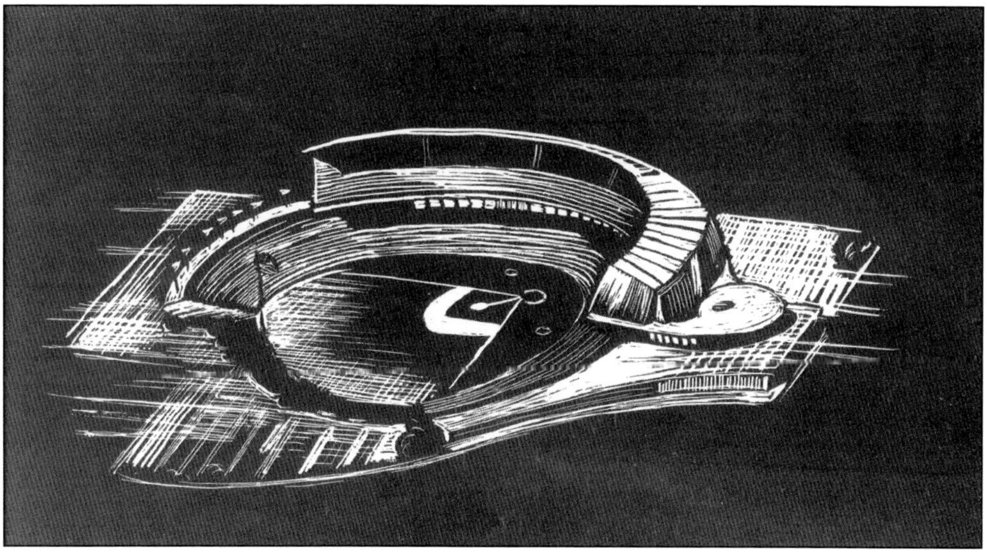

Planning for the bicentennial of the founding of the city of St. Louis included replacing the aging ballpark with a new downtown stadium. In anticipation of a 1964 grand opening, this artists rendering of the new structure appeared in the 1960 Cardinals Yearbook. Bearing little semblance to the final product, which opened two years later than expected, this sketch looks more like the 1944 concept (see page 48). (Image by permission of the St. Louis Cardinals Baseball Club.)

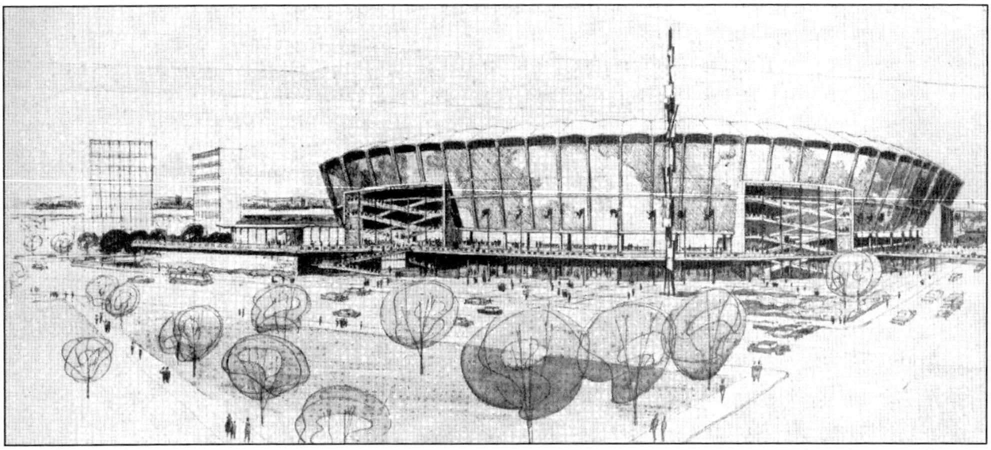

In 1961, the target date for the new stadium still 1964, this concept appeared in the Cardinals' Yearbook. Not exactly the Busch Memorial Stadium that opened in 1966, but similar. (Image by permission of the St. Louis Cardinals Baseball Club.)

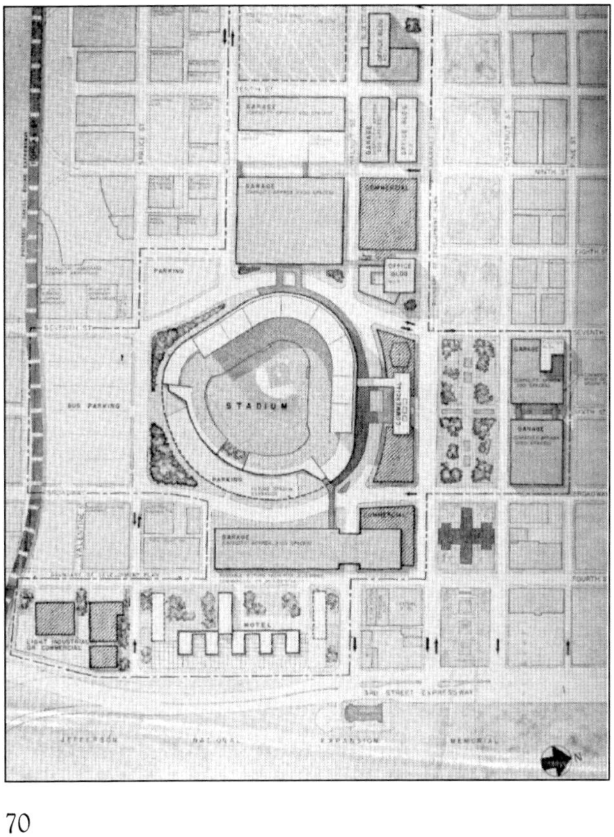

Appearing on the same page as the above image, this map shows the overall layout planned for the new stadium project. Notice that the stadium's shape is more traditional than the circular design of the final product. (Image by permission of the St. Louis Cardinals Baseball Club.)

A former baseball and basketball star for Creighton University who also shot baskets for the world famous Harlem Globetrotters, Bob Gibson pitched for the Cardinals for all 17 years of his big league playing career (1959–1975). Many who witnessed his pitching performance describe the experience almost with reverence. One of the brightest stars to shine at old Busch Stadium, AKA Sportsman's Park, he furnished even more delightful memories to those who saw him play at the new downtown Busch.

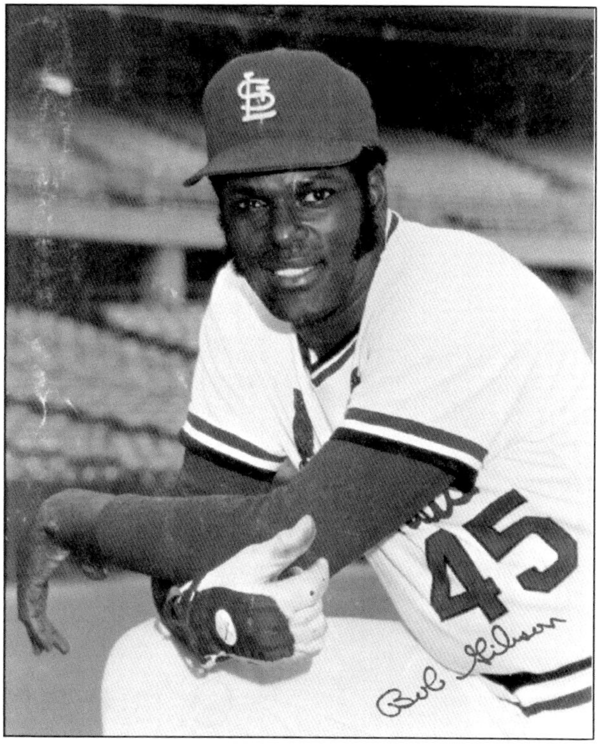

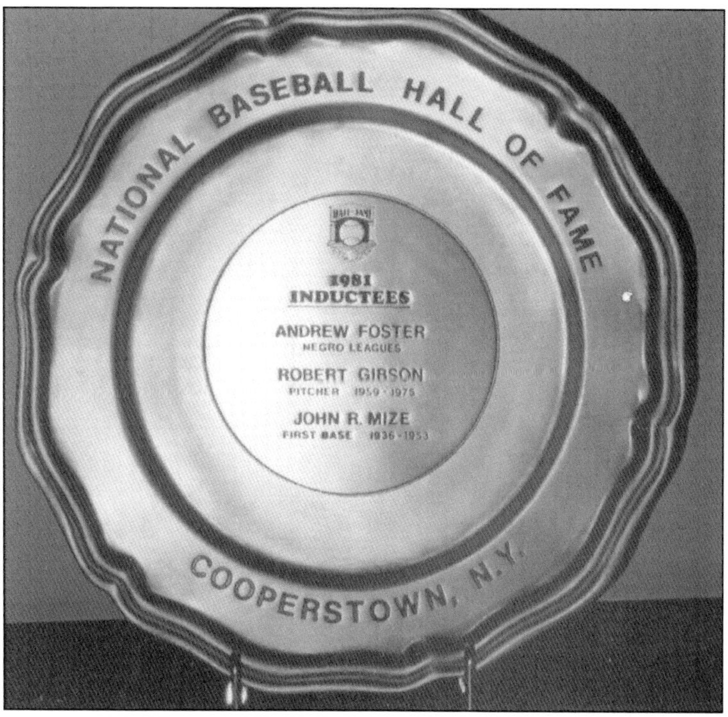

This Baseball Hall of Fame collector's plate records the 1981 inductees. Andrew "Rube" Foster founded the Negro National League in 1920. Both Gibson and Mize played for the Cardinals at old Sportsman's Park. (See Gibson above, and Mize on page 43.)

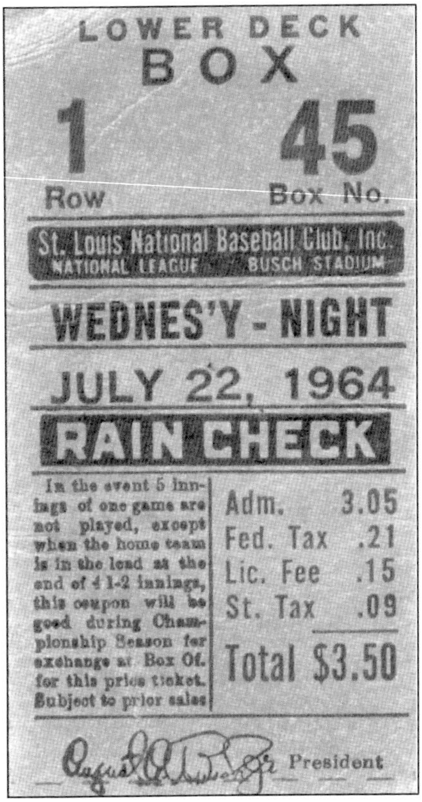

The new park did not reach fruition until 1966, so this stub is a memento of old Sportsman's Park, AKA Busch Stadium. Reflective of the changing times, a July 22, 1964 rain check shows the price of a box seat as $3.50 and the Cardinal president's signature as August A. Busch, Jr. S. Breadon's signature appears on the 1945 stubs pictured on page 51, and those grand stand tickets cost $1.25.

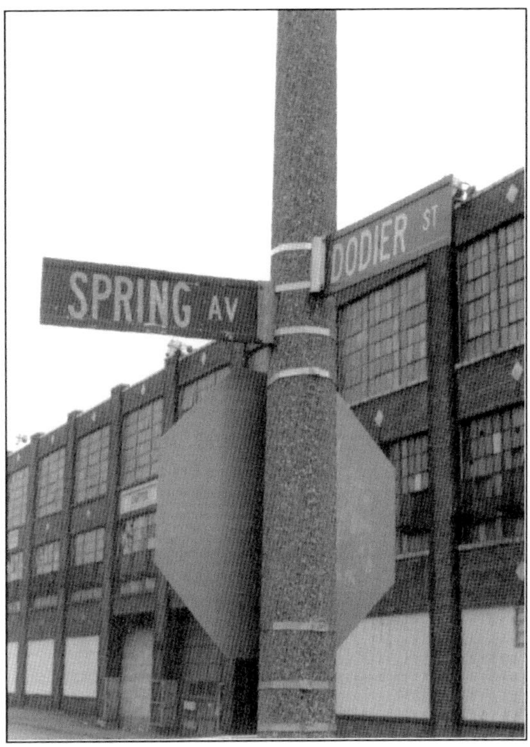

Photographed years after the Cardinals vacated the grounds across from Carter Carburetor, this street sign left little evidence of the rich baseball history of St. Louis baseball across the street. The Cardinals finally got a new stadium downtown, and played the last major league game ever held at Sportsman's Park/Busch Stadium on Sunday, May 8, 1966.

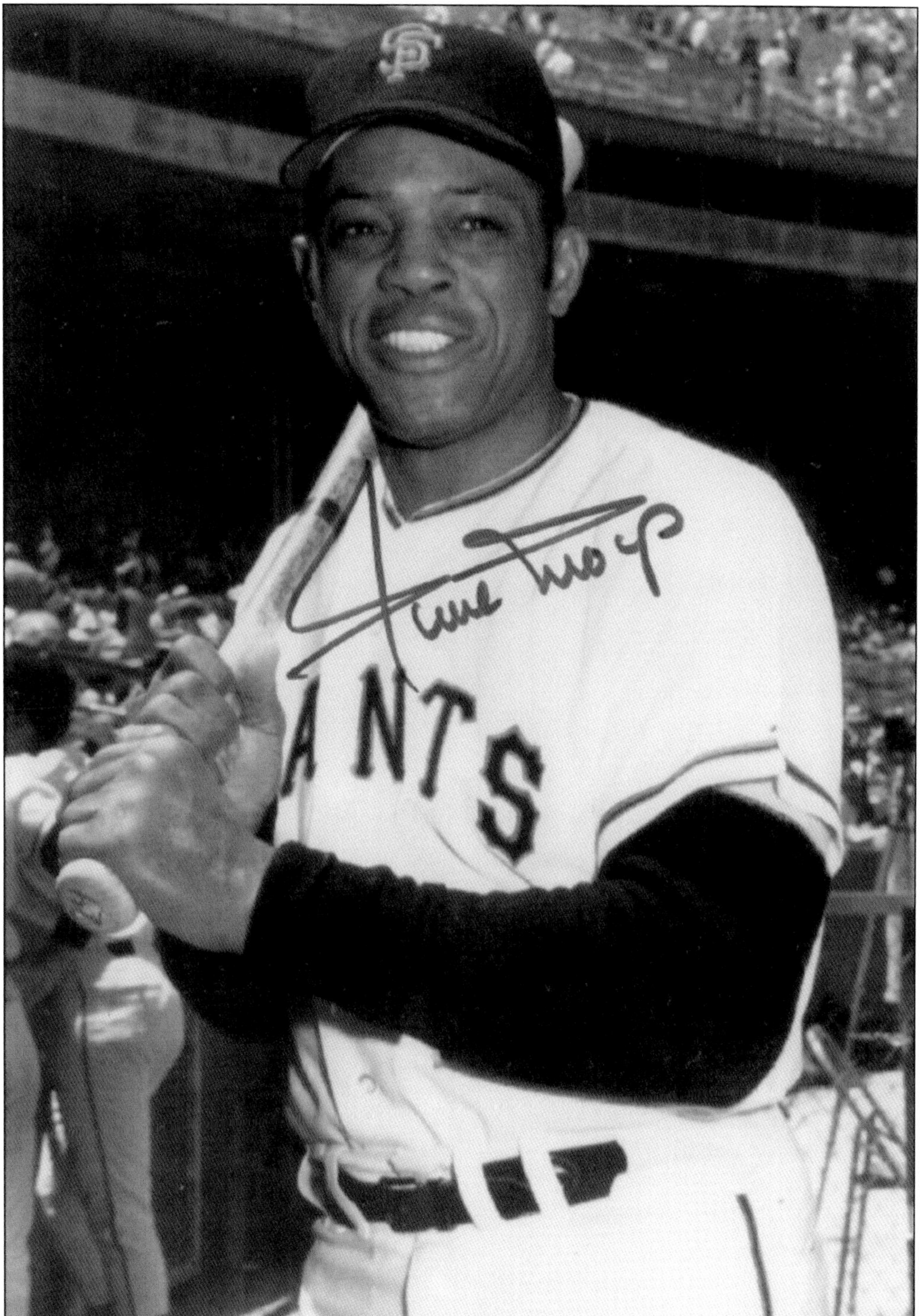

That final game in May at Sportsman's Park/Busch Stadium saw the Cardinals lose to the Giants. In the ninth inning, Giant outfielder and future Hall of Famer Willie Mays smacked the last big league home run ever tallied at the old grounds.

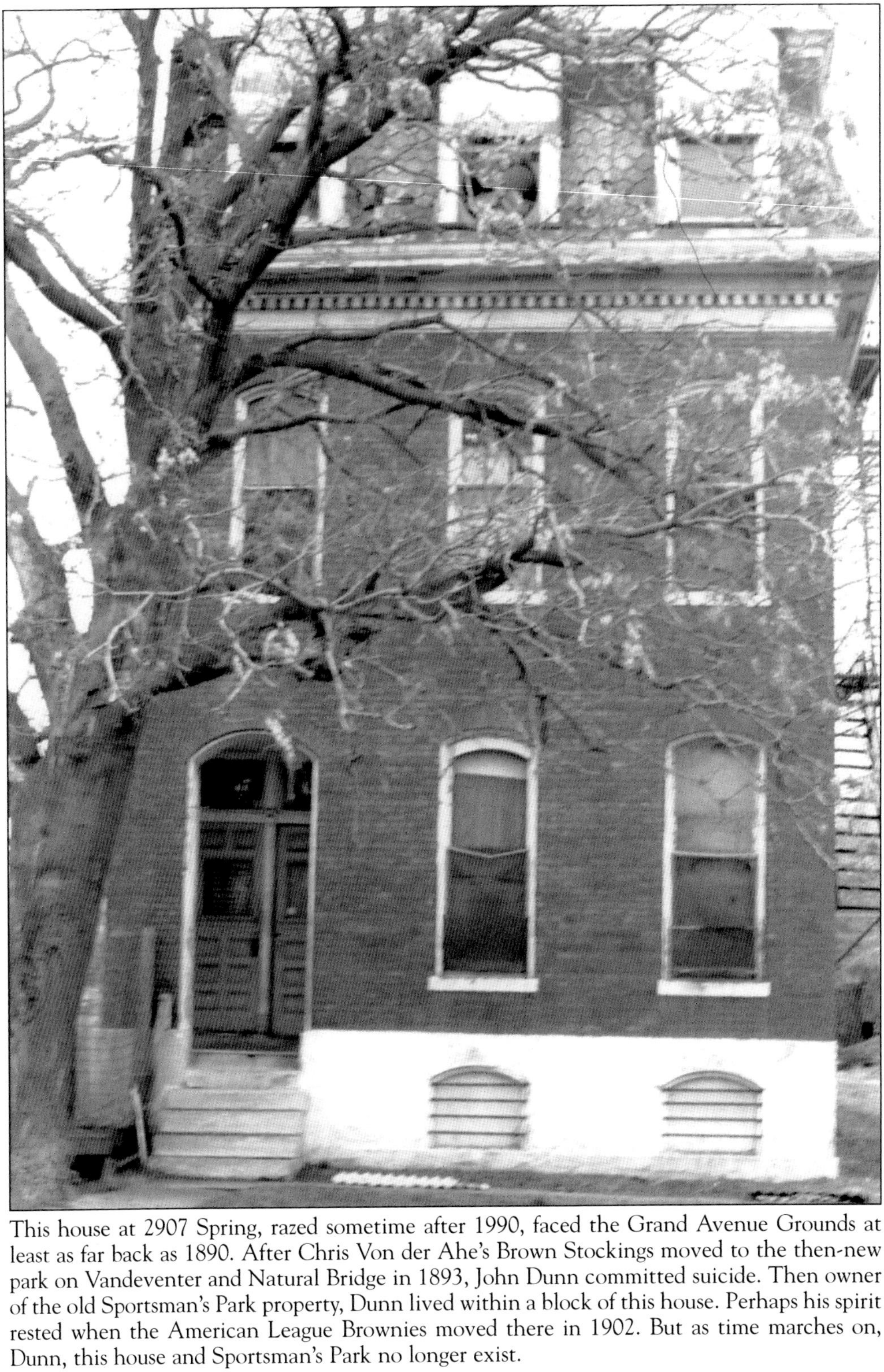

This house at 2907 Spring, razed sometime after 1990, faced the Grand Avenue Grounds at least as far back as 1890. After Chris Von der Ahe's Brown Stockings moved to the then-new park on Vandeventer and Natural Bridge in 1893, John Dunn committed suicide. Then owner of the old Sportsman's Park property, Dunn lived within a block of this house. Perhaps his spirit rested when the American League Brownies moved there in 1902. But as time marches on, Dunn, this house and Sportsman's Park no longer exist.

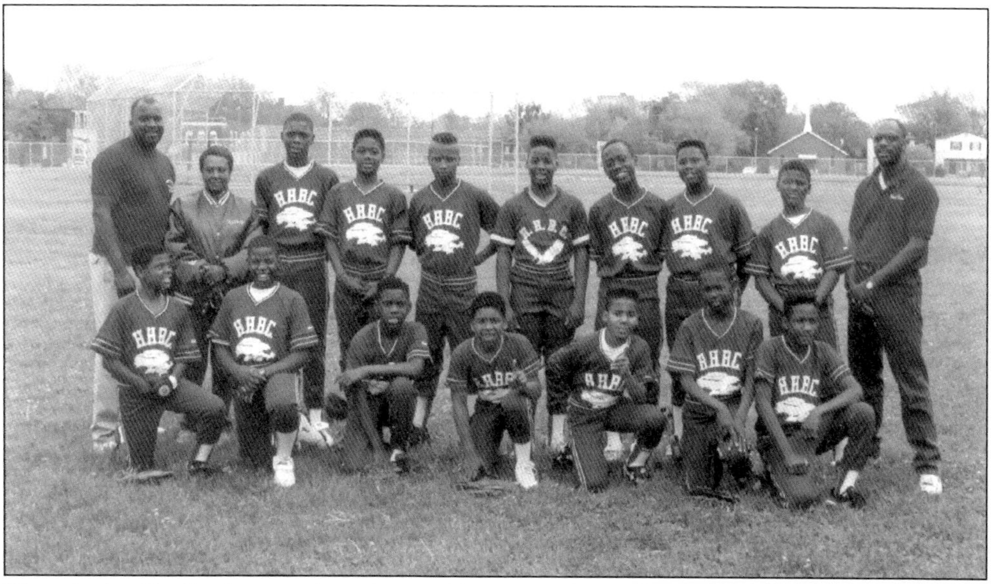

Though the Cardinals moved to the sparkling new Civic Center Busch Memorial Stadium downtown early in 1966, the old Grand Avenue Grounds continued to host the National Game. Soon erected along Dodier, the Herbert Hoover's Boys Club building (now Herbert Hoovers' Boys and Girls Club) serviced the city's youth. This baseball team, sponsored by the club, posed near the lot's playing field on April 27, 1991.

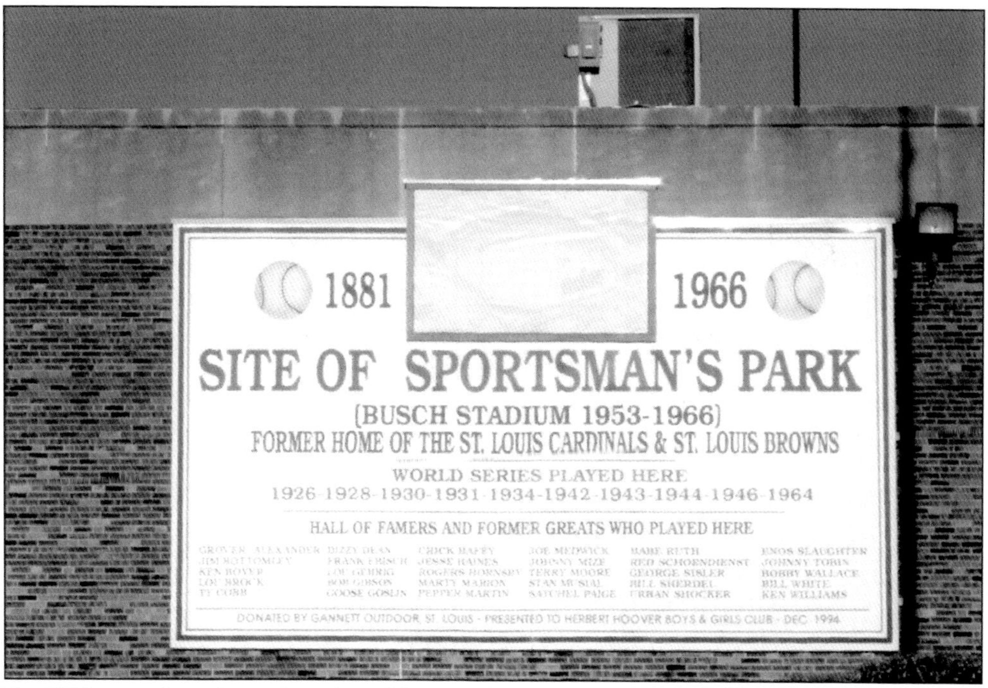

By 2003, travelers along Grand could view this commemorative billboard at the northwest corner of Grand and Dodier. The 1881 date belies the fact that the history of professional baseball there dates back to 1875. Yet the display allows those unaware of the saga of Sportsman's Park an idea of the significance of that corner in St. Louis.

Grand Avenue/Sportsman's Park Big League Teams/World Series & All Star Games

Year	Park Name	Location	Team Name	League
1875	Grand Avenue	Grand & Sullivan	Brown Stockings	National Association
1876–1877	"	"	"	National League
1882–1891	Sportsman's Park	"	"	American Association
1892	"	"	"	National League
1902–1953	"	"	Browns	American League
1920–1953	"	"	Cardinals	"
1954–1966	Busch Stadium	"	Cardinals	National League

Year	Event	St. Louis Club	Opponent	Winner
1885	World Series	Brown Stockings	Chicago NL	Tie
1886	"	"	"	St. Louis
1887	"	"	Detroit NL	Detroit
1888	"	"	New York NL	New York
1926	"	Cardinals	New York AL	St. Louis
1928	"	"	"	New York
1930	"	"	Philadelphia AL	Philadelphia
1931	"	"	"	St. Louis
1934	"	"	Detroit AL	St. Louis
1942	"	"	New York AL	St. Louis
1943	"	"	"	New York
1944	"	Cards/Browns	St. Louis NL/AL	St. Louis NL
1946	"	Cardinals	Boston AL	St. Louis
1964	"	"	New York AL	St. Louis

Year	All Star Game	Grand Ave. Park	Winner	Score
1940	AL vs. NL	Sportsman's Park	NL	4-0
1948	"	"	AL	5-2
1957	"	Busch Stadium	AL	6-5

Four

Busch Memorial Stadium

The final stage in erecting the spectacular Gateway Arch occurred in 1965. Funding for a 34-block downtown improvement plan came from a public bond issue and other sources. After a number of delays, including a fire and several union disputes, Civic Center Busch Memorial Stadium (its official name) finally opened in 1966. Intended for use by both the Baseball and Football Cardinals, the new arena gained financing through private capital. Anheuser-Busch head and Cardinal President August A. Busch Jr. reportedly made the single biggest contribution.

In the closing ceremony immediately following the last game at old Sportsman's Park, a helicopter retrieved home plate and transported it to the new facility. Four days later, on May 12, 1966, the cry of "play ball" resounded throughout the spacious concrete enclosure downtown for the first time.Though ham and cheese sandwiches replaced the traditional hot dogs, because the gas had yet to be connected to the grills, there was little else to complain about on that cool 55-degree spring evening at the Cardinals' new home.

The $1.5 million electric scoreboard, featuring a native cardinal bird designed to flutter and chirp for a home run, thrilled the 46,048 fans in attendance. The opening ceremonies included a helicopter touching down on center field to deliver the American flag. The Cards finally took to the field shortly after eight. Cardinal pitcher Ray Washburn delivered the first pitch, and the redbirds delighted the crowd by defeating the Atlanta Braves, 4-3, in 12 innings.

Thus began the illustrious annals of what we today call Busch Stadium. Designed by internationally known architect Edward Durrell Stone, the huge new amphitheater resembled a masterpiece of ancient engineering, the inimitable Roman Coliseum. Its 70-foot canopy, supported by a row of open arches encircling the top complimented the distant Gateway Arch. A relatively new concept for baseball at the time, instead of the traditional rectangular or oval shape, it used a circular design to accommodate football as well as baseball. Moveable seats could convert the field accordingly. This then was the vision of the future.

By the end of the 2003 season, Busch looked the same on the outside, not counting the statues of former Cardinal players—the first and largest being the familiar representation of Stan Musial unveiled in 1968. Yet, various changes to the interior occurred over time. When the park first opened, the field's natural grass benefited from a soil-warming system called the first in the country. A news report stated that it watered itself electronically. Then, in 1970, a revolutionary new material called Astroturf replaced the grass. The football Cardinals left town in 1988, and St. Louis's revered beer and baseball baron August (Gussie) Busch passed away the following year. Then, in 1995 Anheuser-Busch sold the Cardinals to a group of investors. The new owners made a number of changes, the most notable being the removal of the no-longer-valued Astroturf. Again, the Cardinals could play baseball on real grass like Jeremiah Fruin's nineteenth century Empires. Another change of import made a step backwards in time—the installation of a manually operated scoreboard in center field.

Throughout the years at the downtown Busch Stadium, generations of baseball fans took in its ambiance. Each one of the millions of fans who ever attended a Cardinal game there experienced at least one unforgettable event. Yet, to a true baseball aficionado, every pitch, every inning, every game is a one of a kind happening. When conjured up in one's mind years later, the setting is unmistakable. As with Sportsman's Park, Busch Stadium will live on in photos, documents and living memories.

So many dramatic and remarkable episodes occurred at Busch Stadium over the years, it would be futile to summate in a few hundred words. Like the time in 1988 when non-pitcher Jose Oquendo filled in at the mound for four innings due to a depleted pitching staff. To the crowd's delight, he only allowed two runs. That is just one of countless such unforgettable happenings. But almost everyone remembers the big games. At Busch, the Cardinals played in five World Series, winning twice. There future Cooperstown honorees took to the field in Cardinal uniforms—Orlando Cepada, Steve Carlton, Lou Brock, Bob Gibson and Ozzie Smith. Also wearing the birds on the bat, Red Schoendienst's managed his way to the Hall of Fame. And, the familiar voice of Jack Buck (as well as that of Harry Caray, who ended his career as the Cubs' announcer) live on in the memories of millions, many who never even got the chance to see a game at Busch.

The chart below gives a simple overview of All-Star and post-season play at downtown Busch Stadium. One can check the record books for statistics on individual achievements. Since St. Louis has been blessed with so many great players, it would take a much larger work to describe them all. The few images and descriptions of individuals in this book are just tantalizing snippets that allow some insight into the reason why baseball is still our National Game, and why St. Louis is called a Baseball Town.

Year	Event	St. Louis Stadium	Opponents	Final
1966	All Star Game	Busch Memorial	NL vs. AL	NL 2-1
1967	World Series	"	St. Louis/Boston	St. Louis 4-3
1968	World Series	"	St. Louis/Detroit	Detroit 4-3
1982	NLCS	"	St. Louis/Atlanta	St. Louis 3-0
1982	World Series	"	St. Loius/Milwaukee	St. Louis 4-3
1985	NLCS	"	St. Louis/Los Angeles	St. Louis 4-2
1985	World Series	"	St. Loius/Kansas City	KC 4-3
1987	NLCS	"	St. Louis/San Francisco	St. Loius 4-3
1987	World Series	"	St. Louis/Minnesota	MN 4-3
1996	NLDS	"	St. Lois/San Diego	St. Loius 3-0
1996	NLCS	"	St. Louis/Atlanta	Atlanta 4-3
2000	NLDS	"	St. Louis/Atlanta	St. Louis 3-1
2000	NLCS	"	St. Louis/New York	NY 3-1
2001	NLDS	"	St. Louis/Arizona	Arizona 3-2
2002	NLDS	"	St. Louis/Arizona	St. Louis 3-0
2002	NLCS	"	St. Louis/San Francisco	SF 4-1

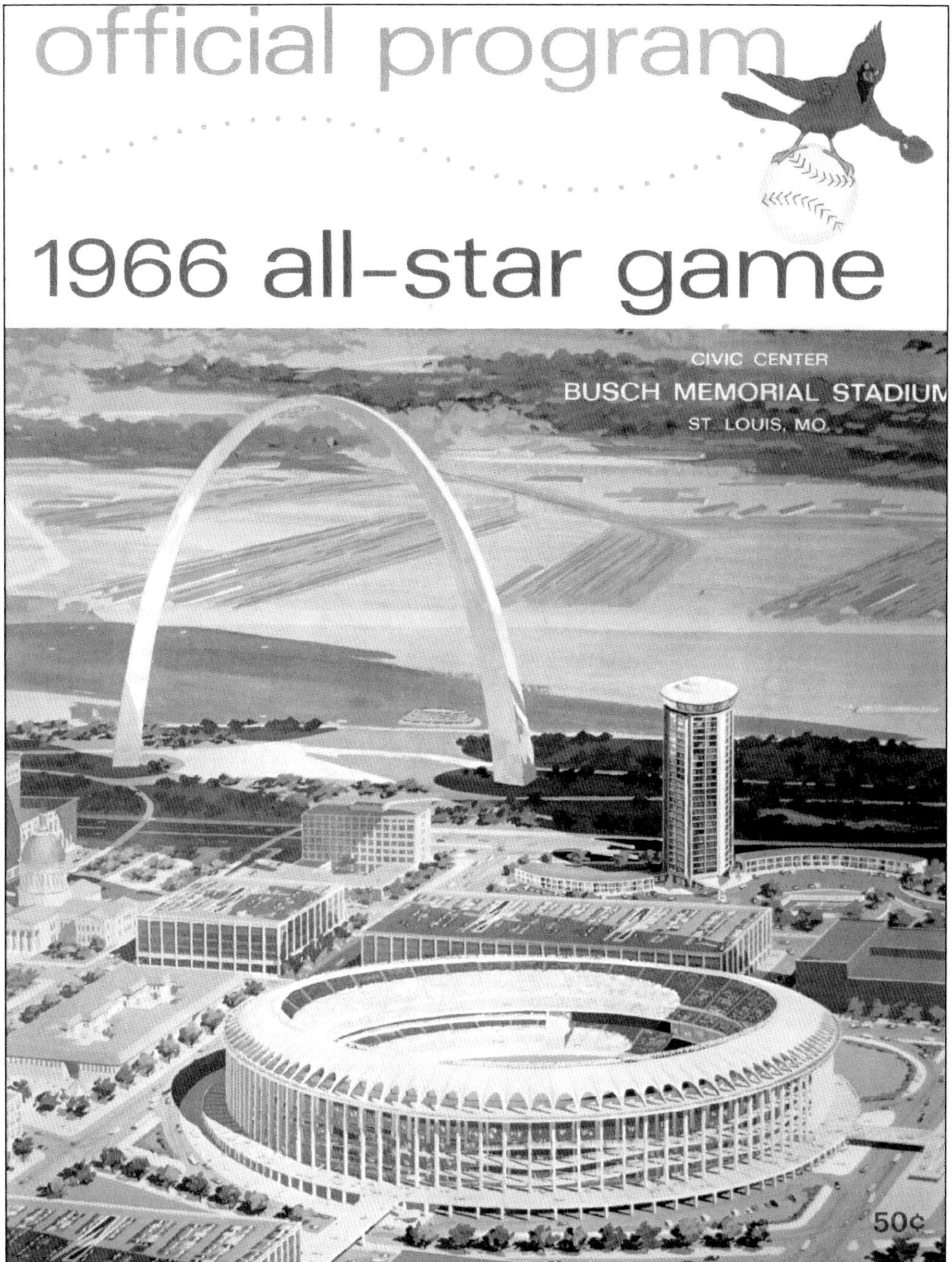

An image that soon became the universal snapshot of St. Louis included the Gateway Arch and Busch Stadium. Probably one of its first renderings appeared on the official program of the first and only All-Star Game held at Busch. Occurring July 12, 1966, the event offered a taste of summer in the city of St. Louis.The thermometer recorded 106 degrees that day, and of the 49,936 people in attendance, some 135 fans suffered heat prostration. It's hard to say how many sweltering ticket holders remained at the game's tenth inning conclusion—the Nationals won, 2-1.

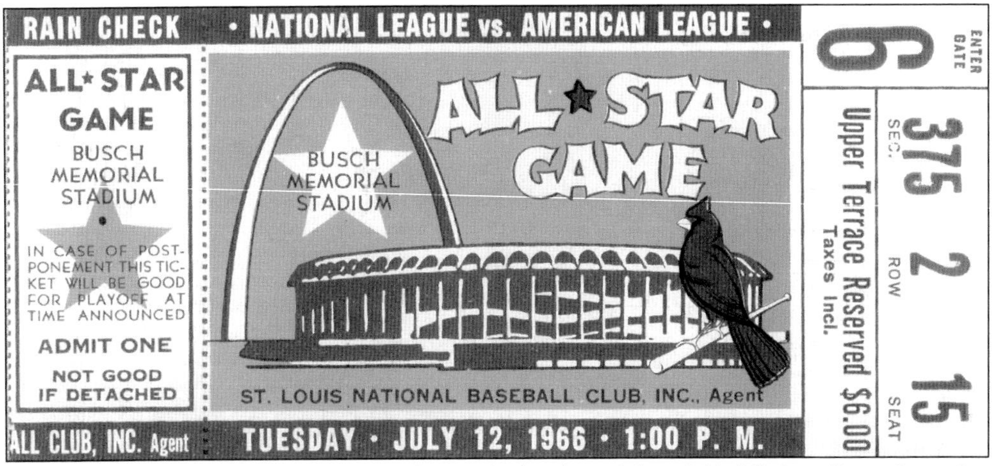

A survivor of the boiling weather inside Busch the day of the 1966 All-Star Game kept this rain check as proof of acclimatization. A sports announcer from another city once said about Busch that it holds heat well.

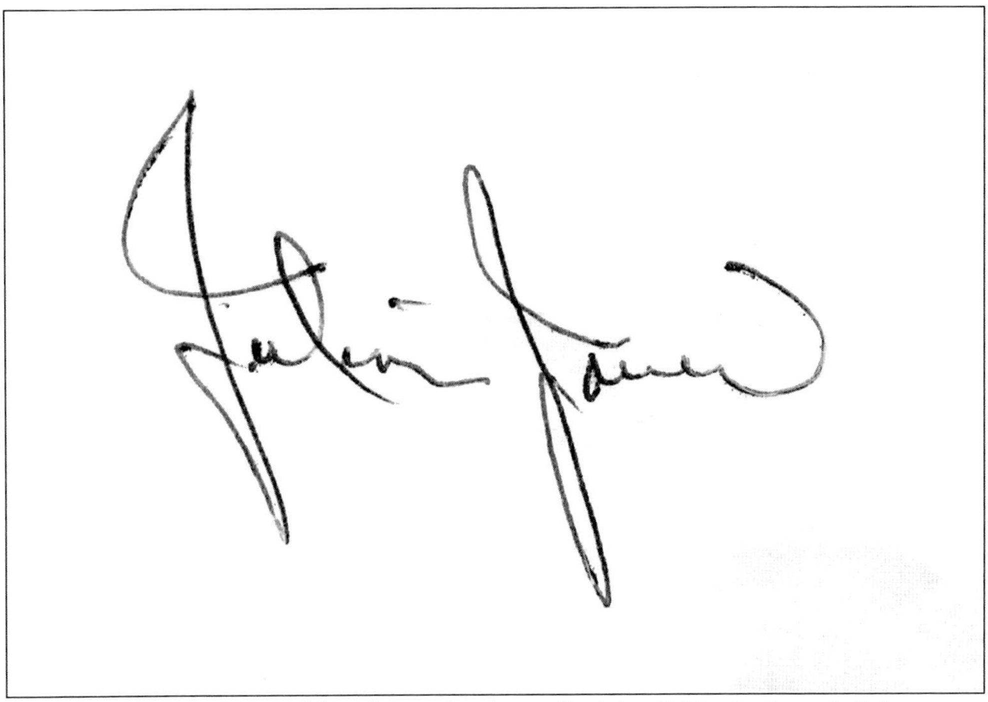

Rewarded for home team fidelity during the dry spell of the 1950s, St. Louis ball fans again enjoyed post season play in the '60s. And during the season buildup, they saw a number of rising Cardinal stars. Julian Javier (Cardinal second baseman, 1960–1971), who penned the above autograph at a private party, was a fan favorite.

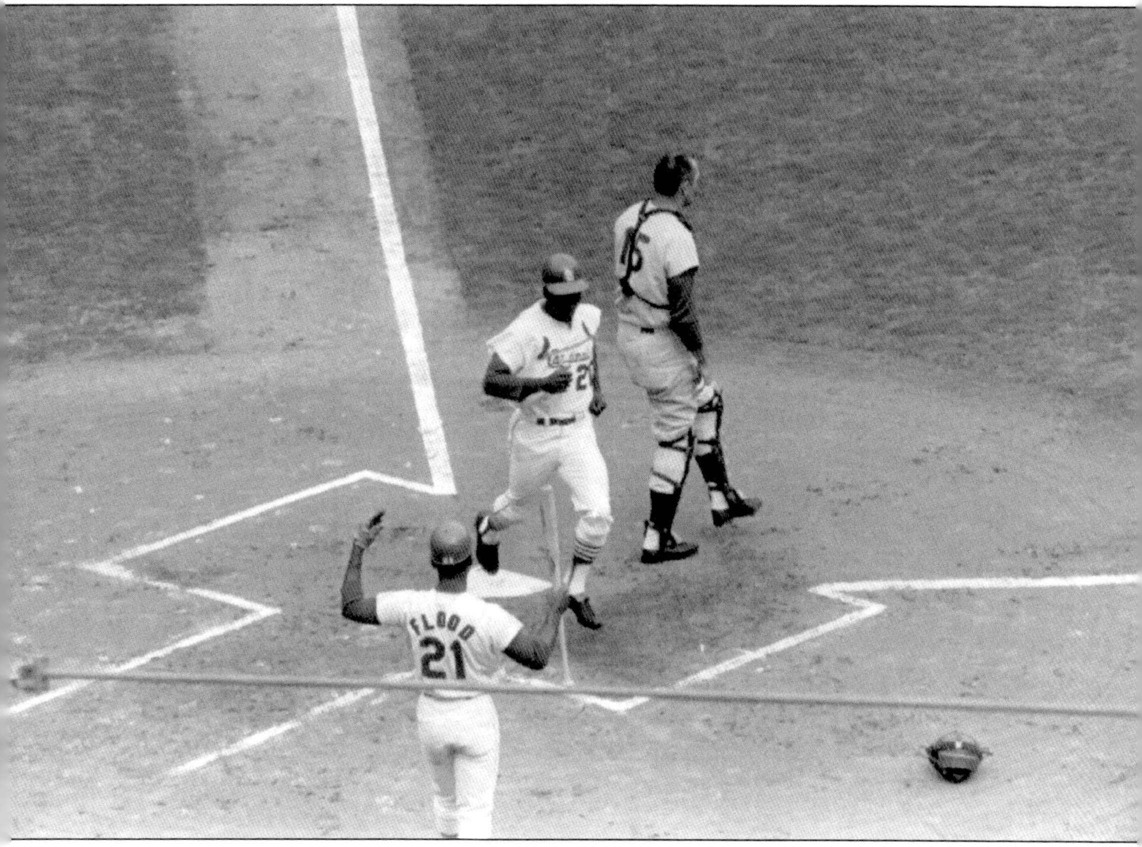

In this 1968 photo taken at Busch during a Cardinal-Dodger game, Lou Brock crosses the plate while Curt Flood welcomes him with open arms. Dodger catcher Tom Haller steps toward the pitcher's mound. A great outfielder, Flood played in the '66 All-Star Game. He later made history by challenging the reserve clause when the Cardinals traded him to the Phillies after the '69 season. Although his antitrust litigation failed, it ultimately led to the clause's demise. So, one man, who once called Busch Stadium home, accomplished the purpose of both the Union League of 1884 and the Brotherhood of 1890 (See pages 22–23 and 35).

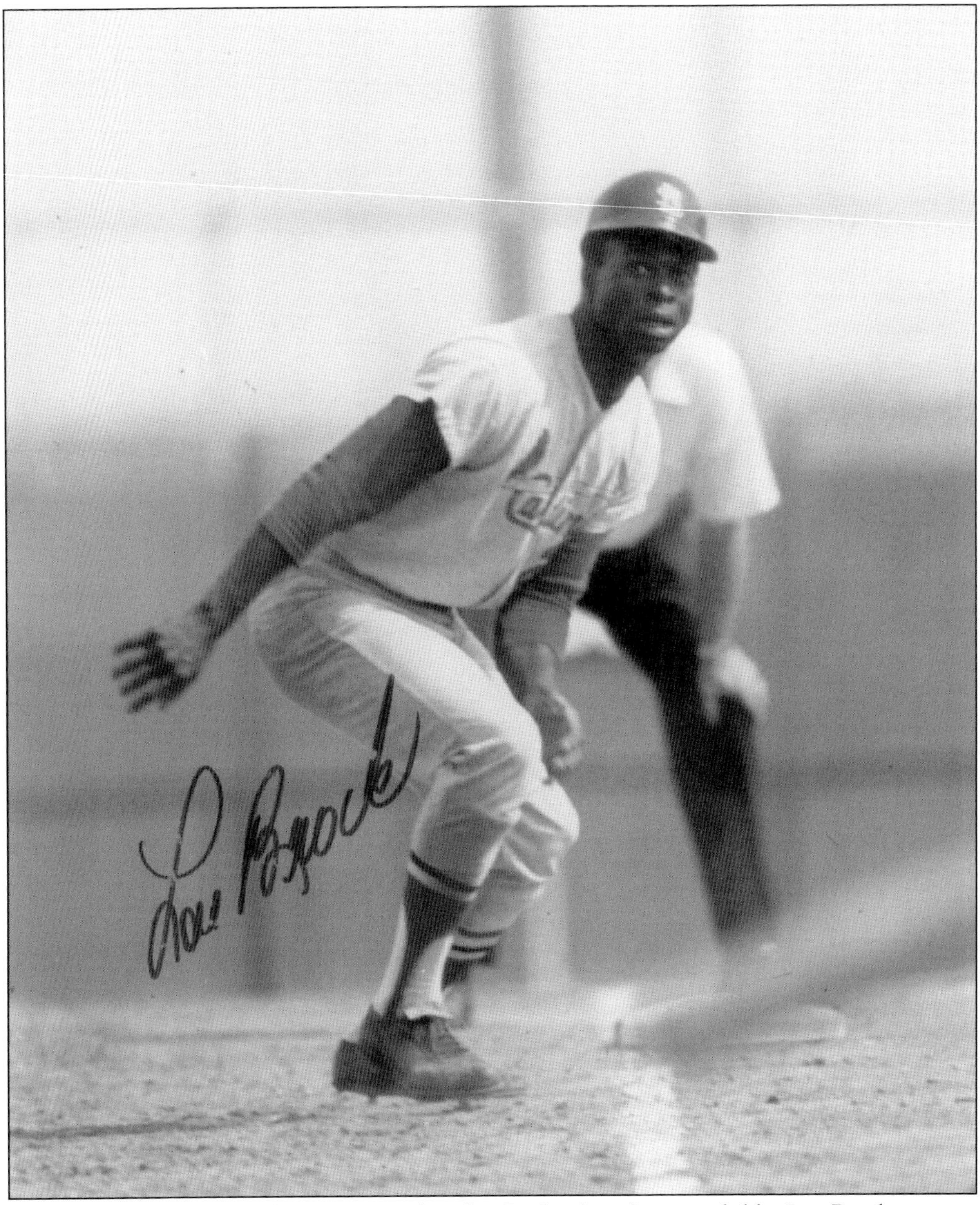

One of the most exciting players ever to don the Cardinal uniform, outfielder Lou Brock came to St. Louis as the result of a trade that infuriated the fans. Popular pitcher Ernie Broglio went to the Cubs in that 1964 deal, but in time Cardinal fans thanked the baseball gods. Remaining with the Cards through '79, Brock ended his career a member of the "3,000 Club" with a grand total of 3,023 hits. More significantly, his intelligent and swift base running allowed him to break the stolen base record of the times. At this writing, he is number two on the all time list, with 938.

This keepsake image of the plaque honoring Lou Brock displayed at the Baseball Hall of Fame in Cooperstown evidences the value of the 1964 acquisition from Chicago.

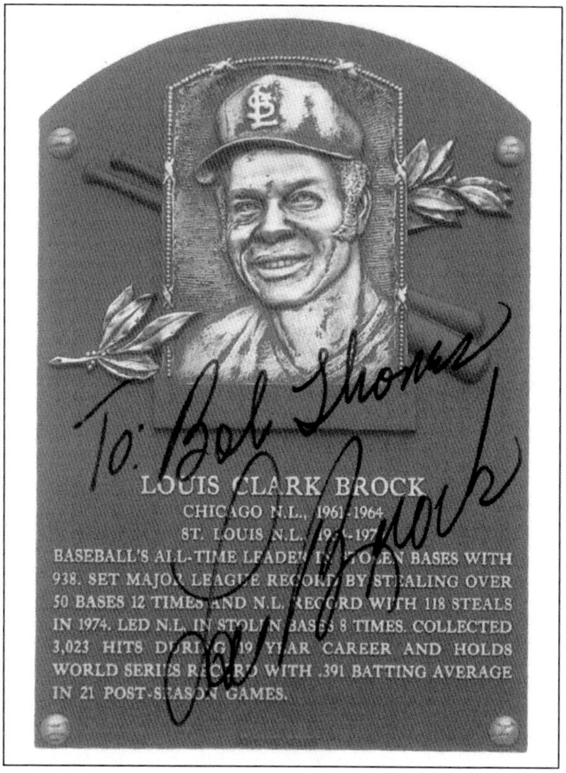

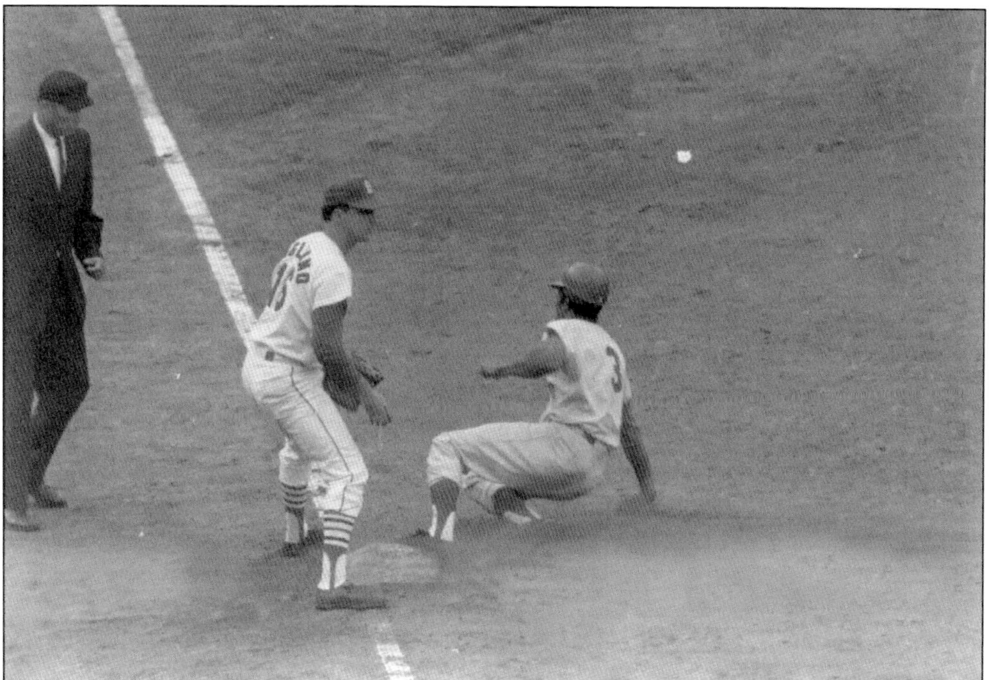

In this series of photos taken during a 1968 game with the Dodgers, Cardinal second baseman Phil Gagliano poises for the catch while Dodger Willie Davis slides in to the bag.

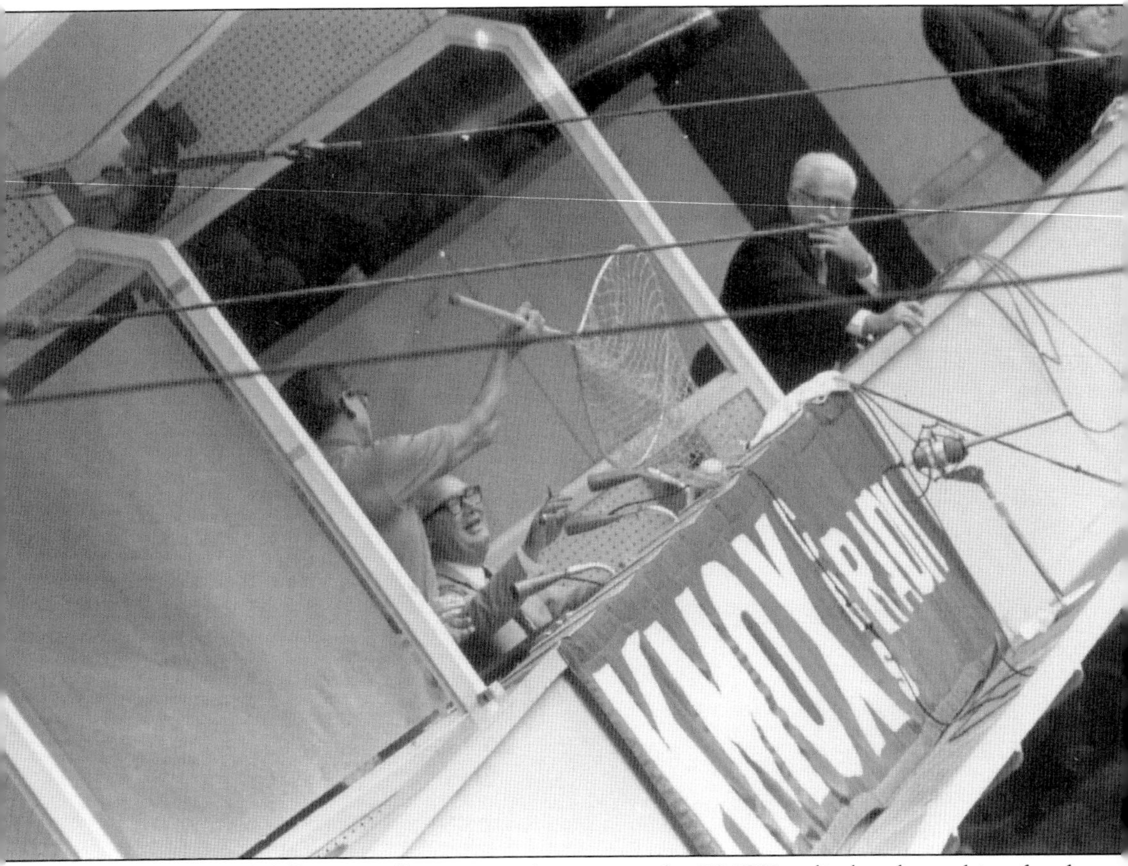

Most baseball followers will recognize the man in the KMOX radio booth reaching for the ball caught in the net. Now remembered most as the "Take Me Out to the Ballgame" singing voice of the Chicago Cubs, Harry announced for the Cardinals from 1945 through 1969. Jack Buck (not seen in this photo), who joined Caray in the booth in 1954, stayed with St. Louis to become the most renowned voice of the Cardinals. Well known St. Louis sports writer Bob Broeg is seen in the upper right corner of this image.

Dodger Zoilo Versalles crosses the plate as seen in this view from above. In addition to the legendary Cardinal-Cub rivalry, most St. Louis baseball lovers of old recall a long-standing competition with the Dodgers. At many games like this, the crowd in attendance included almost as many Dodger rooters as Cardinal buffs. Often, families split allegiances, adding plenty of good-natured jibbing at Busch Stadium.

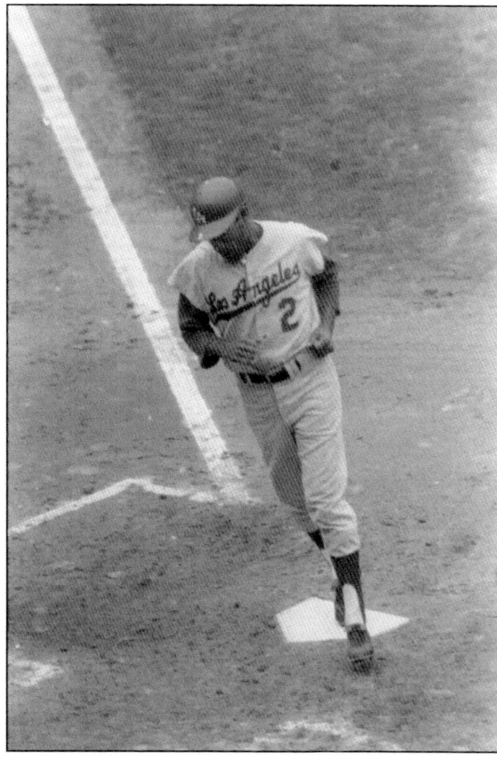

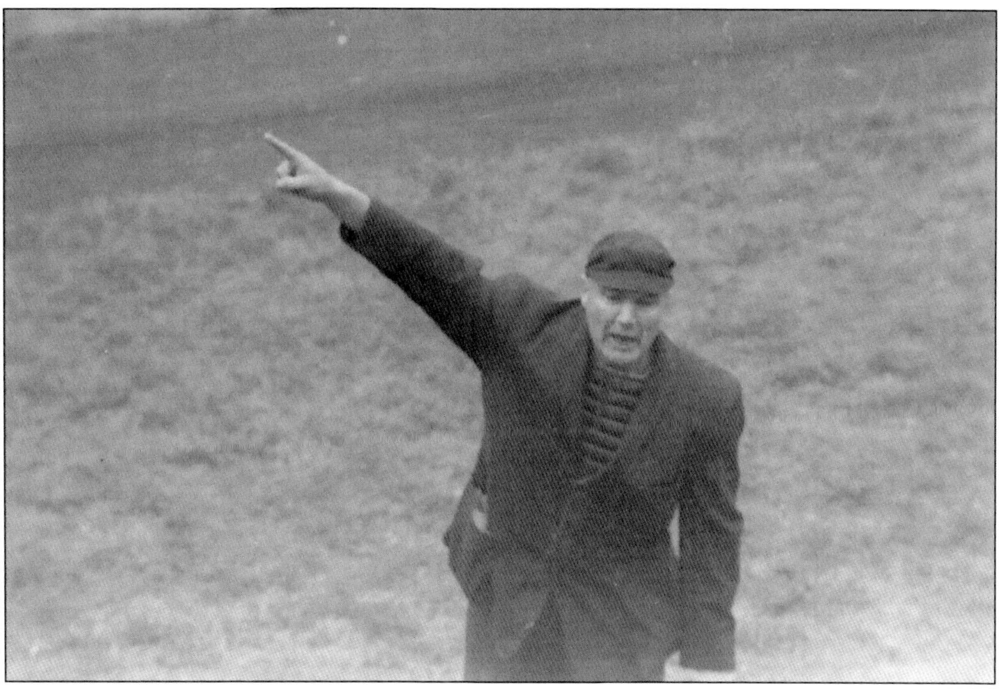

Here the stereotypical stone-face umpire barks with authority. In this series of photos, the stadium's natural grass is obvious. Several seasons passed before the Busch got the Astroturf that finally grew unpopular. By the time the new millennium, real grass replaced the green outdoor carpet.

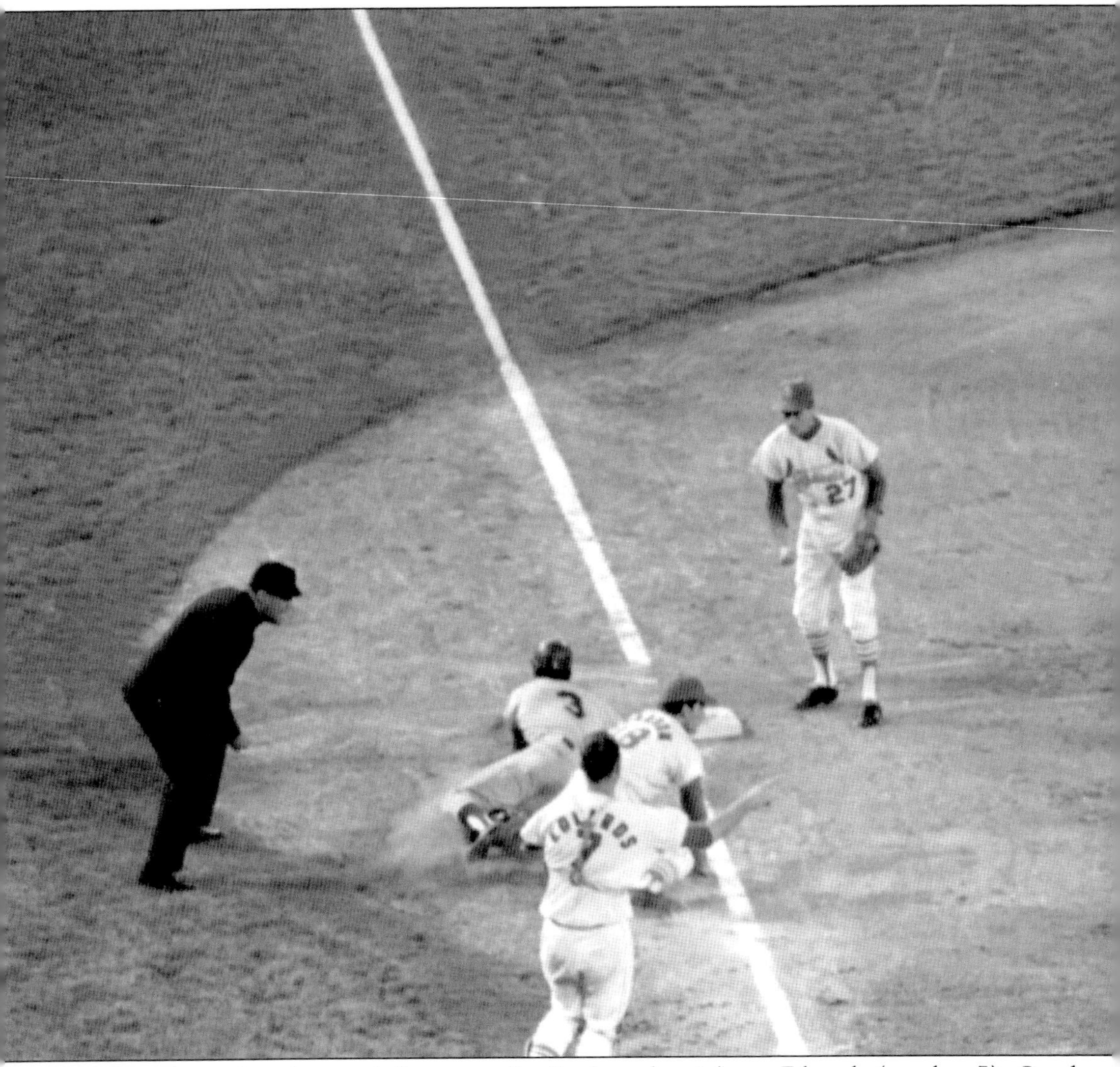

Seen here, from bottom left up, are Cardinal catcher Johnny Edwards (number 7), Coach Milliken, Dodger Willie Davis, and Cardinal Dal Maxvill (number 27). Any Cardinal fan of the '60s will remember Maxvill, who played short for the Cardinals from 1962 to 1972.

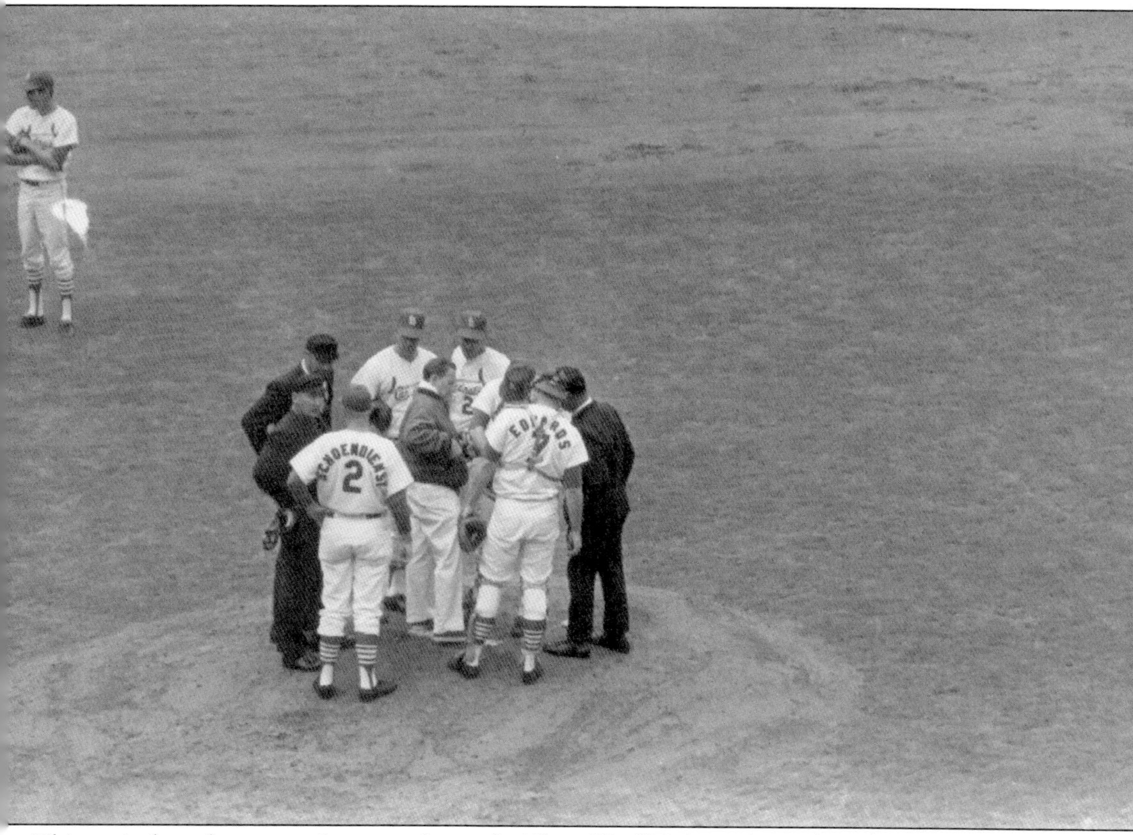

This typical conference at the mound reveals Albert "Red" Schoendienst (number 2) speaking with the umpire. Red managed the Redbirds during fourteen seasons (1965–1980 and 1990), two in which he led the Cardinals to the World Series. This followed a stellar playing career of 19 years, mostly with the Cards.

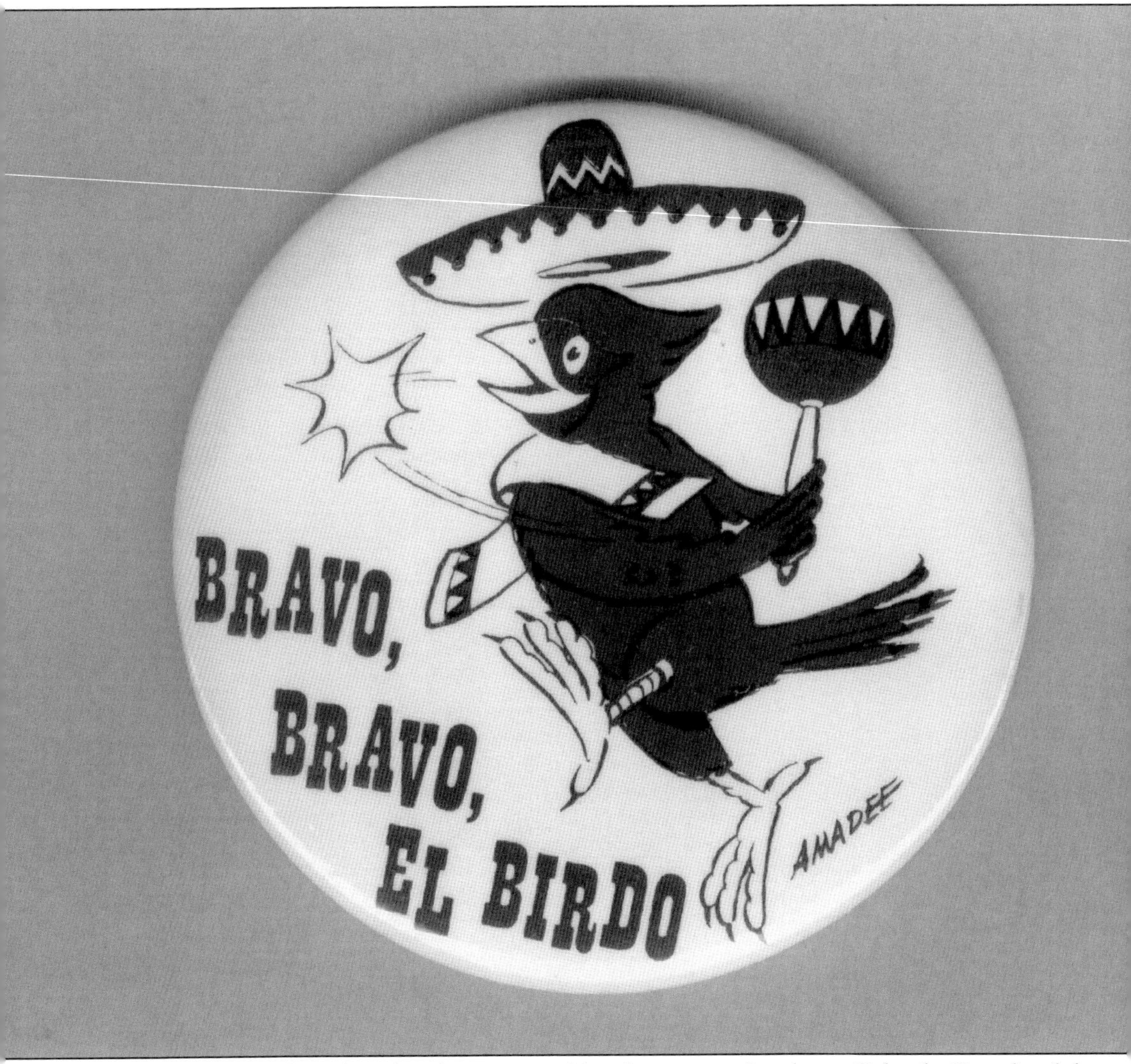

"Bravo, Bravo, El Birdo," the phrase coined by charismatic first baser Orlando Cepeda of the champion Cardinal 1967–1968 seasons, resulted in this collector's pin. His nicknames, "Baby Bull" and "Cha Cha," added to his fetching persona.

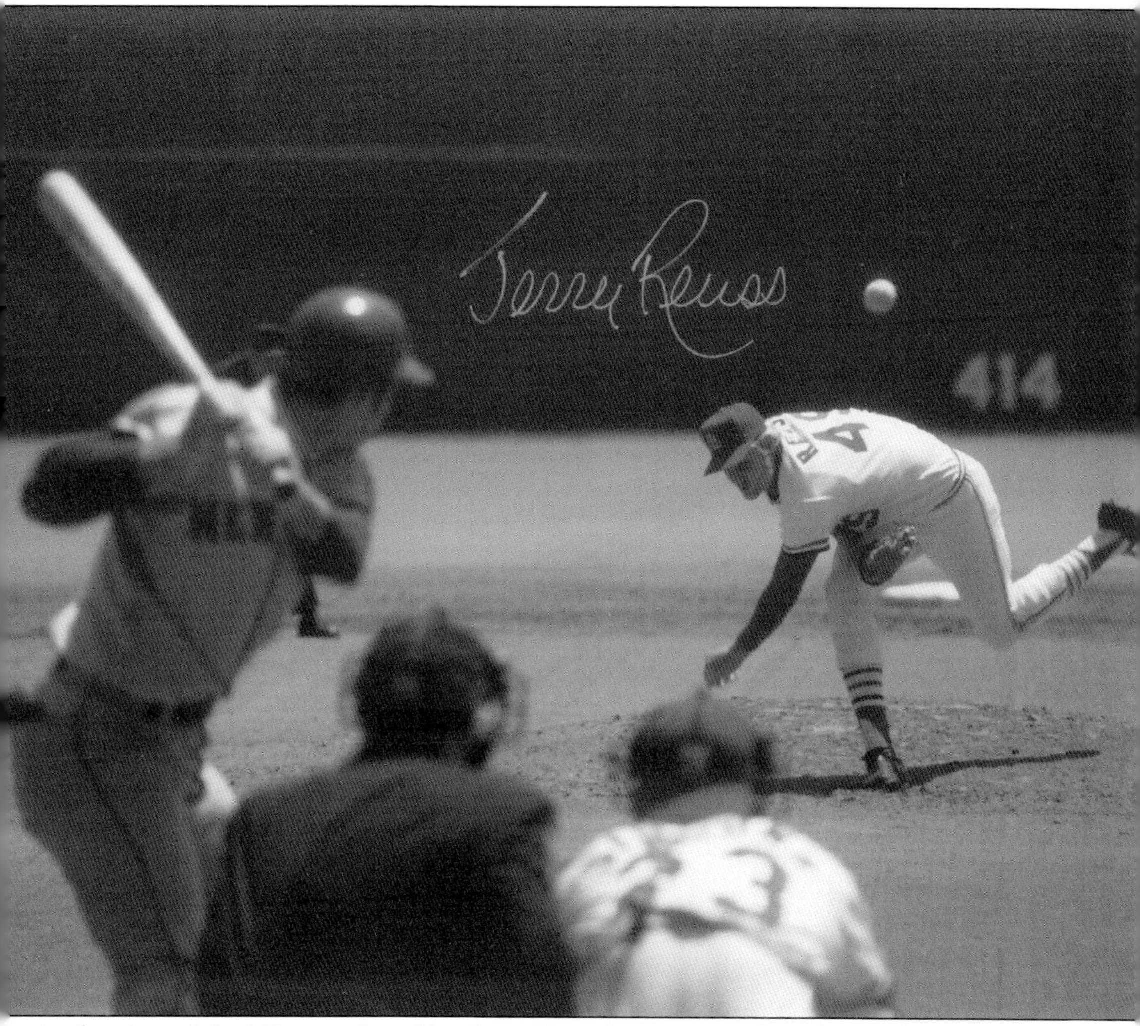

At the close of the '60s, new faces like that of Jerry Reuss appeared on the Cardinals' team. Beginning his big league career in St. Louis in '69, Reuss left after the '71 season. But his major league career stretched over 22 years with eight different clubs.

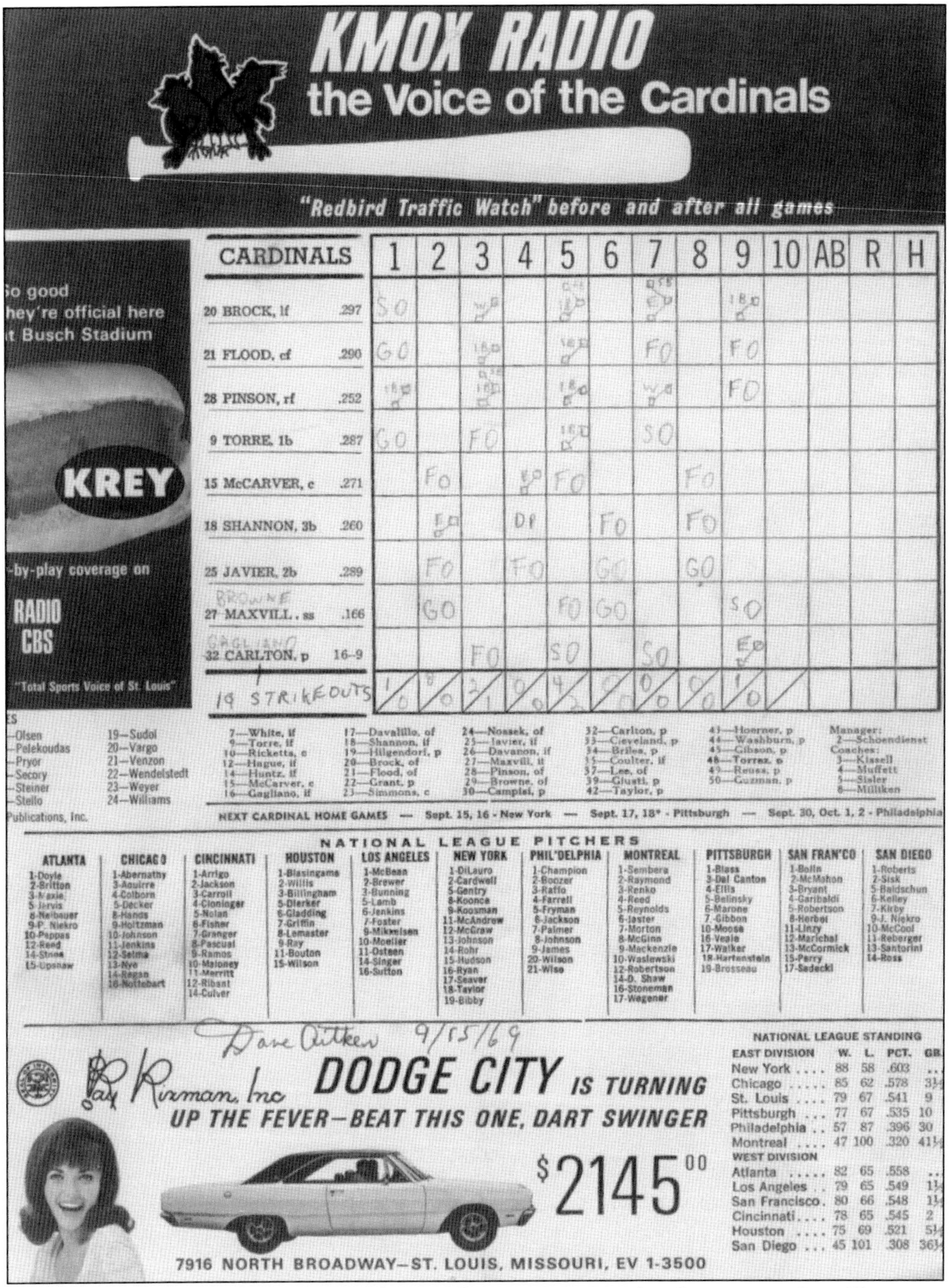

A scan of this September 15, 1969 lineup shows some very familiar names. In addition to some mentioned in the previous pages, Pinson, McCarver, Torre, Shannon and Carlton stand out. Vada Pinson's stint in St. Louis only lasted one year. Tim McCarver, Joe Torre, and Mike Shannon stayed longer, and all later gained widespread recognition in other baseball capacities. Steve Carlton went to the Phillies in 1972, and got elected to the Hall of Fame 22 years later.

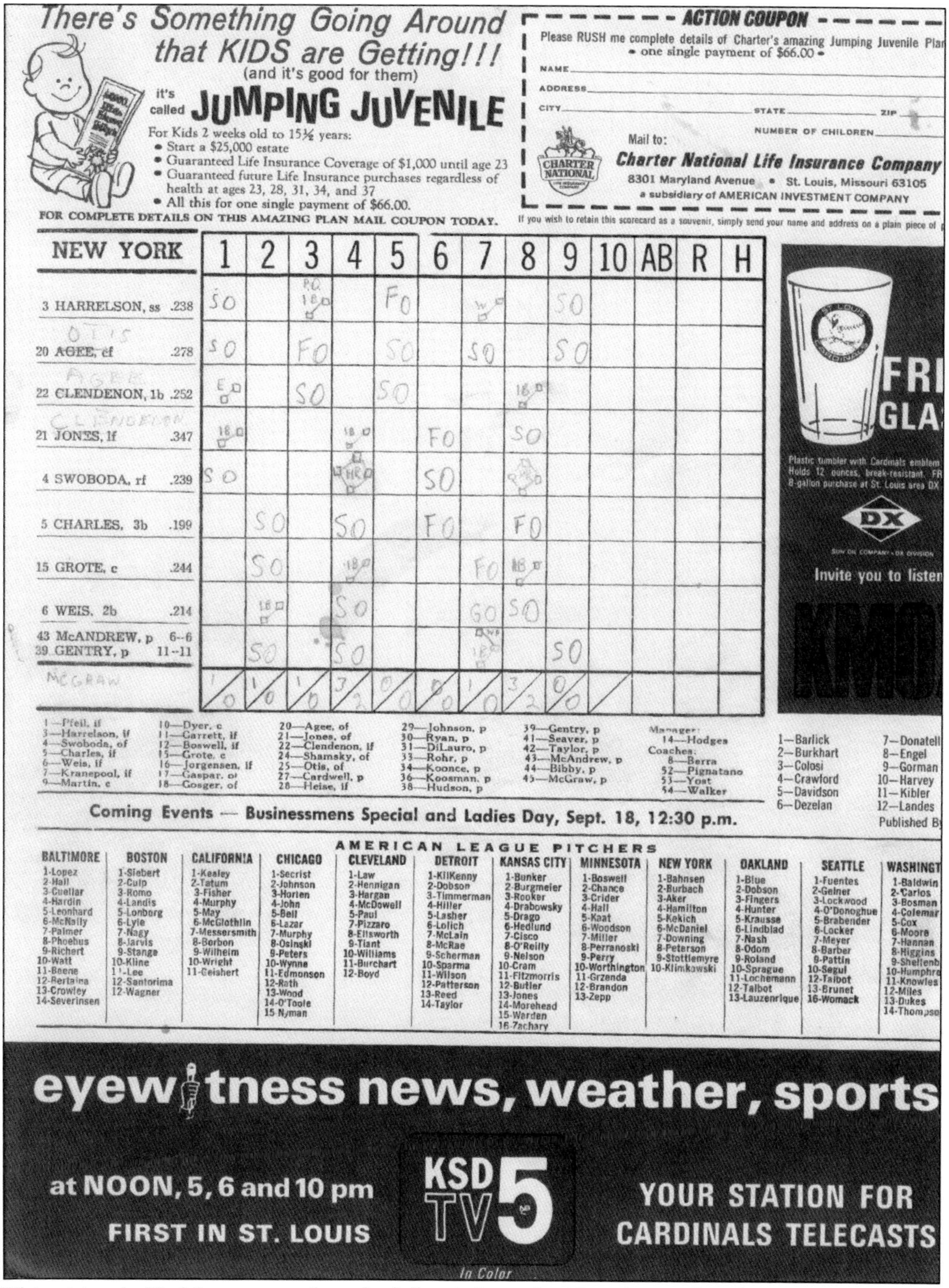

This visitor half of the scorecard on the left validates the 19 strikeouts hand printed by Cardinal fan Dave Aitken below Carlton's name (see page 90).

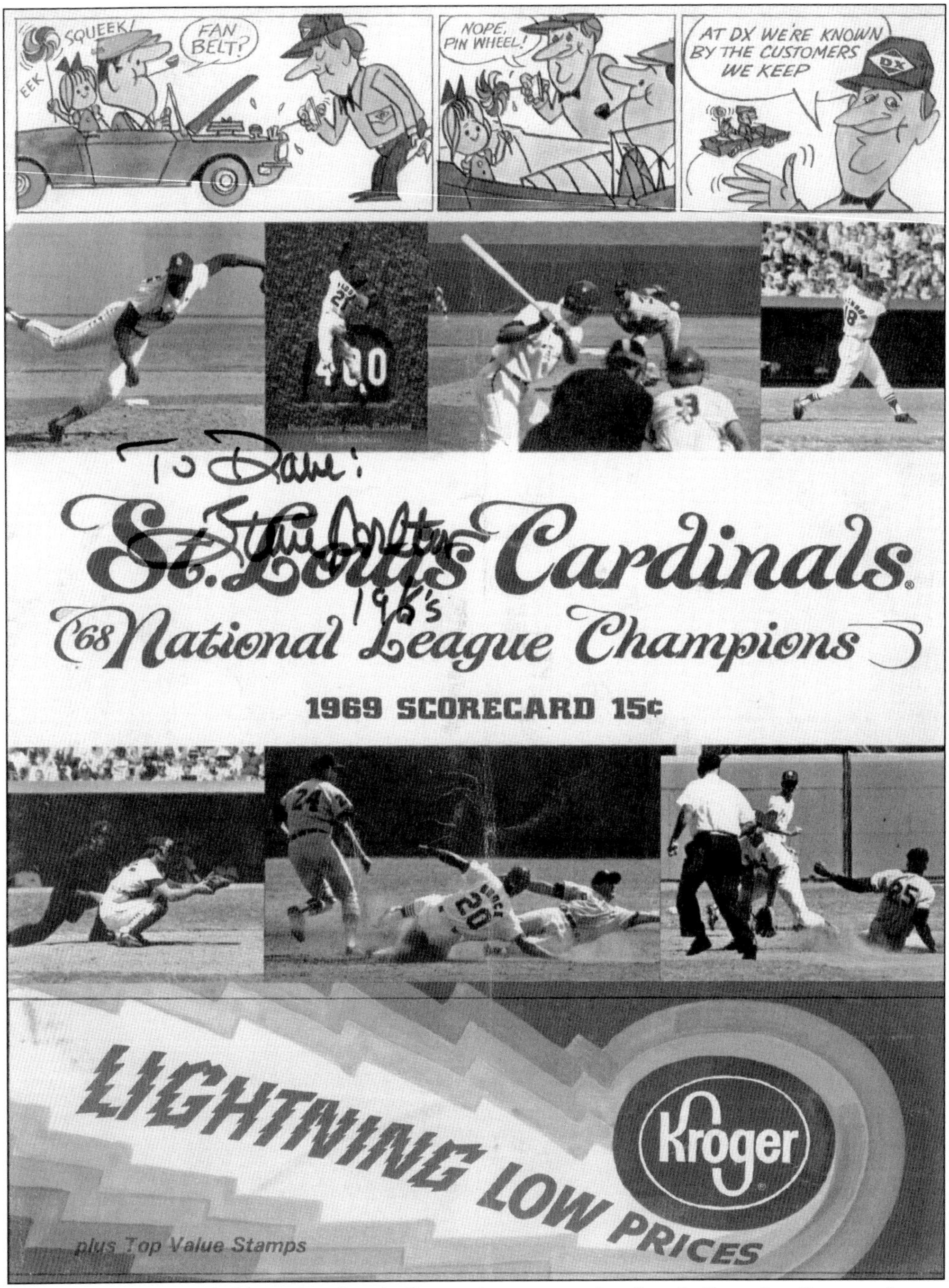

After Carlton retired, like other baseball men he appeared at baseball card collectors shows, signing autographs. When approached to sign this cover of the card shown on pages 90 & 91, he immediately remembered the event. Though he tallied 19 Ks, he lost the game. Notice the player pictured on the left upper side of this cover—a most familiar sight to those who saw Bob Gibson's Hall-of-Fame style of pitching. It always looked as if he would topple over when he released the ball. But Gibbie was always in control.

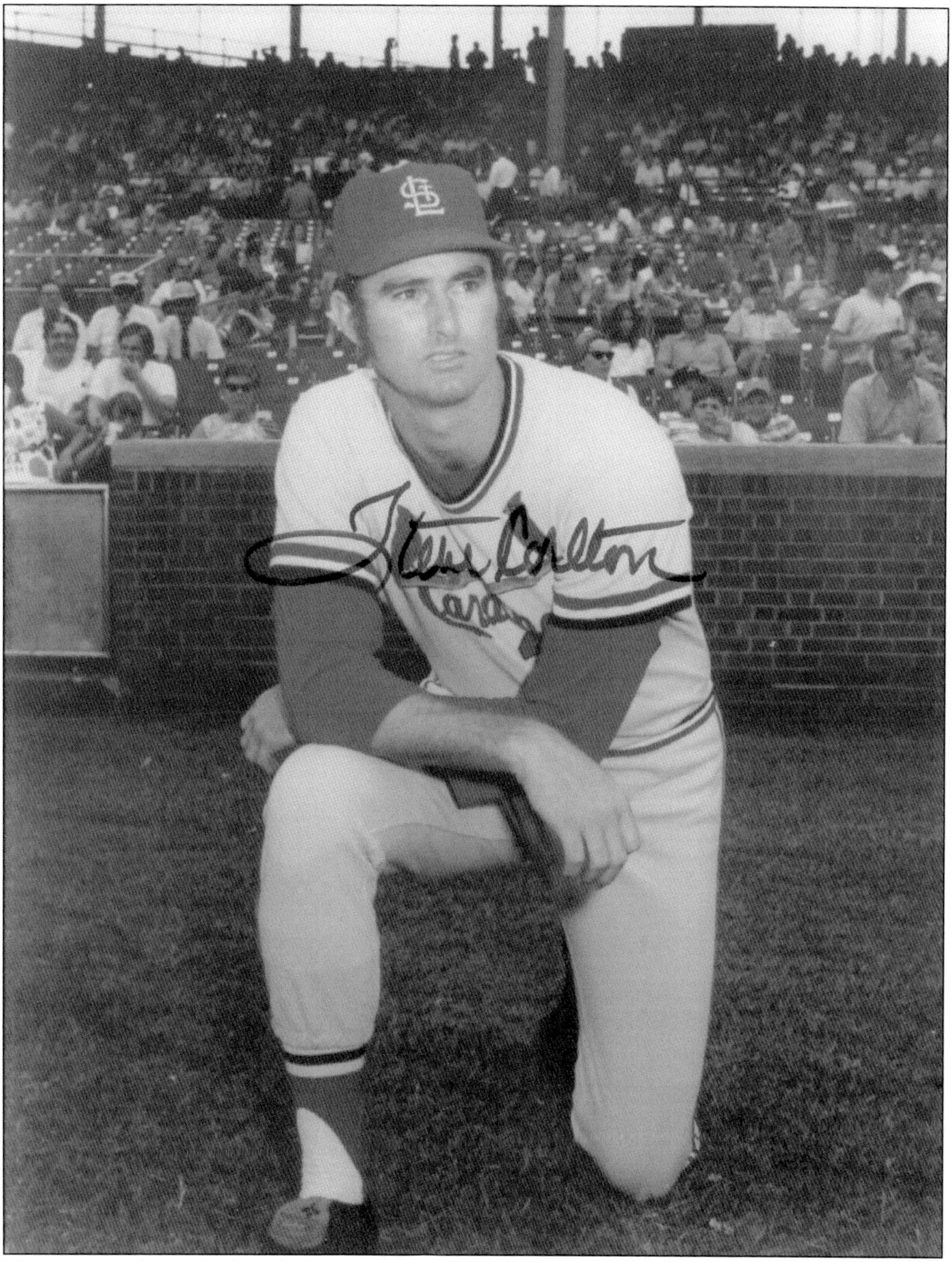

This is lefty Steve Carlton before he went to Philadelphia, San Francisco, and Cooperstown. Cardinal Fans still lament his departure from St. Louis.

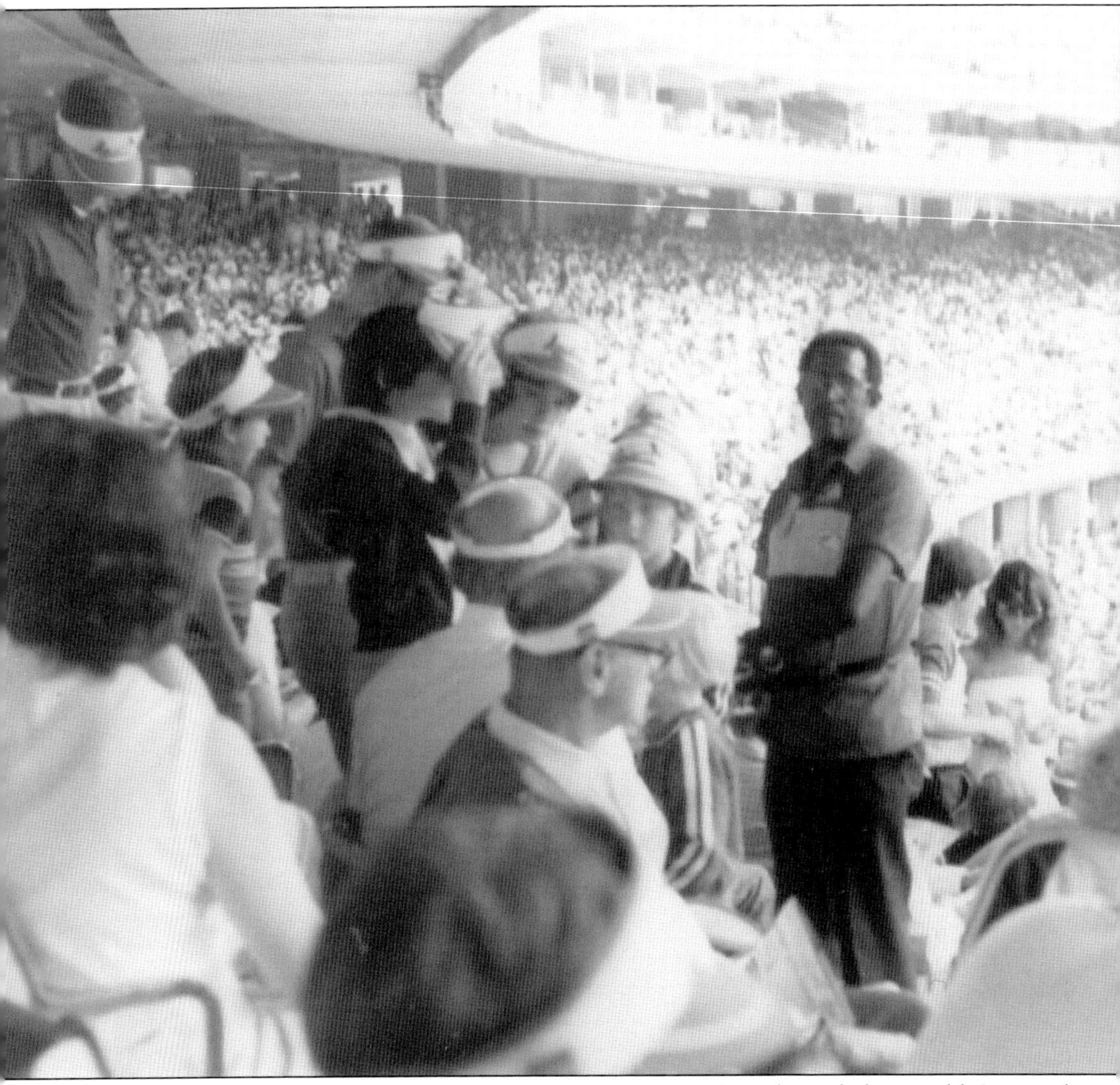

Although a dozen summers had passed since Busch Stadium hosted the World Series, the masses still packed the stands for this Cardinal game in 1981. Promotions, such as the visor giveaways worn by fans here drew some, but the game itself attracted the majority. During this typically sizzling summer day in St. Louis, a crowd gathers around the beverage vendor.

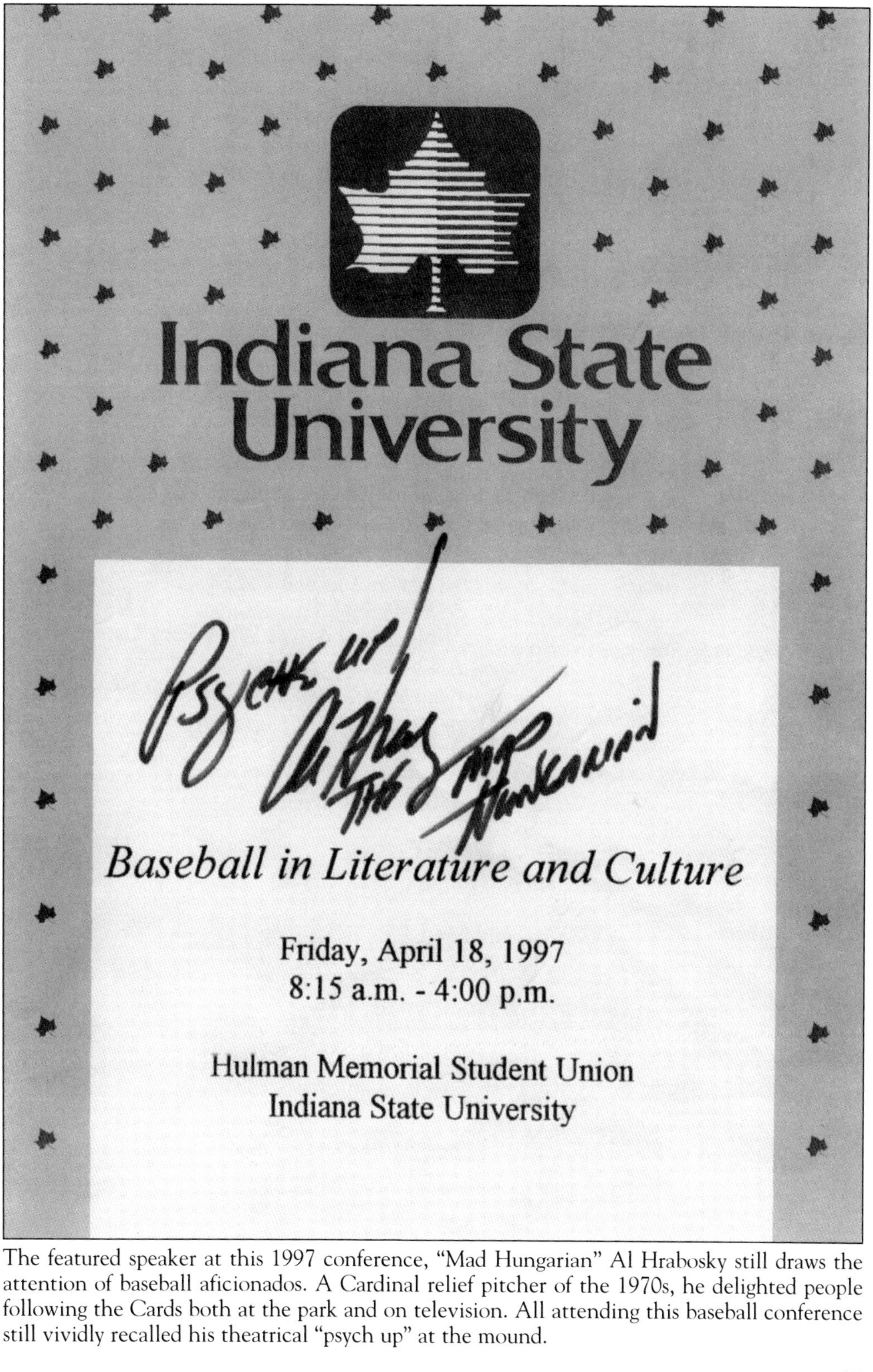

The featured speaker at this 1997 conference, "Mad Hungarian" Al Hrabosky still draws the attention of baseball aficionados. A Cardinal relief pitcher of the 1970s, he delighted people following the Cards both at the park and on television. All attending this baseball conference still vividly recalled his theatrical "psych up" at the mound.

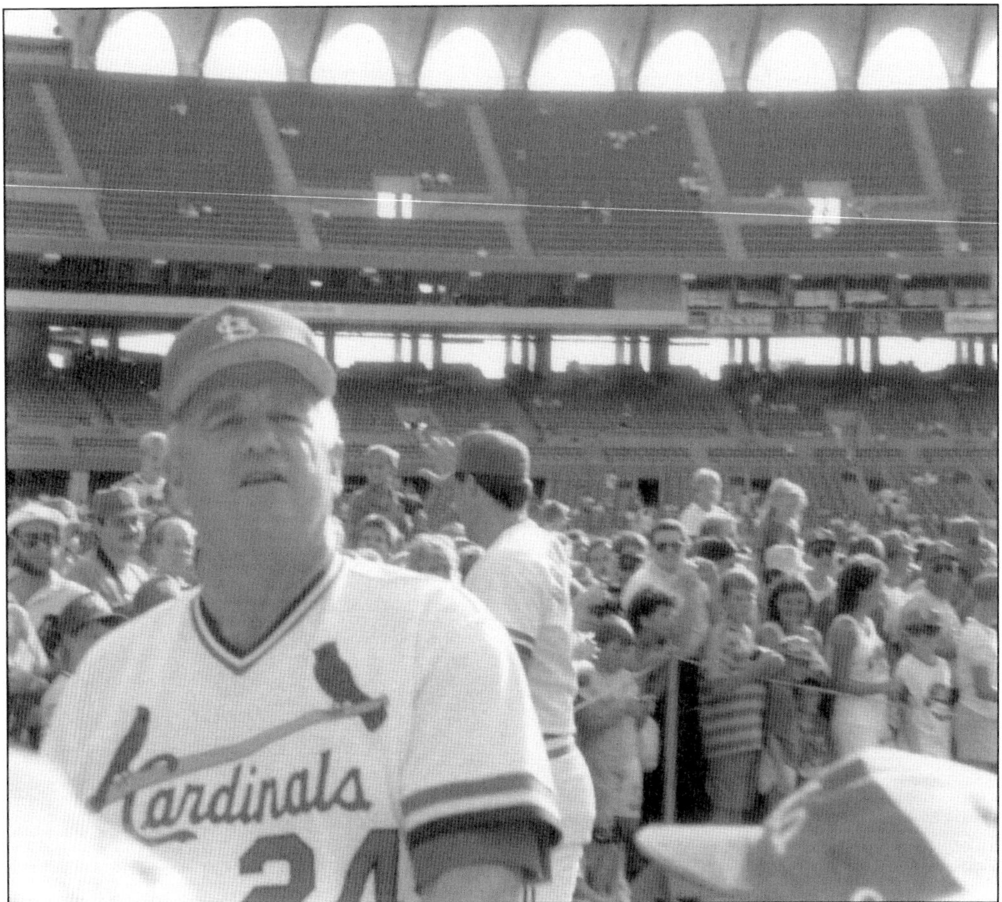

Still a well-known face in St. Louis, Whitey Herzog, often called the "White Rat," managed the Cardinals for a little more than a decade. In 1980, he came to St. Louis from the Kansas City Royals and took the Cards to three World Series. Here he poses for fans during an annual pre-game Camera Day at Busch.

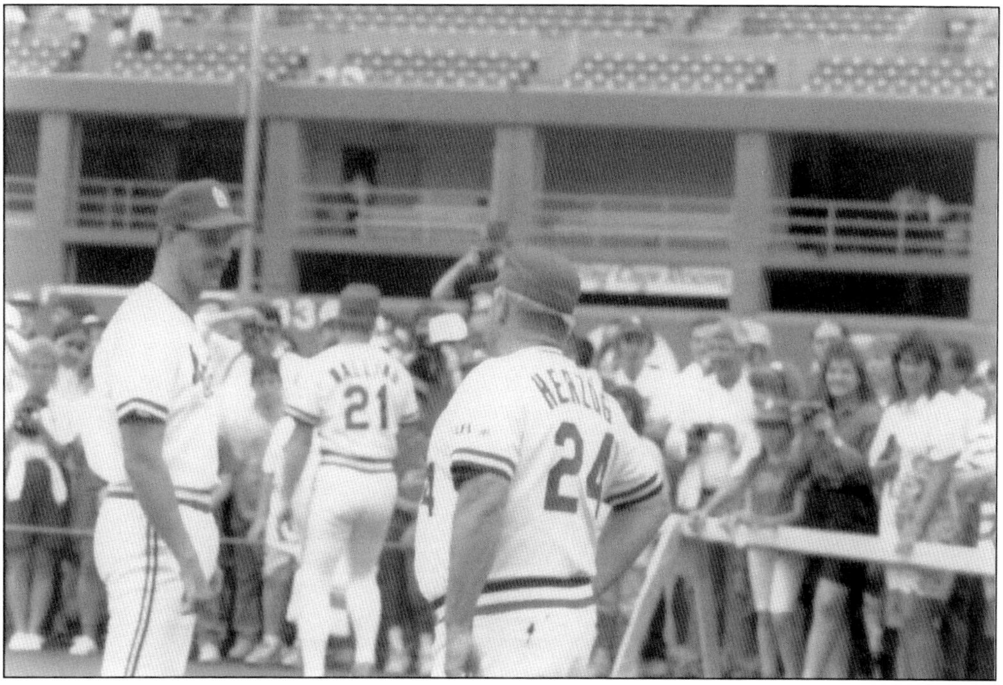

During camera day, fans can walk down on the field to meet and photograph their favorite players. Here Todd Worrell (left) has a word with the White Rat (right). Six-foot five-inch tall Cardinal reliever Worrell earned 36 saves in 1986, and played with the '88 All-Stars.

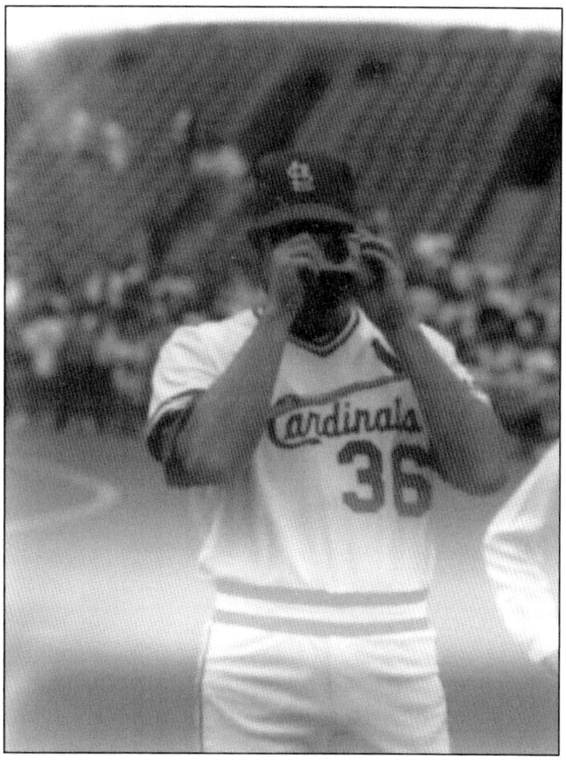

Even the ballplayers get into the act during Camera Day at Busch Stadium. Here Cardinal pitcher Brynn Smith trades shots with a picture-snapping fan. Acquired from Montreal in 1990, Smith stayed with the St. Louis club for three seasons.

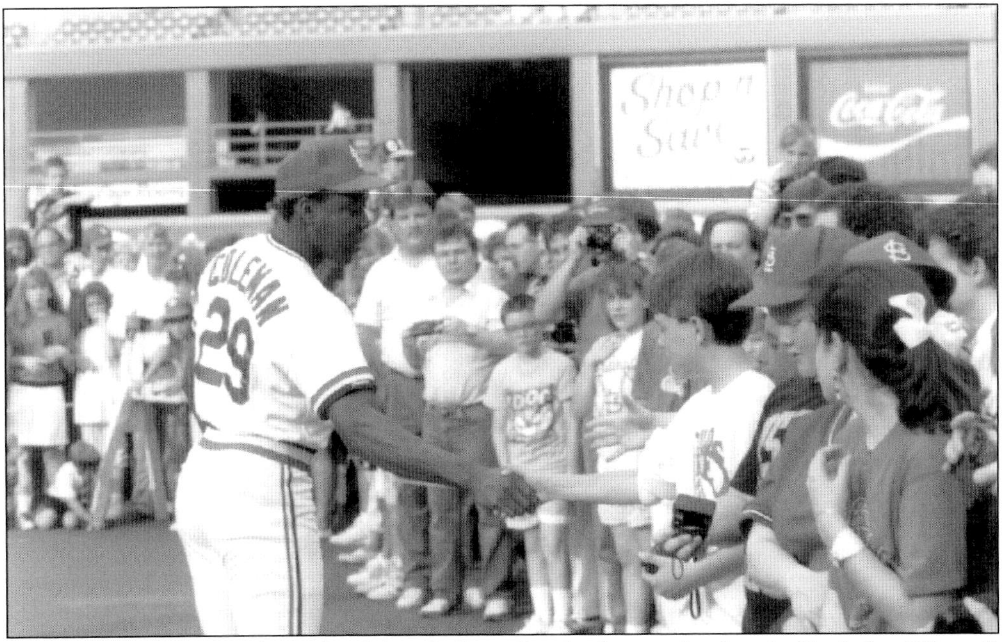

Anyone who witnessed Cardinal baseball at Busch during the last half of the '80s will recognize this man. In this Camera Day shot, swift base-runner Vince Coleman shakes hands with awed youngsters.

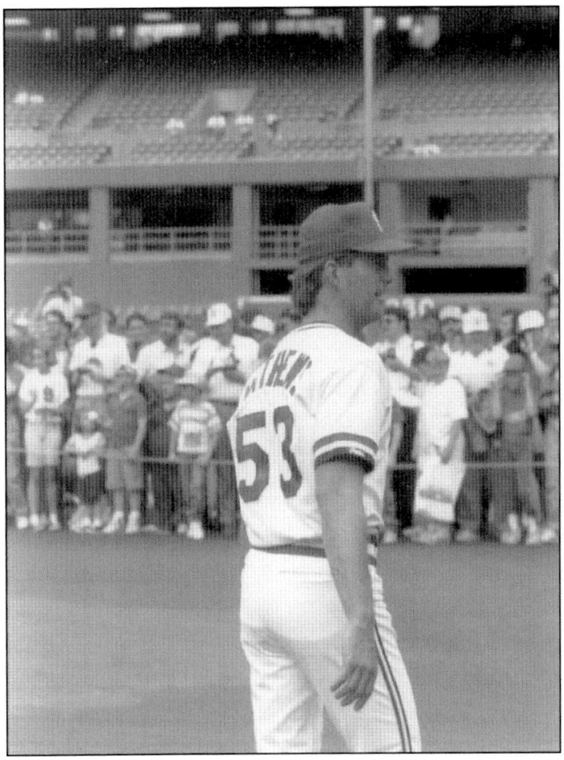

A teammate of Coleman's, Greg Mathews pitched for the Cardinals for four seasons (1986–1990). He won eleven games during the '87 National League Championship season.

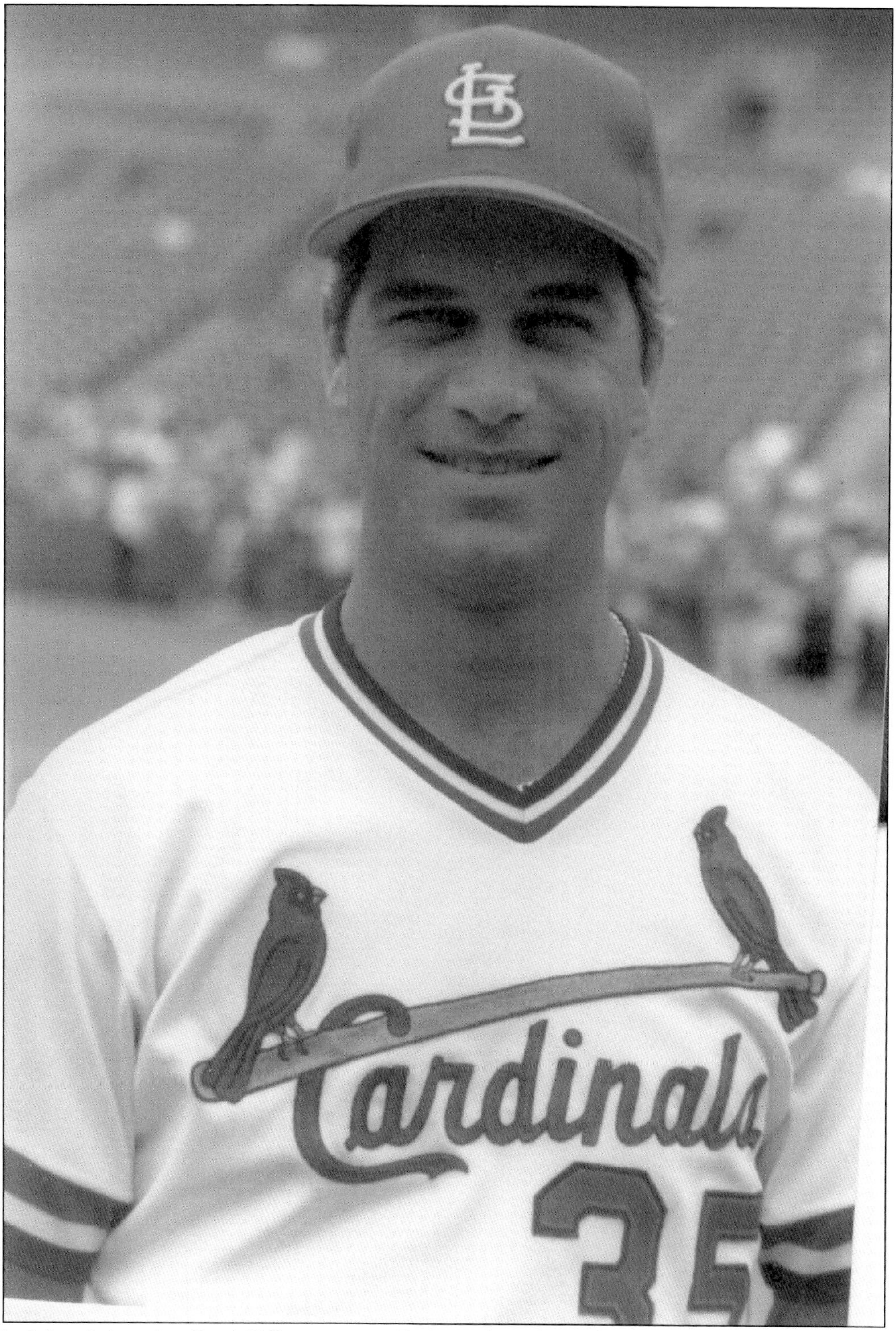

Left-handed pitcher Frank DiPino came to St. Louis from the Cubs in 1989, turning in a win-loss record of 9-0 that season. Here he gives a congenial smile for a Busch Camera Day fan.

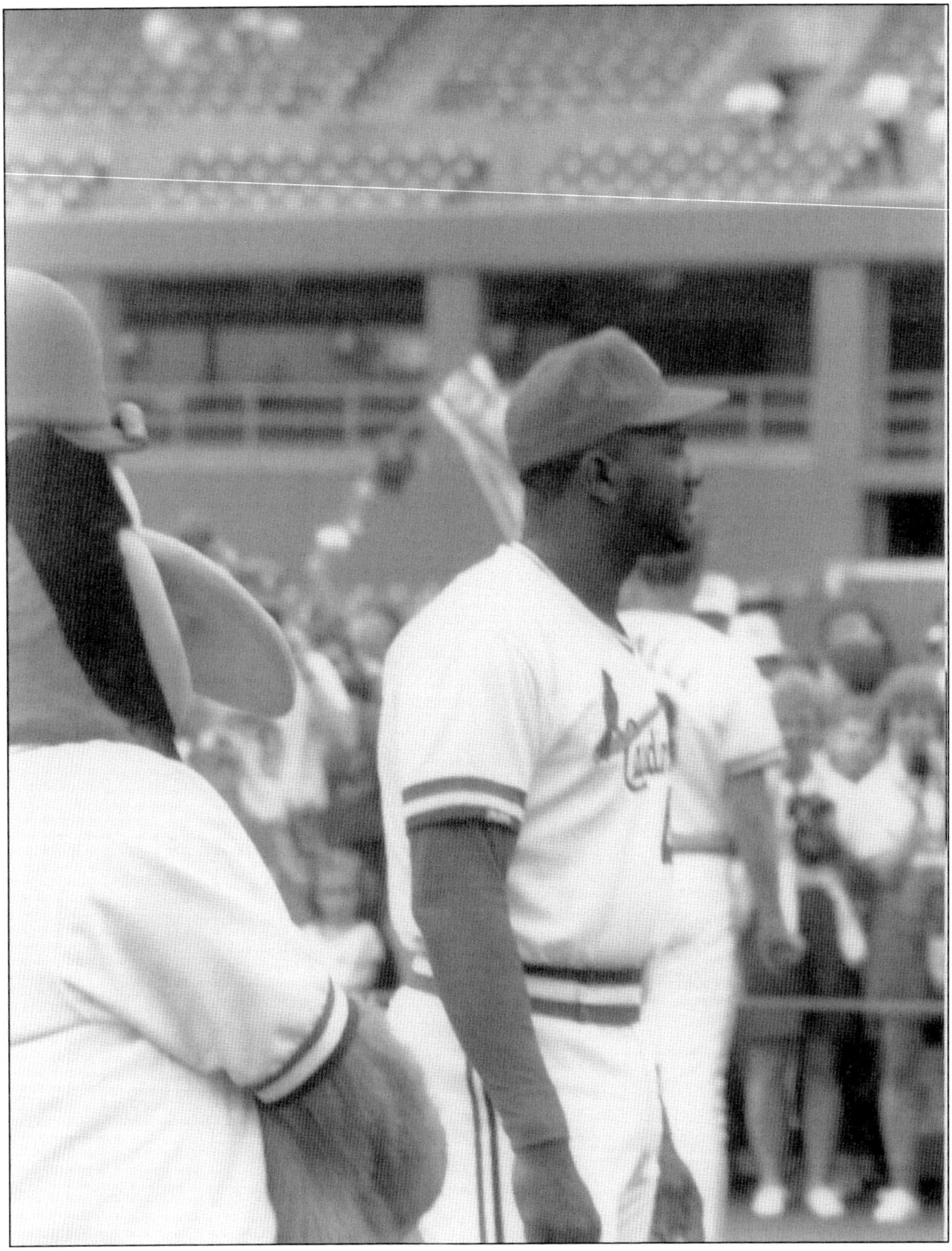

Here the ubiquitous Fredbird dares to approach the man who inspired fear in the heart of batters, "Big Lee" Smith. His gentle demeanor with the fans during Camera Day belies his menacing appearance on the pitcher's mound. First with the Cubs, Smith came to St. Louis after two and a half seasons with Boston. That was in 1990, and the following season he earned an outstanding 47 saves for the Cards. After turning in two more strong seasons, he went on to other clubs before retiring in '98. Of 43 major league relievers with 150 or more career saves, he heads the list with 478. Fredbird, already a standard element of the Busch Stadium experience, still entertains the baseball crowd.

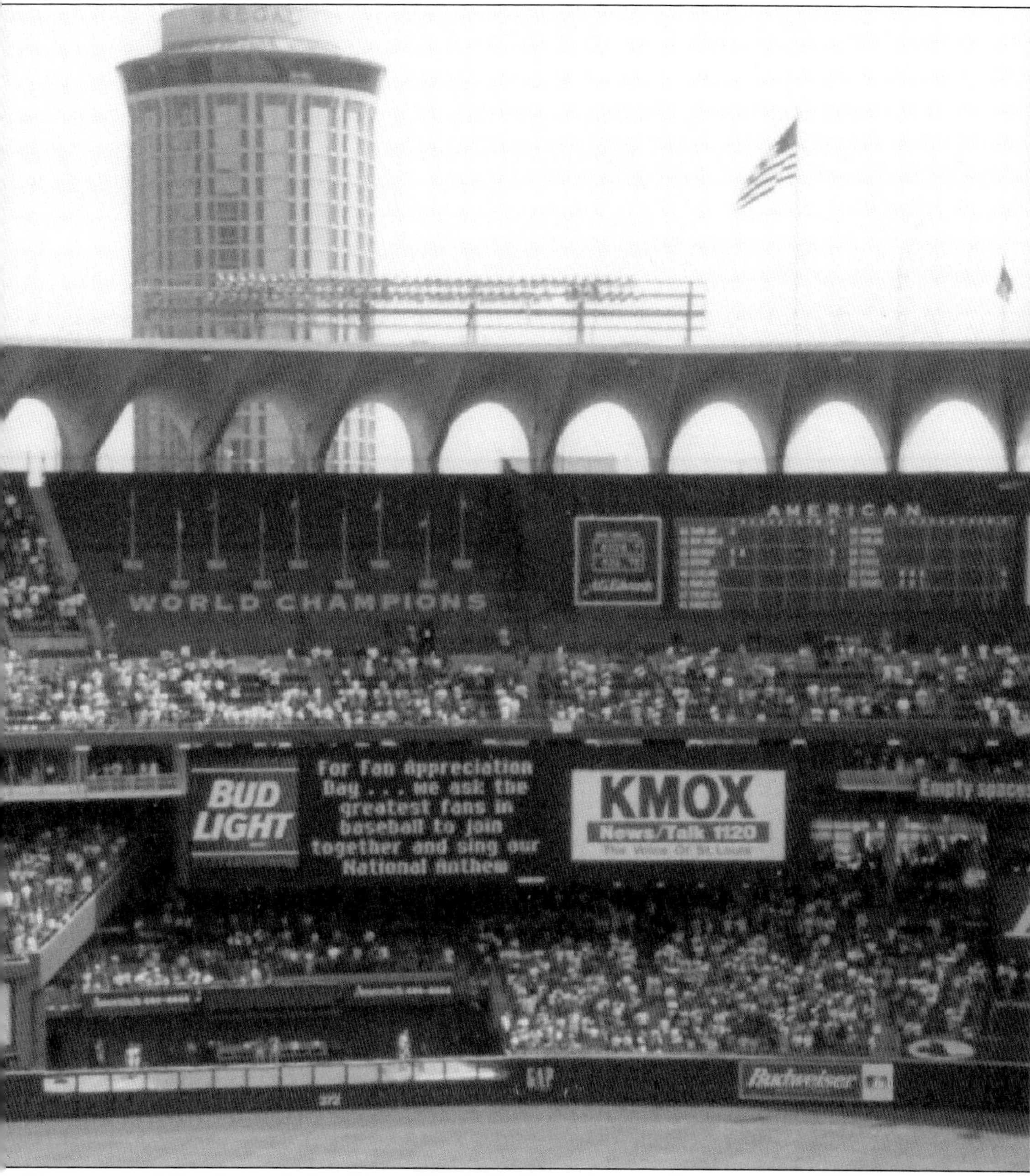

On an annual Fan Appreciation Day at Busch Stadium, the crowd rises to sing the National Anthem. On this occasion of the last day of the season, those with purchased tickets get free admission to a game the following year.

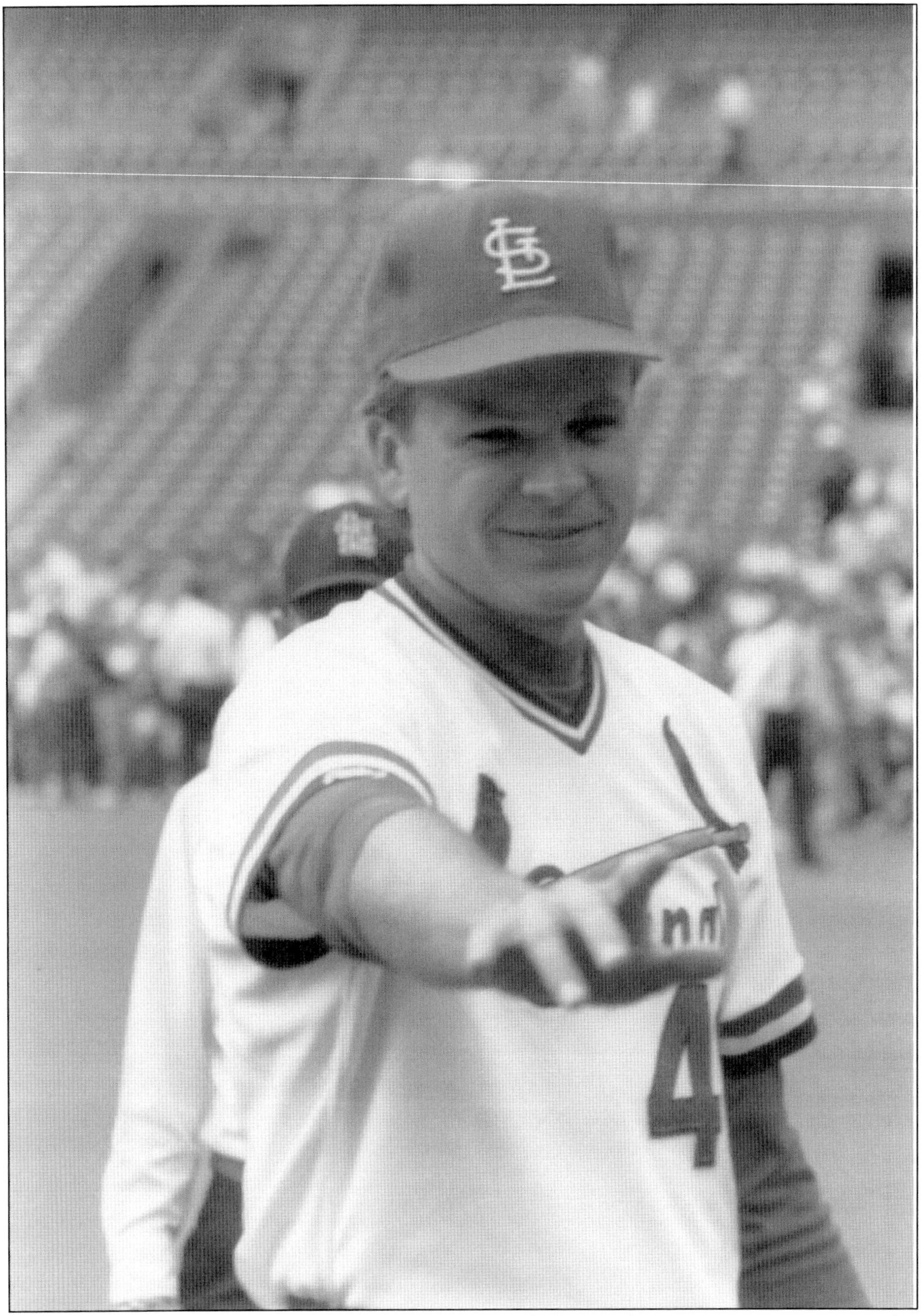

Another left-handed pitcher, Ricky Horton started with the Cards in 1984. Participating in the post-season play of '85 and '87, he then served brief stints with the White Sox and the Dodgers and returned to St. Louis to finish his big league career in 1990. Seen at Camera Day, he reaches out to shake hands with fans.

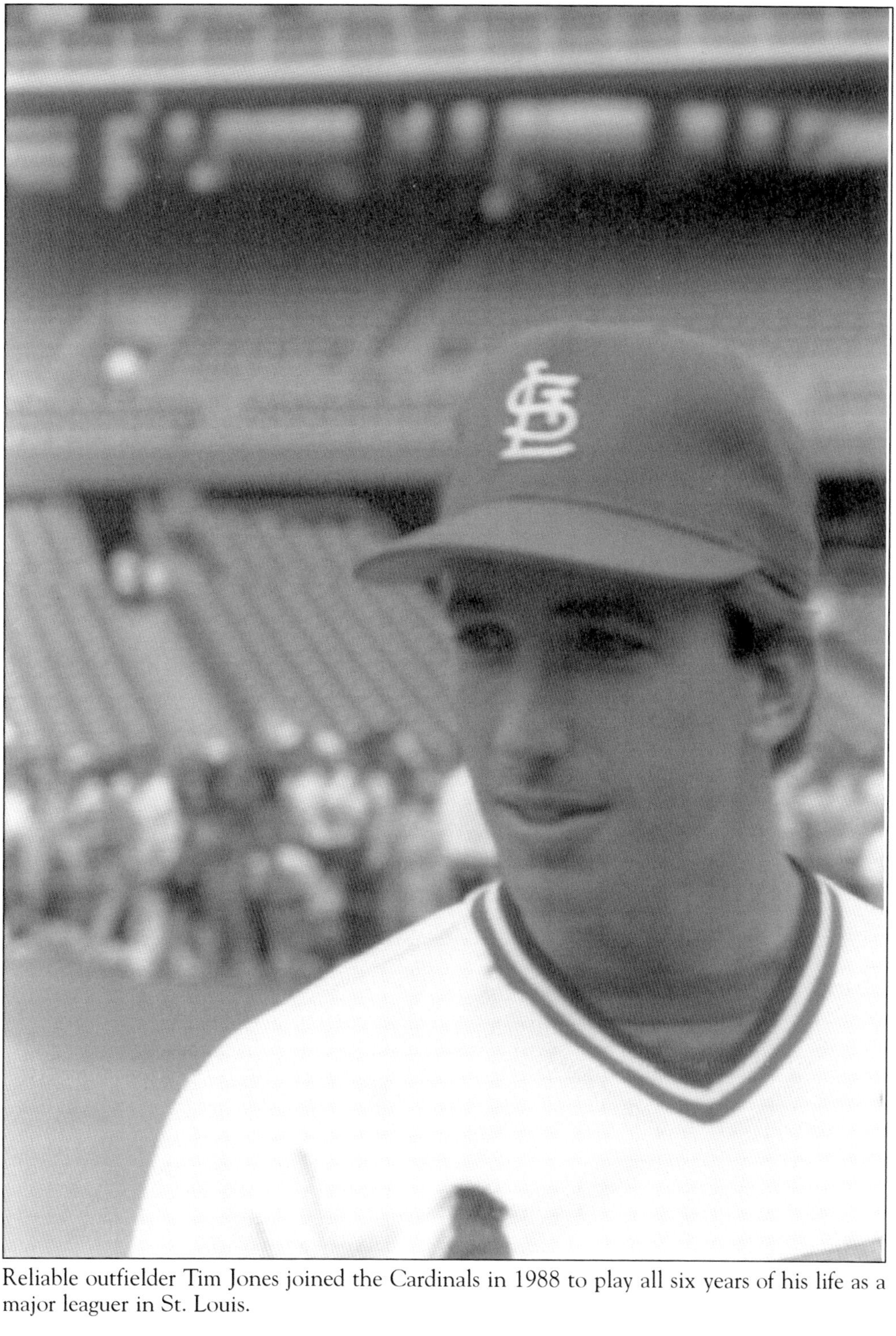

Reliable outfielder Tim Jones joined the Cardinals in 1988 to play all six years of his life as a major leaguer in St. Louis.

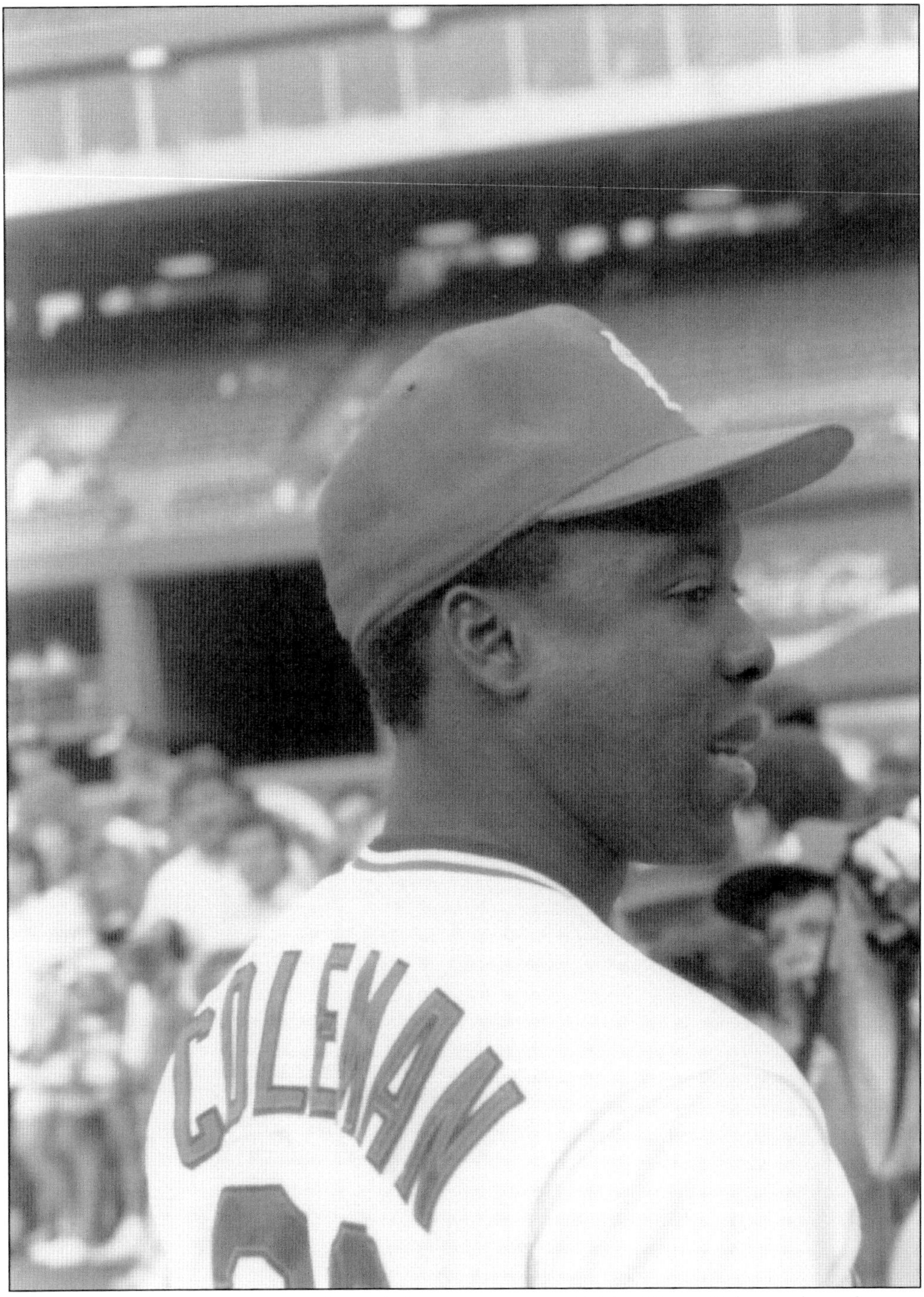

The swiftest of an exciting trio of speedy base runners, outfielder Vince Coleman kept fans on the edge of their seats with his daring base robbing. In each of his first three years with St. Louis, he stole more than 100 bases. He holds the record for most stolen bases in a rookie season, at 110. With the Cards from 1985 through 1989, he made the NL All-Star Team in both '88 and '89. After leaving St. Louis, he played for seven more seasons.

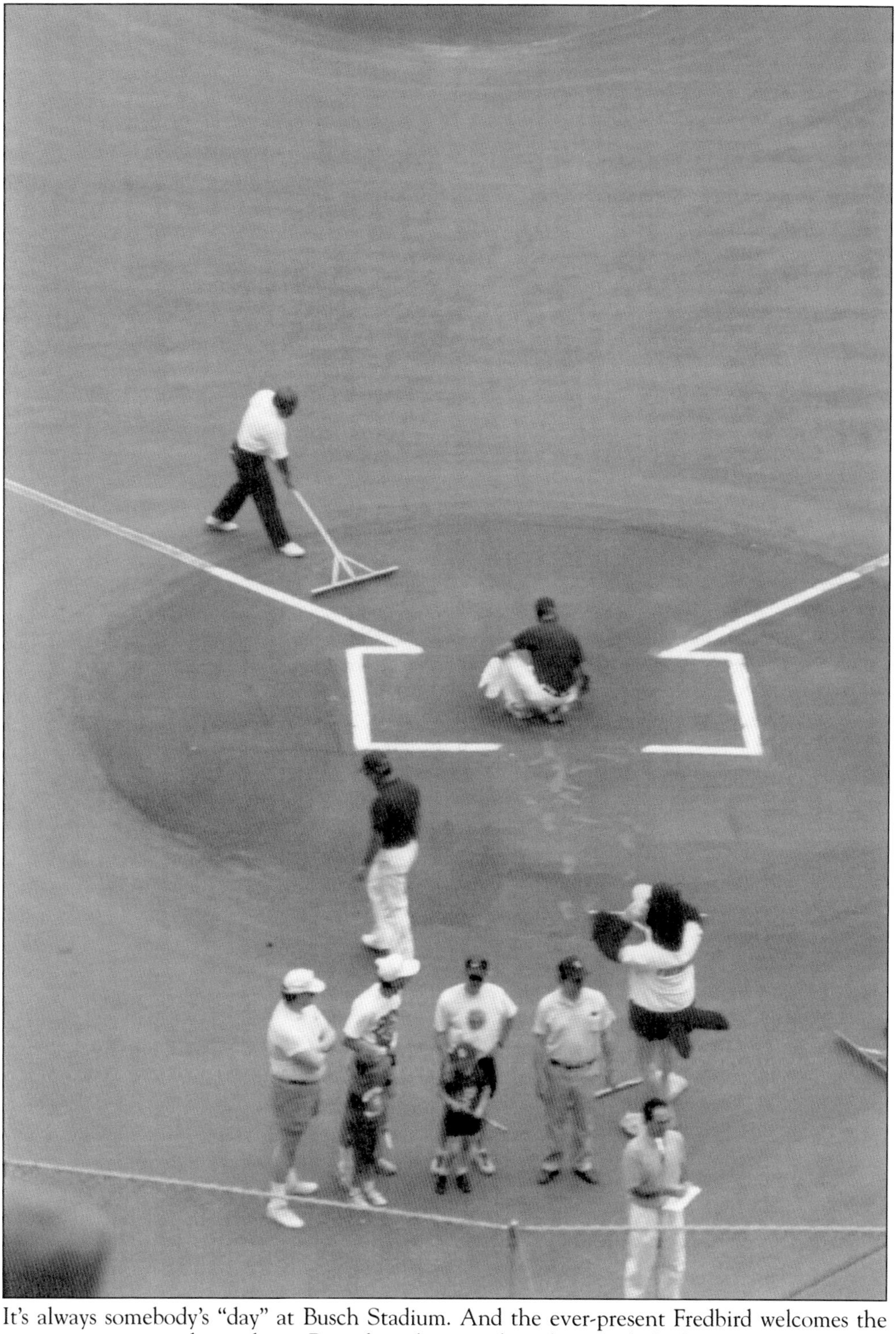

It's always somebody's "day" at Busch Stadium. And the ever-present Fredbird welcomes the guest or guests, as shown here. But often the crowd in the stands find more amusement by watching the groundskeepers prepare the field.

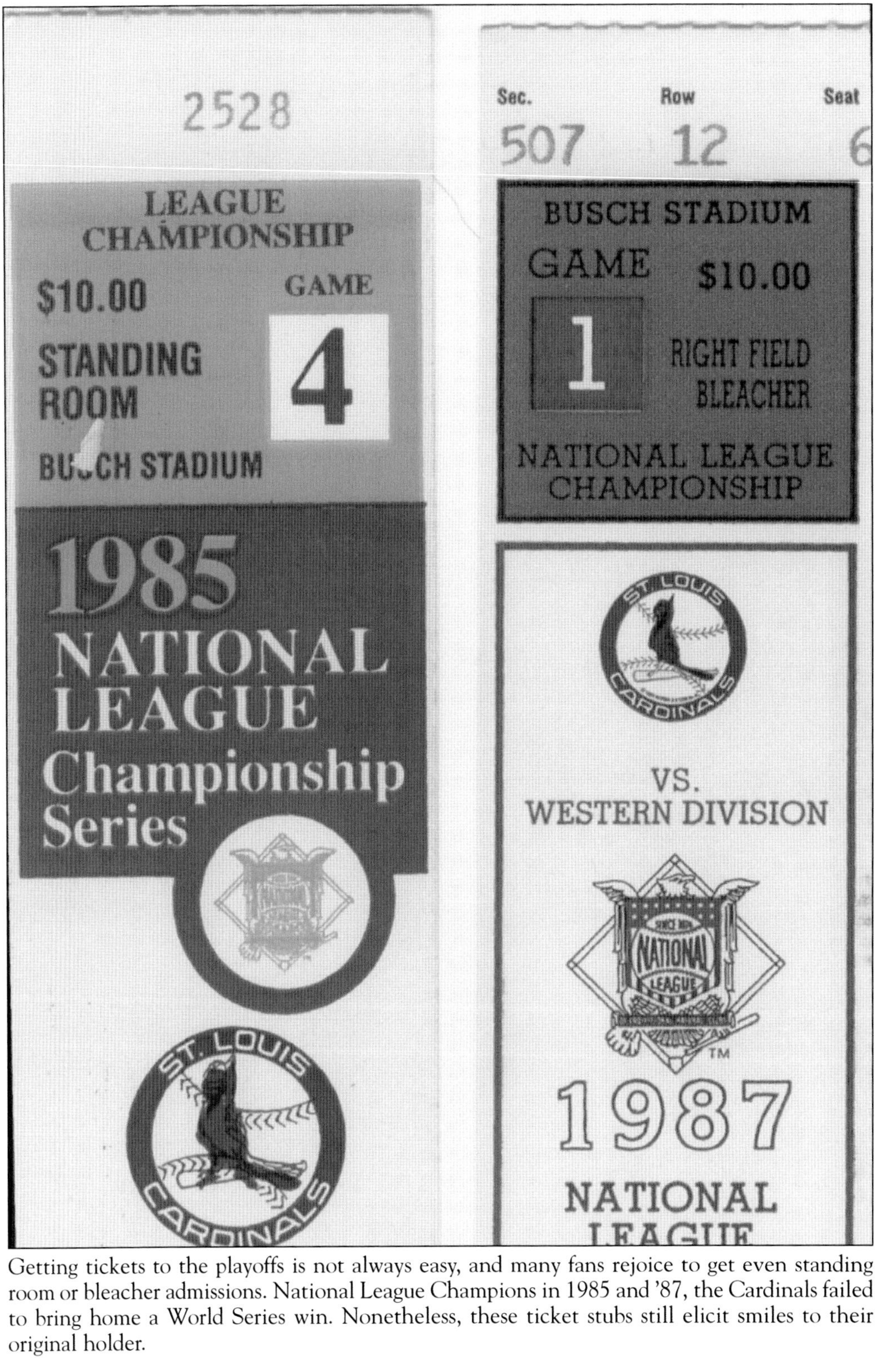

Getting tickets to the playoffs is not always easy, and many fans rejoice to get even standing room or bleacher admissions. National League Champions in 1985 and '87, the Cardinals failed to bring home a World Series win. Nonetheless, these ticket stubs still elicit smiles to their original holder.

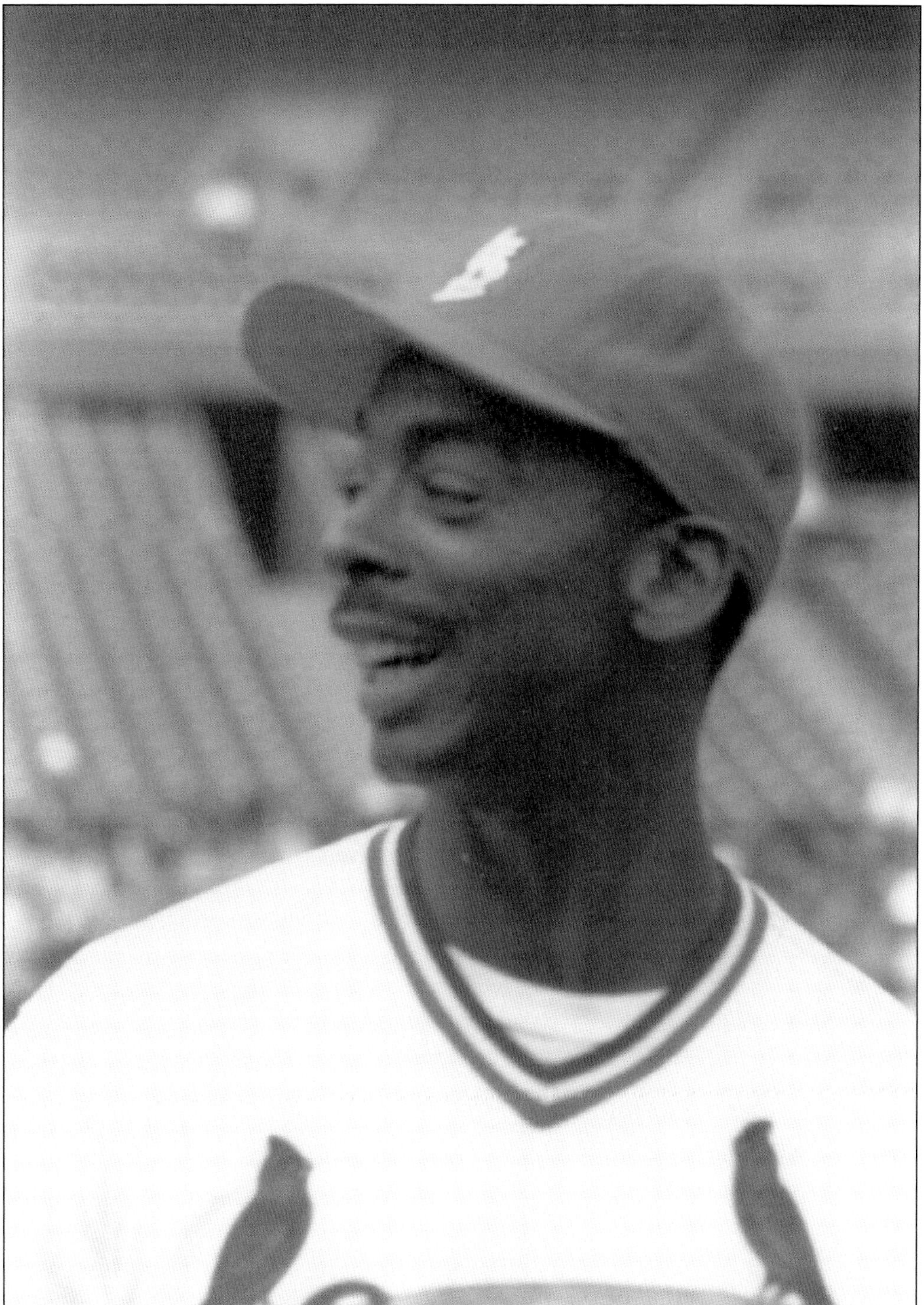

Fans shouted "Willie McGee, hit one for me" when this guy picked up the bat at Busch. Starting 13 of his 18 major league seasons (1982–1999) with the Cardinals, he earned his best stats in 1985 with 56 stolen bases and a batting average of .353. He played in four All-Star Games during his time with the Cards.

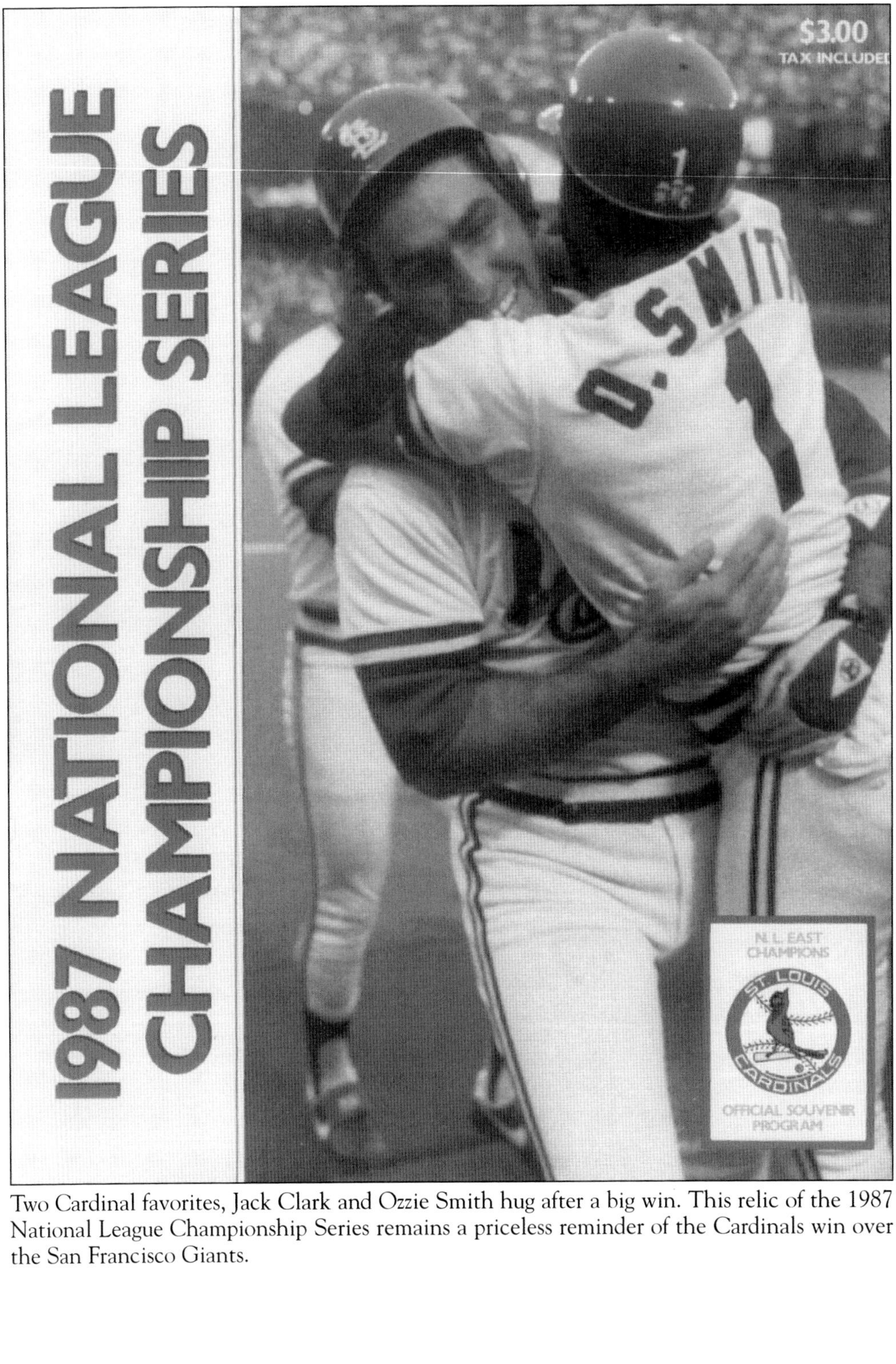

Two Cardinal favorites, Jack Clark and Ozzie Smith hug after a big win. This relic of the 1987 National League Championship Series remains a priceless reminder of the Cardinals win over the San Francisco Giants.

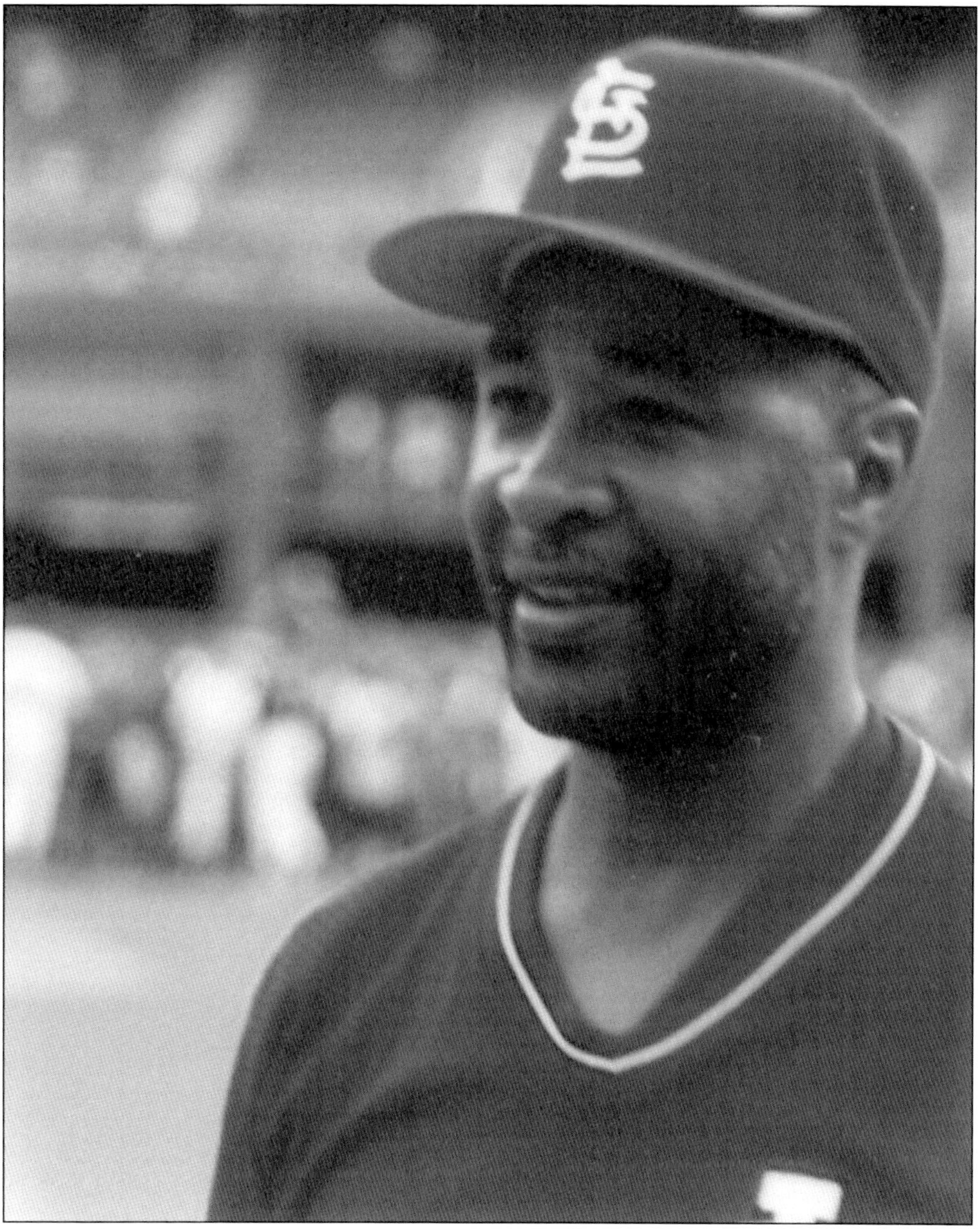

One need not be a baseball fan to recognize the face of Ozzie Smith. Just viewing his picture conjures remembrances of the "Ozzie! Ozzie!" chant at the ballpark. The last Cardinal inducted in baseball's Hall of Fame, Smith came to St. Louis after four seasons with San Diego. That was in 1982, and the acrobatic shortstop spent his remaining fifteen star-studded years in a Cardinal uniform, retiring after 1996.

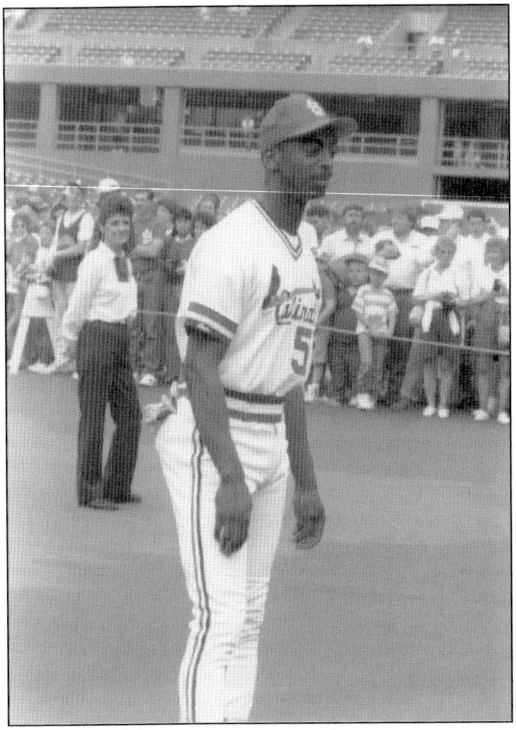

Rangy Willie McGee (see page 107) draws admiring glances from the crowd behind the ropes during Camera Day.

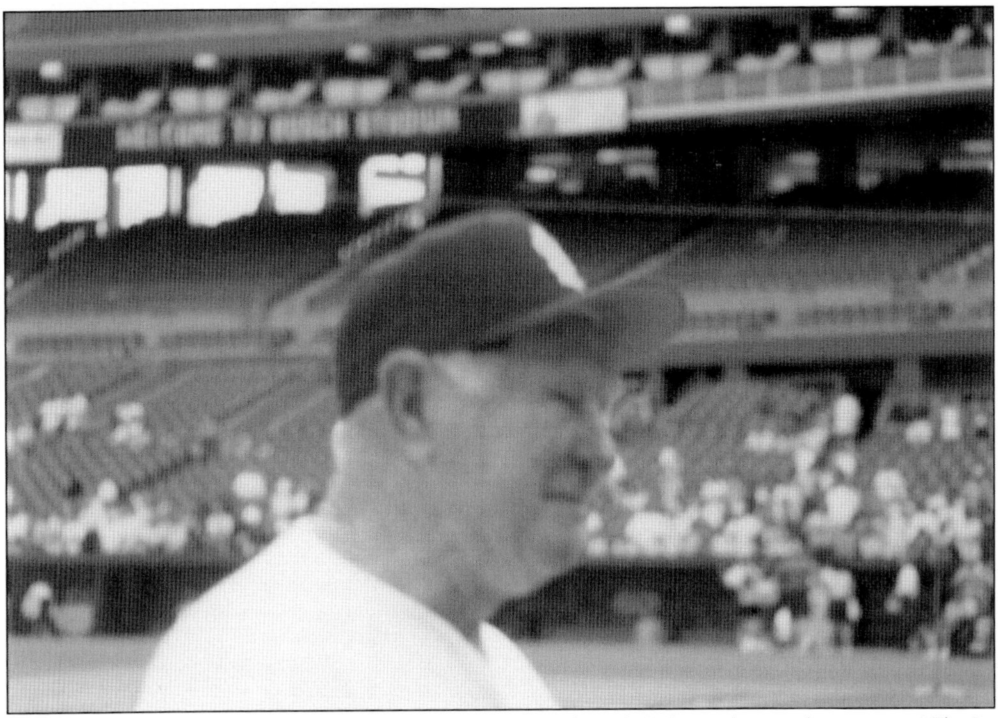

This blurred image fails to obscure the identity of Red Schoendienst (see page 87). In addition to his years as player and manager, Red coached in the majors for 17 years, the last eleven with the Cards.

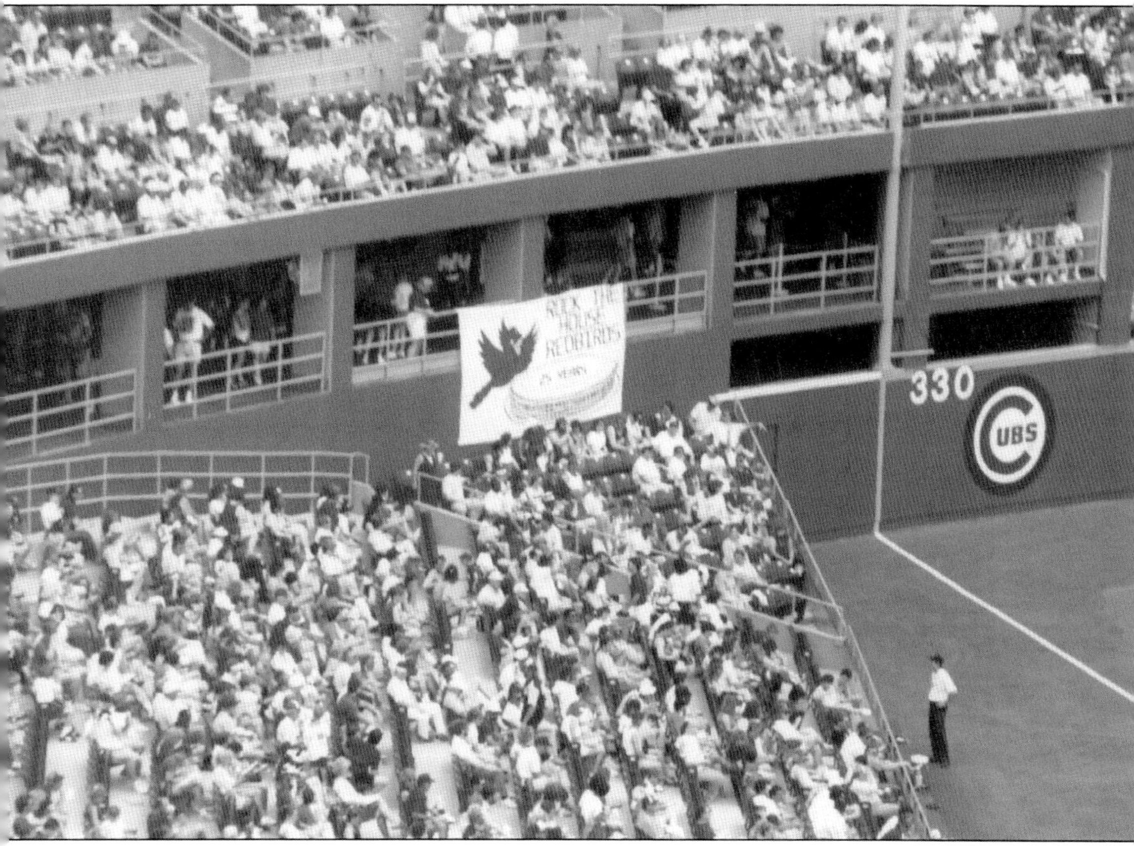

This view of the left field corner at Busch reveals the year that these fans gathered for a day at the ballpark as 1991. The temporary sign hanging from the rails reads "Rock the House Redbirds—25 years." The house being Busch Stadium at the age of 25.

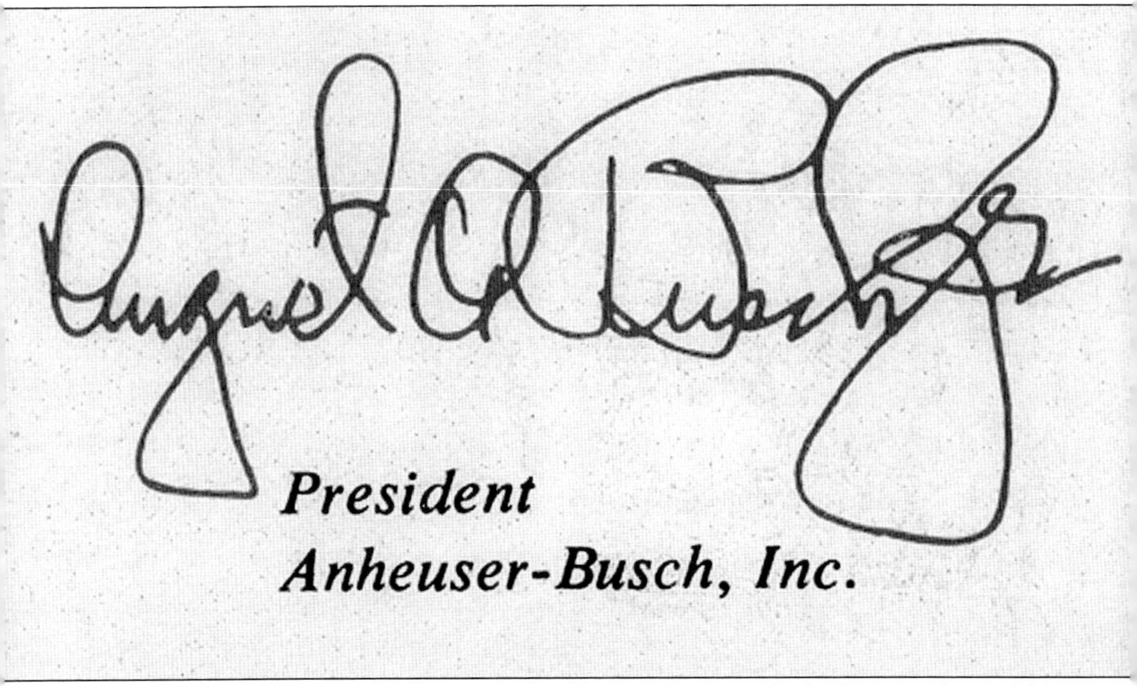

This famous signature followed a message to the fans shown on the back cover of a World Series program. In 1989, all of St. Louis mourned the death of August A. Busch Jr. as the passing of an era. Generations of baseball fans associated their beloved Gussie steering the magnificent Clydesdales onto the field as part of the Cardinal Baseball experience. Accompanied by the rousing strains of "Here Comes the Big Number One" Budwieser song, that tradition lives on in the fondest memories of all baseball fans of modern times.

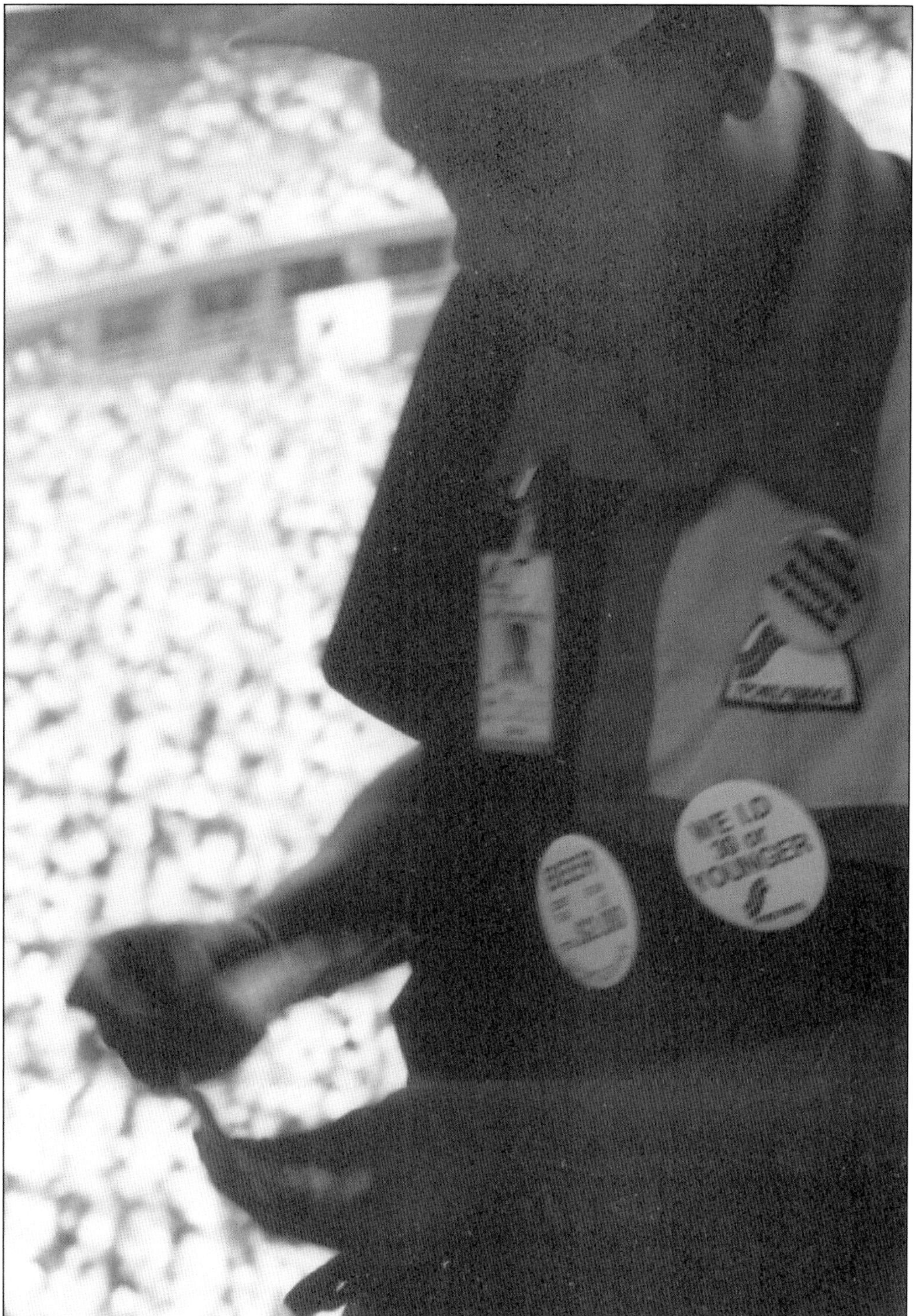

As essential to Cardinal baseball as the grounds' crew, beer vendors honor the tradition begun more than a century earlier. Saloon owner and beer brewer Chris Von der Ahe (see Chapter Three's introduction on page 33) would be envious.

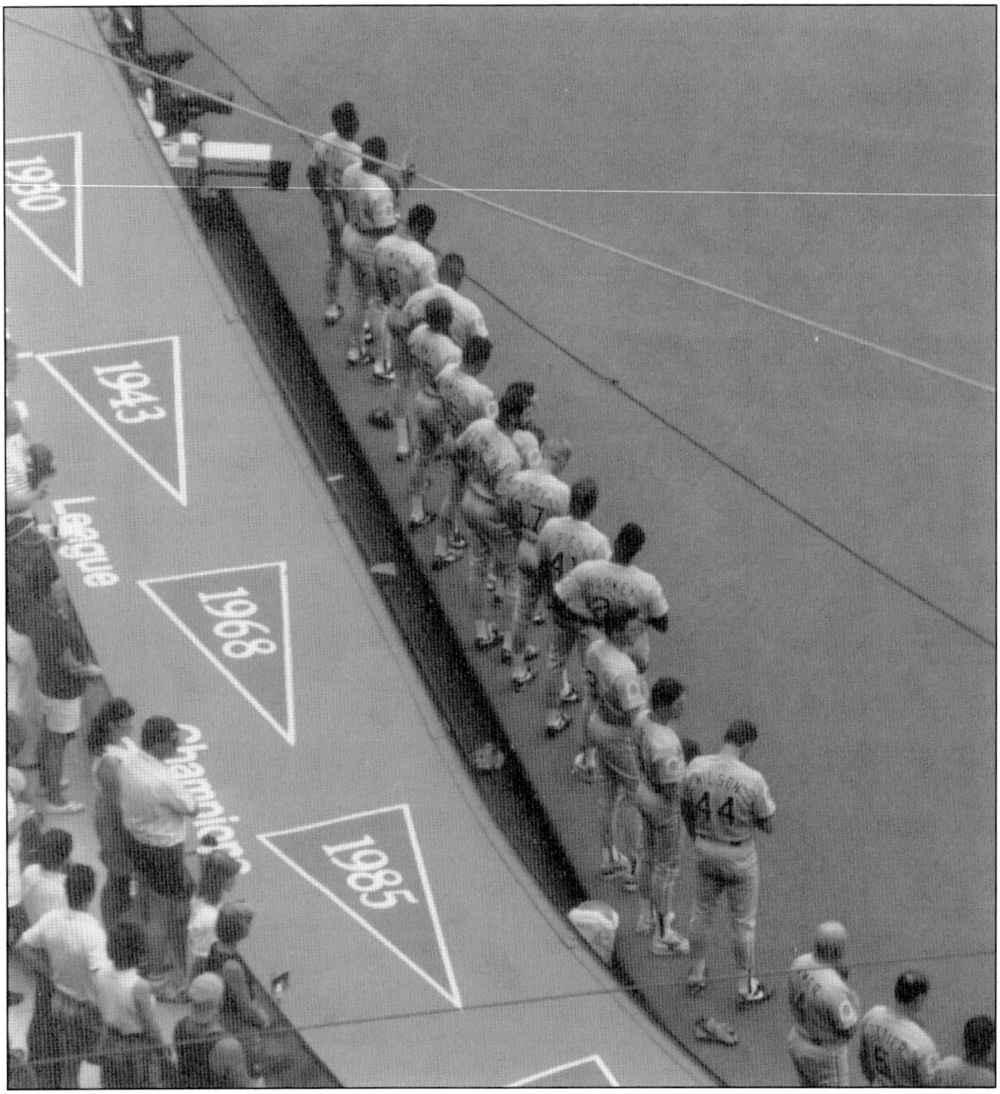

Playing to a packed house at Busch on June 3, 1990, the Chicago Cubs remove their caps for the singing of the National Anthem. The arena and the numbers of fans in the stands differ from that first National League game played in St. Louis on May 5, 1876 (see chapter three). Yet the Chicago-St. Louis rivalry, and the game of baseball, remains much the same.

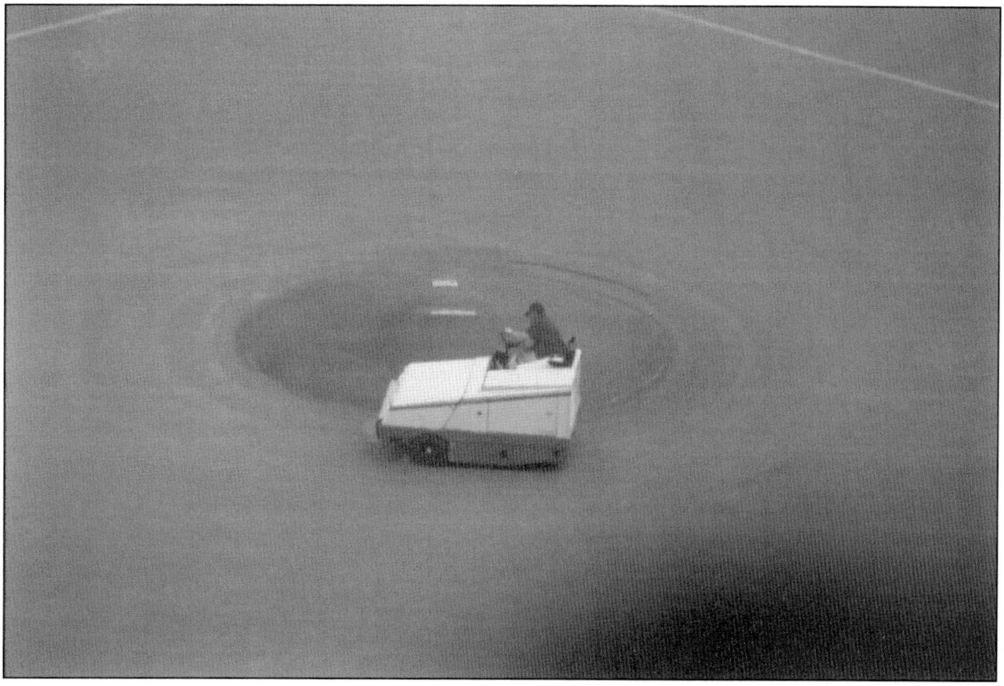

This twentieth-century machine would confound base ball devotees of the early days. Yet, the Zamboni became yet another interesting aspect of the total major league baseball experience at Busch Stadium during the era of the Astroturf.

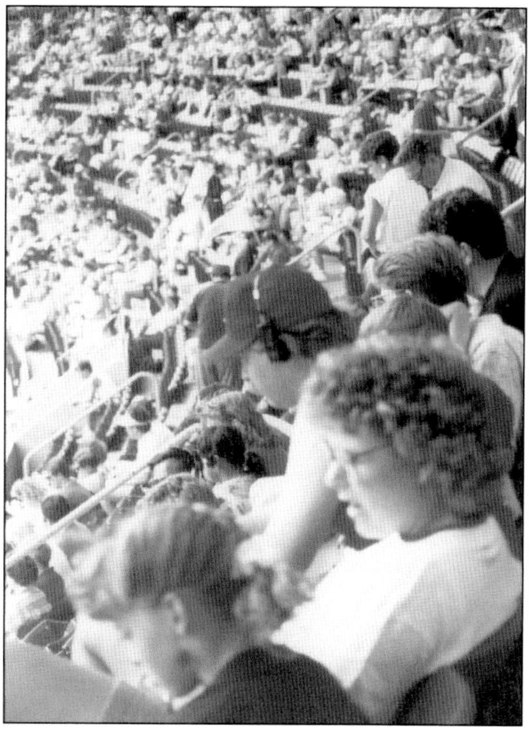

This typical ballgame crowd at Busch endures the glaring sun to see the Cards and the Cubs compete on a field measurably hotter than the temperature in the stands.

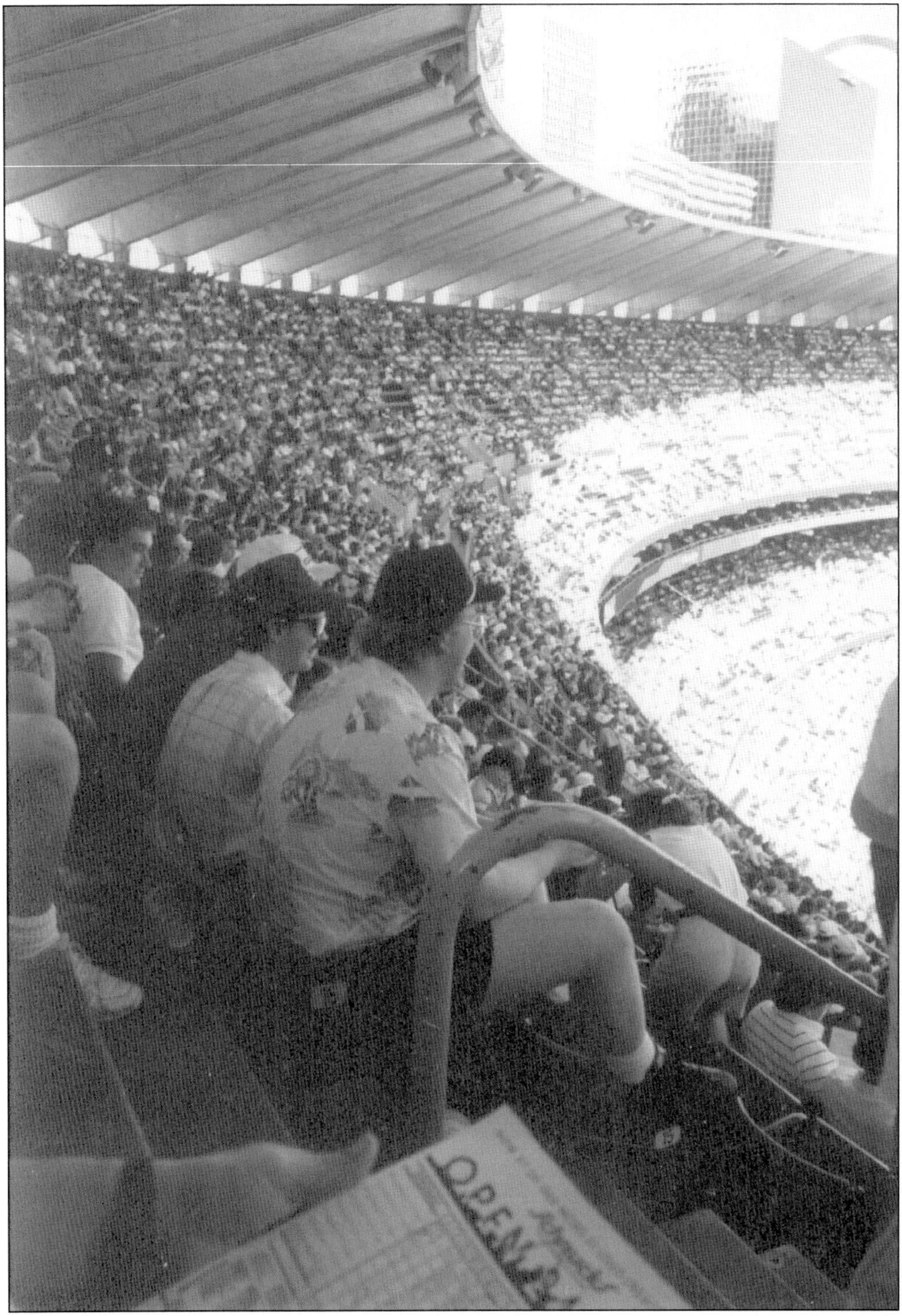

The shadows cast by the searing sun compliment the distant Gateway Arch, and provide welcome shade to fans filling the nosebleed section. During a contest between "arch" rivals (the Cubs and the Cards), the weather doesn't matter. It's a great day for a ballgame.

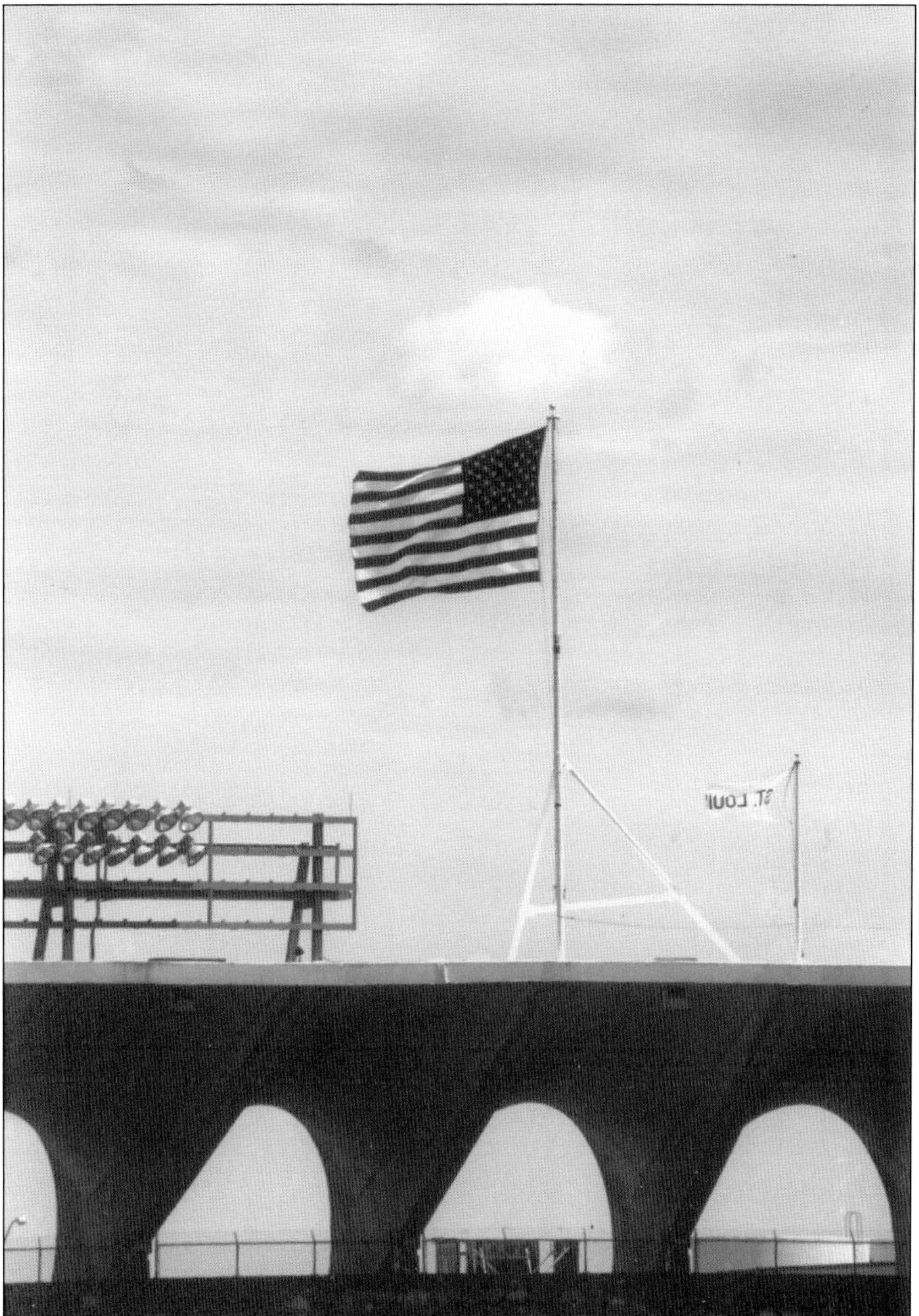

The summer wind persuades Old Glory's billowing motion above the arched canopy of Busch Stadium. St. Louis baseball fans relish this sight, as a listless flag on a hot day spells extreme discomfort below.

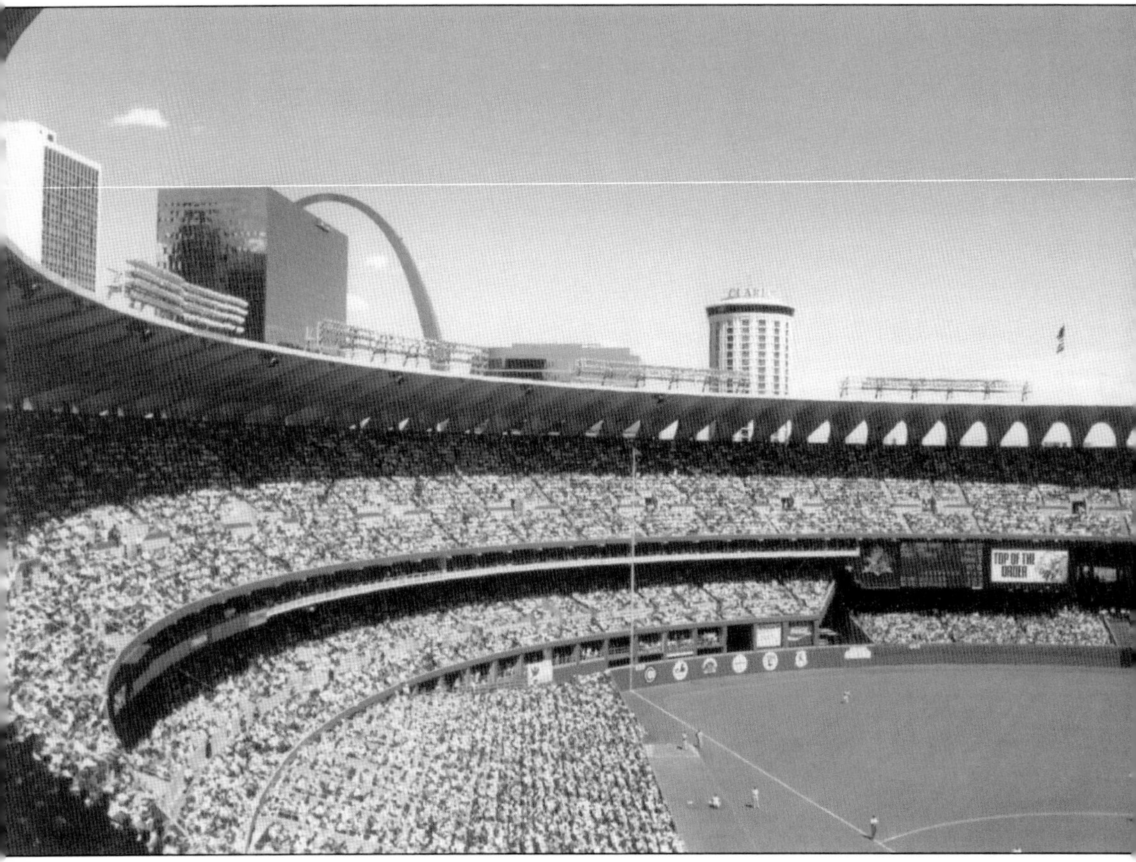

This left field view from the upper deck shows the score at the top of the seventh—Cubs 1 and Cards 7. Also, notice the Budweiser Eagle sign to the left of the scoreboard, shades of Sportsman's Park.

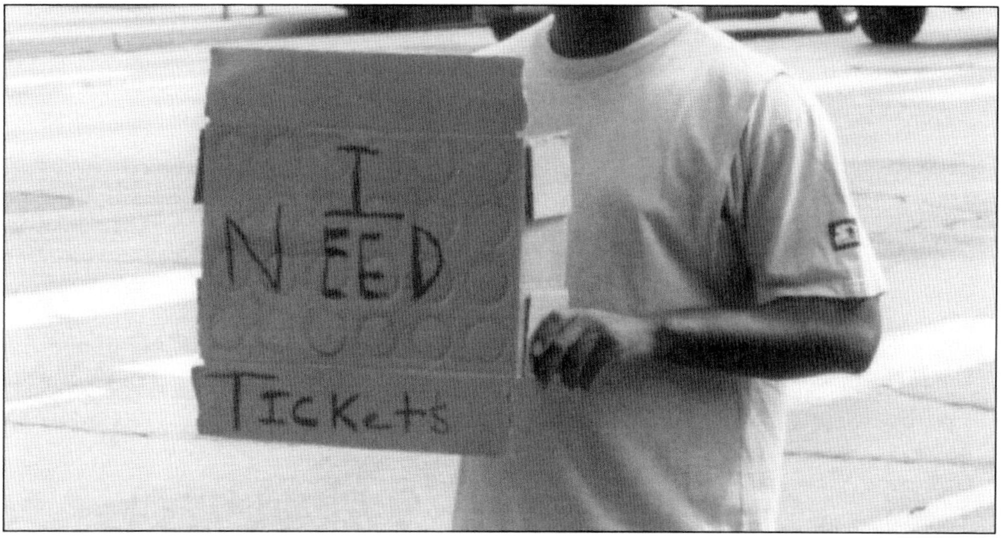

Sunday morning, September 27, 1998, ticket-toting Cardinal fans walked toward Busch Stadium to see this usual site during that epic season. Hopefully, the man holding this sign got what he wanted.

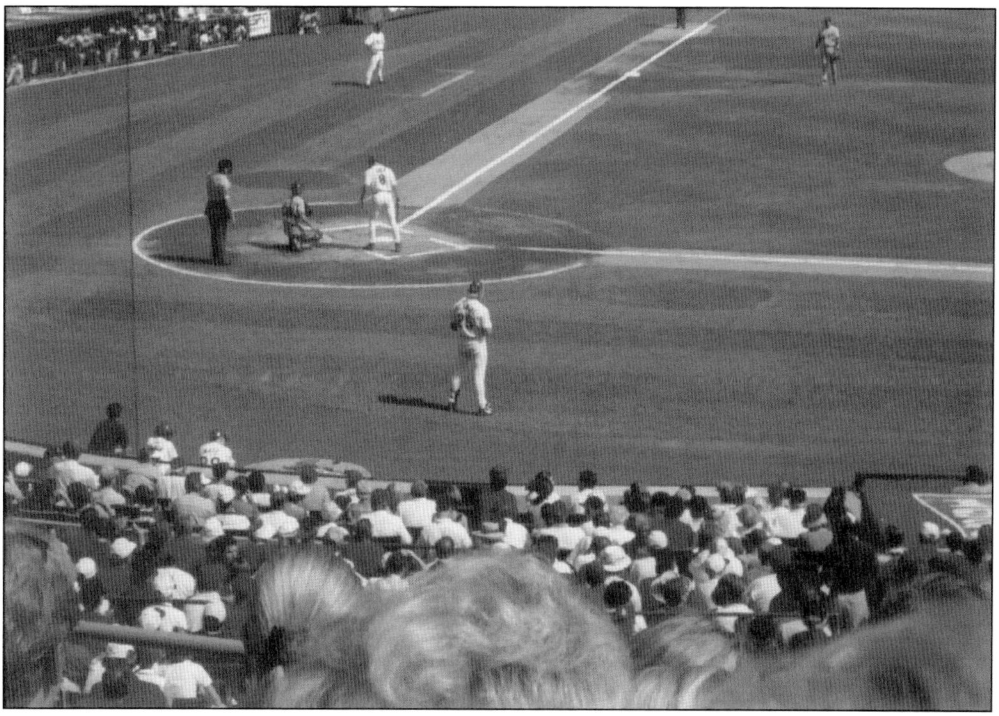

The famous Cardinal player wearing number 25 awaits his turn to bat.

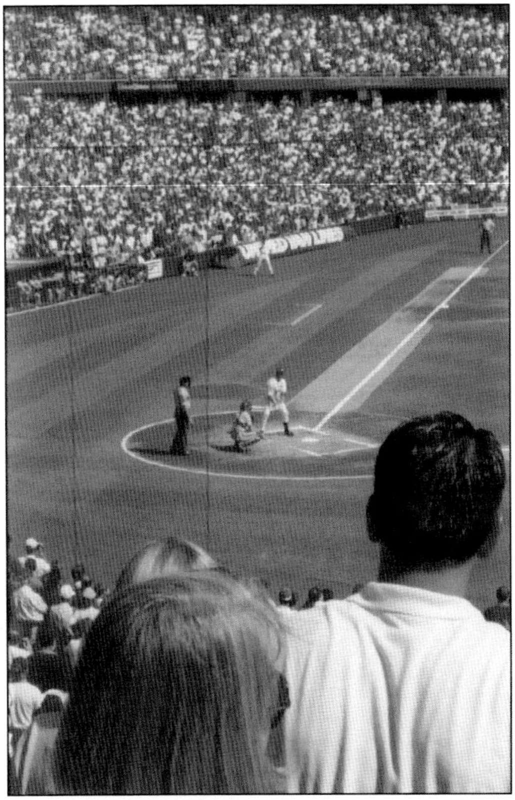

He gets ready.

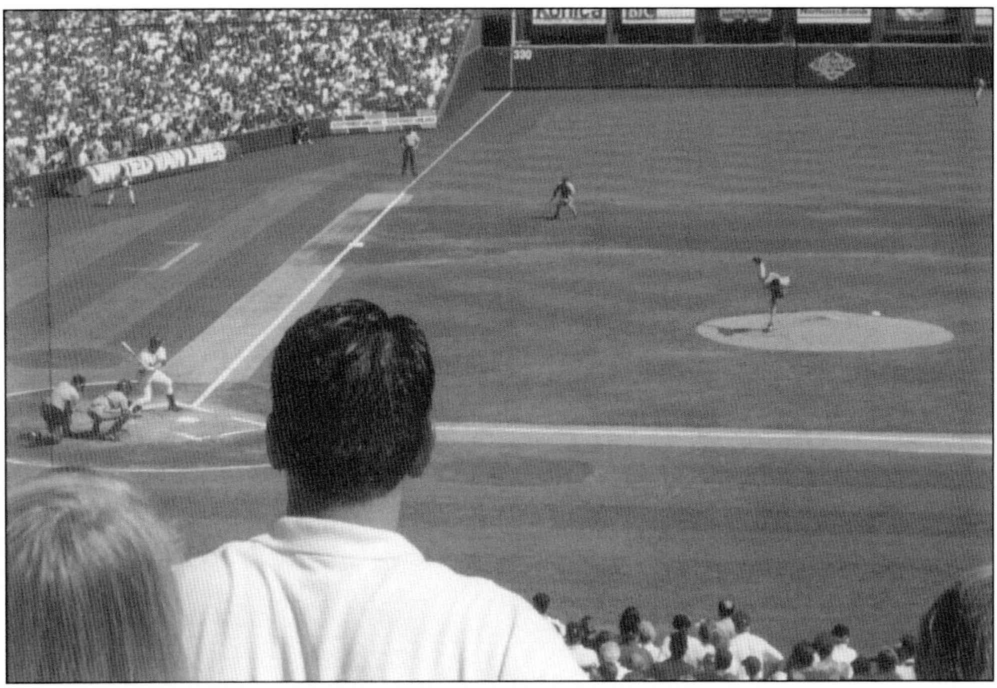

The Expo pitcher releases the ball.

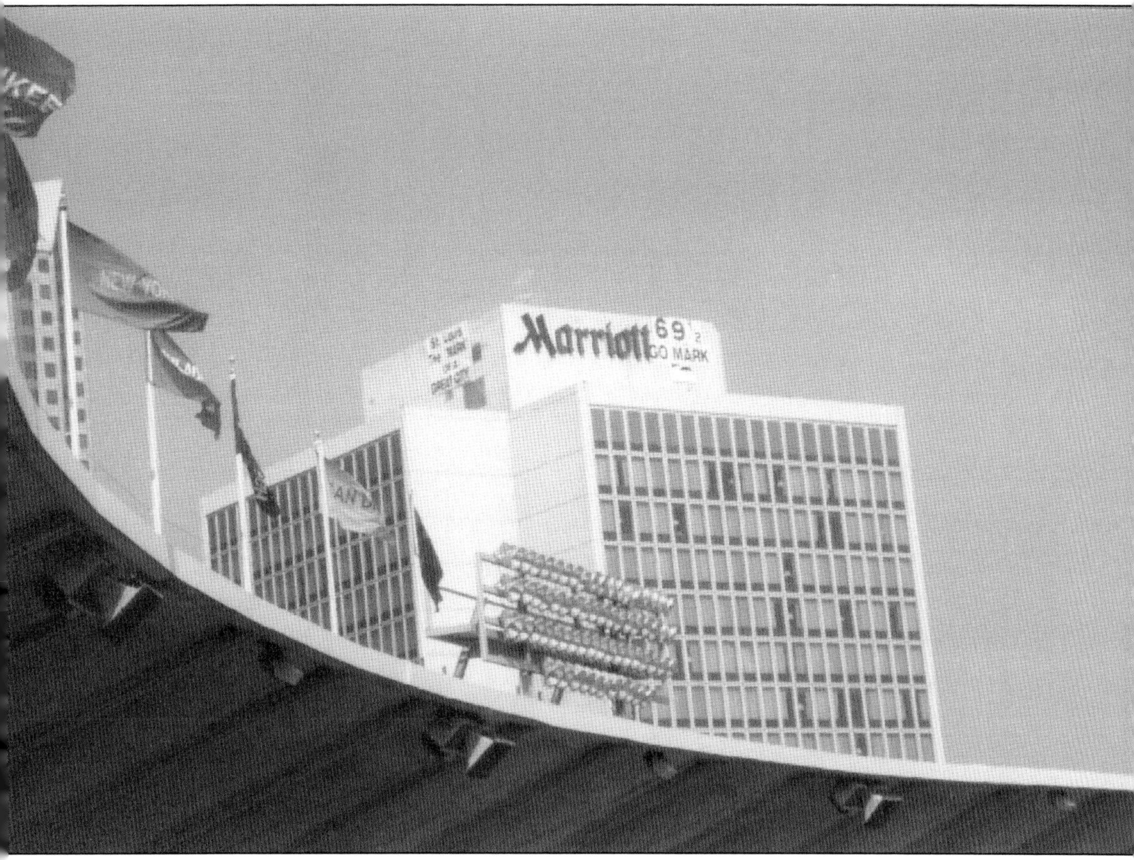

Displayed at the top of the nearby Marriott, a makeshift banner alludes to Mark McGwire's 69th home run, plus a questionable call not counted as a homer.

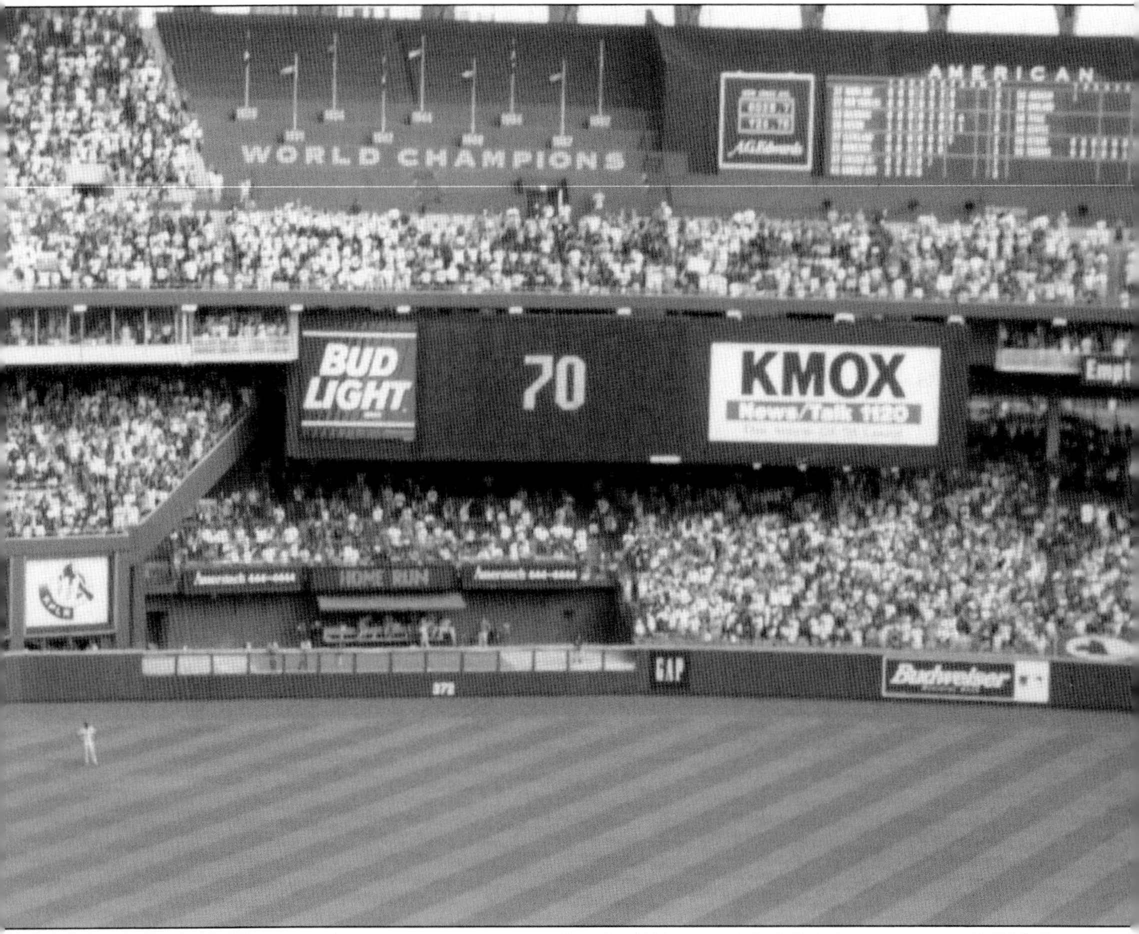

Expo outfielders stand in resignation immediately following Mark McGwire's record 70th home run of the 1998 season. Though San Franciso's Barry Bonds would surpass that with 73 just three years later, joy enveloped Mudville on September 27, 1998. The Mighty Mac slammed two that day.

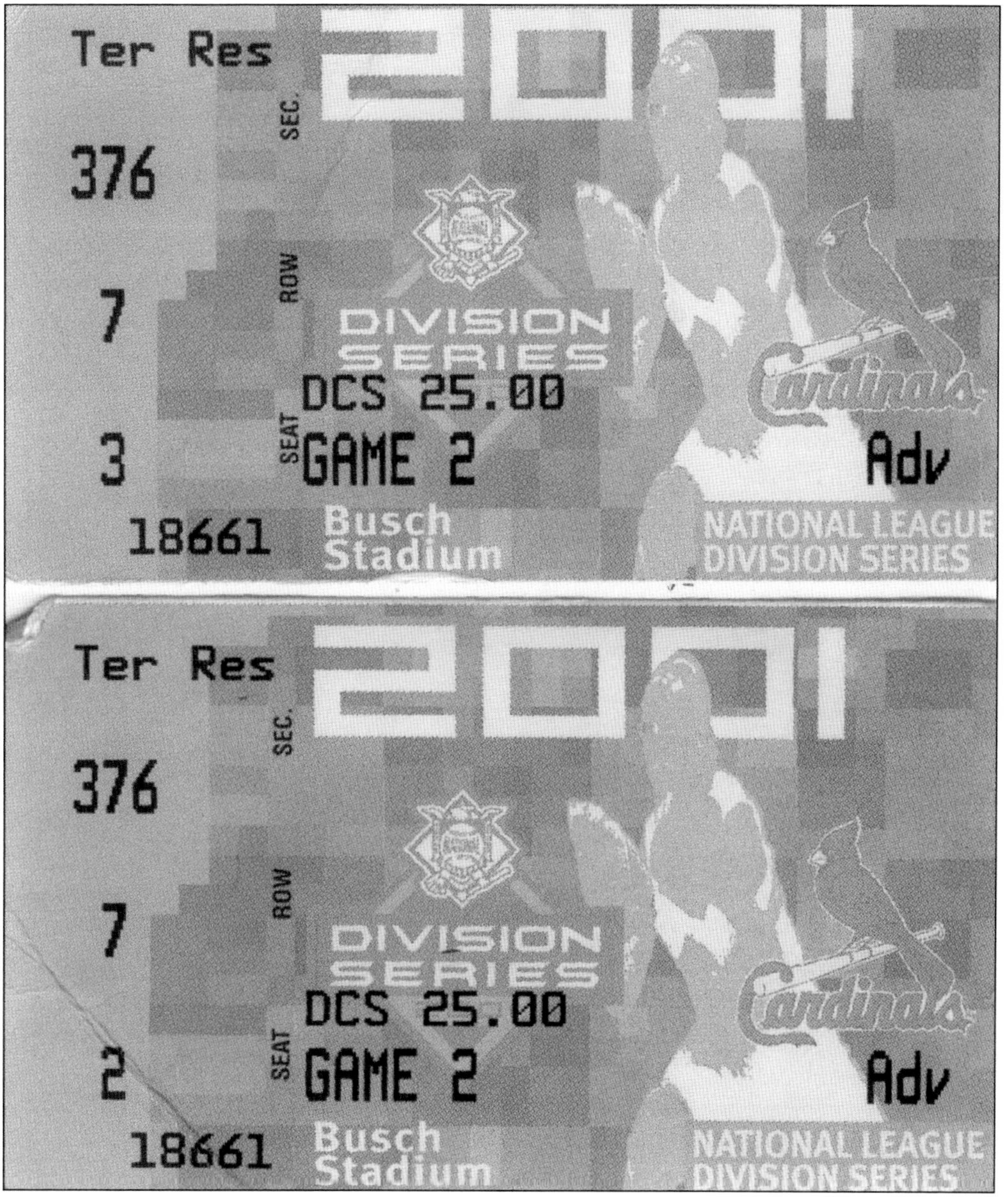

With Tony La Russa managing the Cardinals since 1996, St. Louis again saw post season play. Three times the club advanced to the National League Championship Series (1996, 2000, and 2002), and in 2001 to the Division Series. By 2004 new heroes like Albert Pujols inspired the eternal hope for next year. As always with baseball, the holders of these stubs hope to add more to their collection.

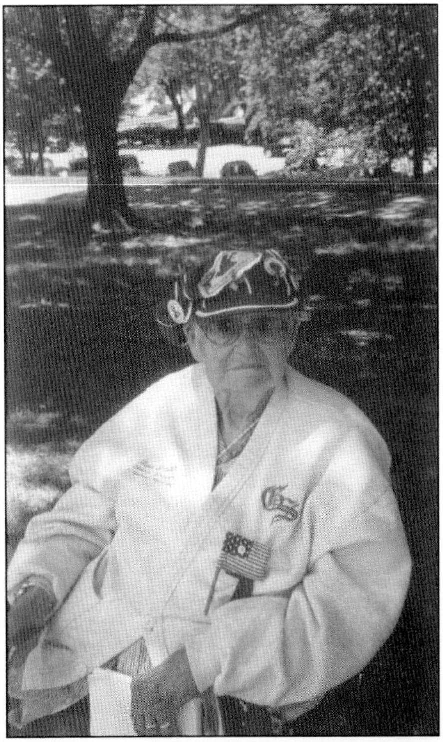

Though most baseball spectators prefer the big stadiums like Busch to see a ballgame, the simple summer pastime still lures fans to the city parks. Watching a match between the VBBA St. Louis Perfectos and Rock Springs Ground Squirrels, vintage fan Rubie Longbons relaxes under a shade tree at Lafayette Park in June 2003. Recognized as the "Official Grandmother of Vintage Base Ball" at an annual base ball festival held at Columbus, Ohio, Longbons comes prepared for the twin bill.

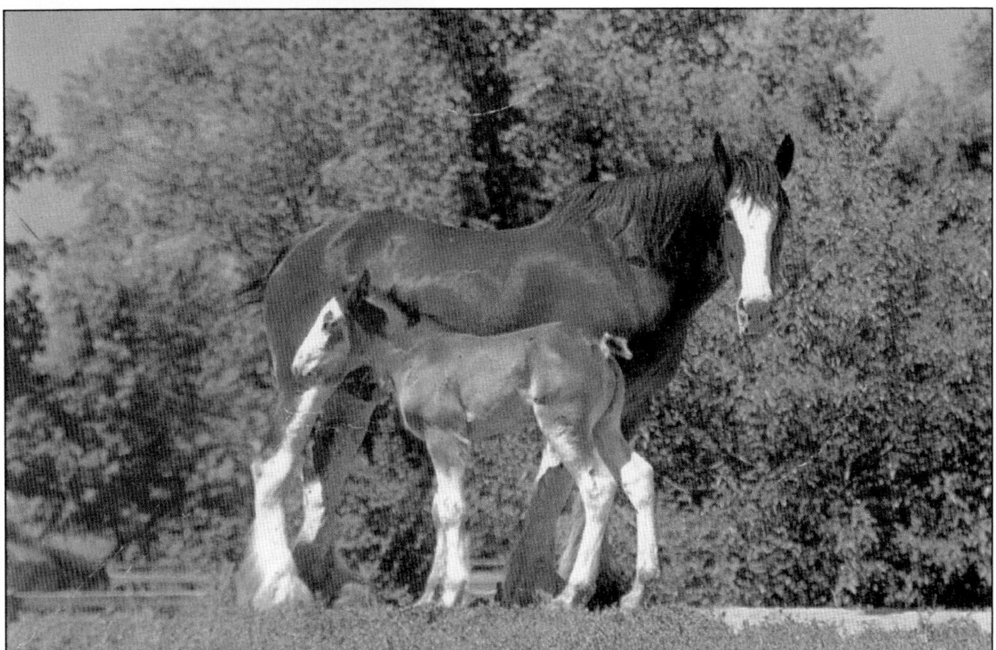

Even the world famous Clydesdales enjoy the natural setting. Though this postcard image makes no illusion to baseball, millions of Americans associate these remarkably handsome horses with beer and baseball. From this book's thematic perspective, the adult and youngster seem to symbolize baseball's eternal promise of next year.

Serious followers of baseball find their seats before the game begins, and never leave till the fat lady sings. Here the fans in the top row of section 350 settle in to watch the day's contenders' warm up exercises. A few rows down, baseball purist Bob Thomas fuels up with peanuts and Coke in anticipation of possible extra innings.

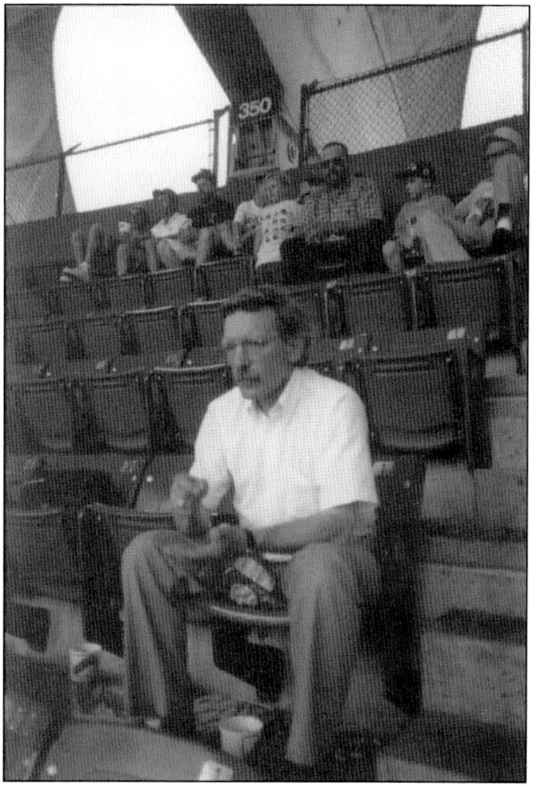

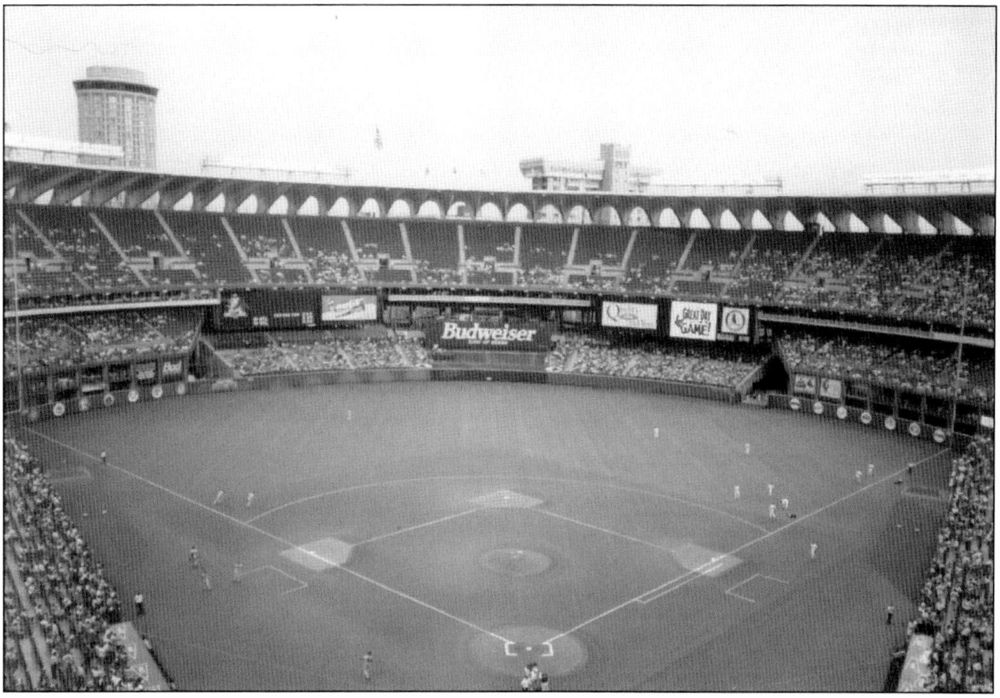

The people in the above photo have this bird's eye view of the field inside Busch Stadium. The many baseball fans of yesteryear would be more than amazed.

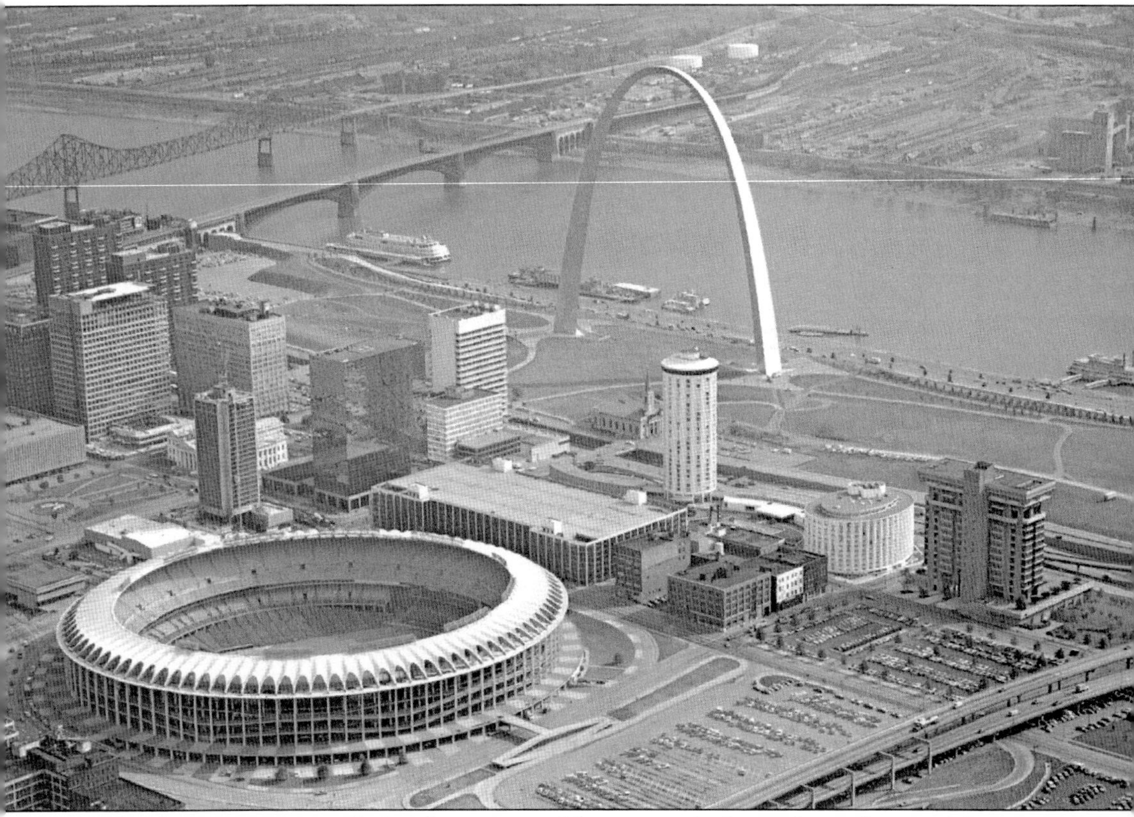

On this picture postcard, the classic view of downtown St. Louis shows the equal dominance of the Gateway Arch and Busch Stadium. That image is soon to change, and one might consider how authors of the future will relate the history of Busch.

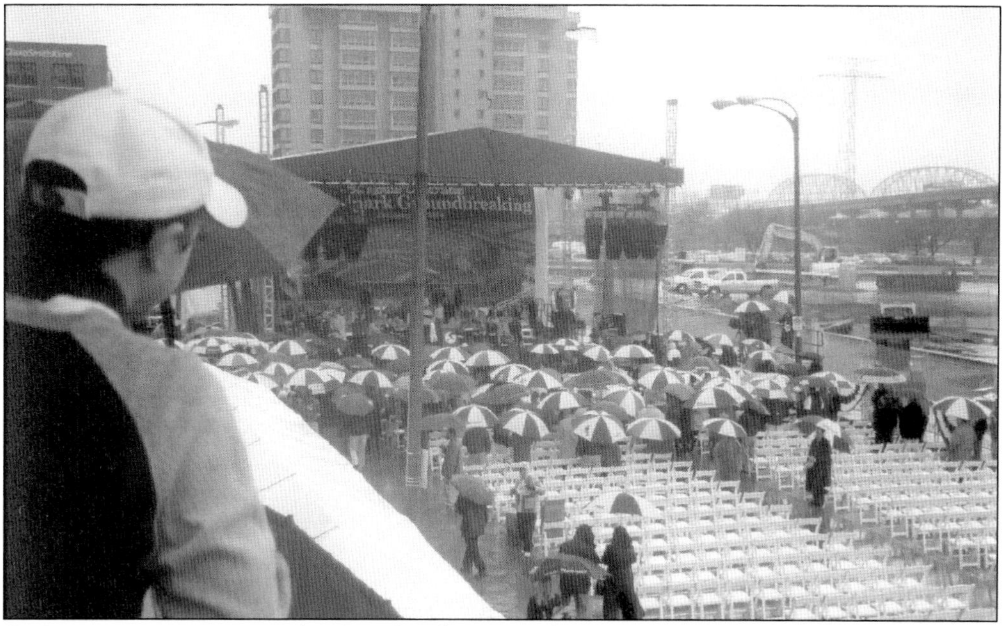

On January 17, 2004, a crowd gathered in the rain and cold to witness the official groundbreaking of yet another baseball stadium in St. Louis. The young man in the forefront views the event from stadium plaza, seeing construction equipment in the rear.

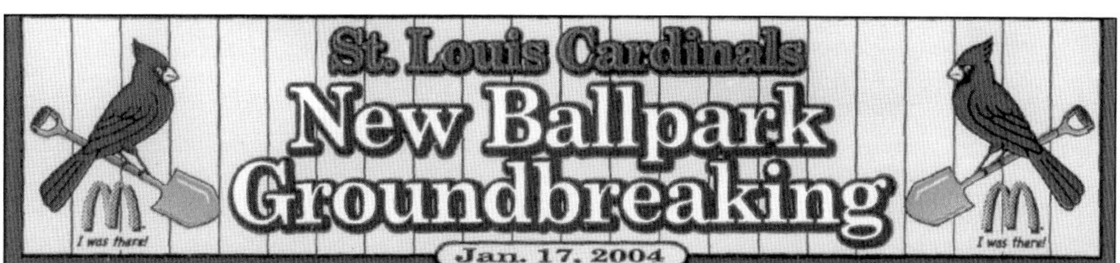

Youngsters in attendance at the official groundbreaking ceremonies received yellow hard hats. Everyone there got a decal like this. Hopefully, the centuries to come will not render this the only remaining evidence of the stadium built in 2004.

Suggested Reading

Atlas of St. Louis 1883, G.M. Hopkins, CE.

"The Background of Professional Baseball in St. Louis," Anthony B. Lampe, *Missouri Historical Society Bulletin*, Vol 7, 1950.

"Baseball in Saint Louis, 1867-1875: An Historical Case Study in Civic Pride," *Missouri Historical Society Bulletin*, Gregg Lee Carter, July 1975.

"Black Baseball Teams in St. Louis," *St. Louis American*, Normal (Tweed) Webb, April 1970.

"A Century of Baseball," *St. Louis Commerce*, Robert E. Hannon, May 1966.

Fru-Con: 125 Years of Performance and Achievement, Fru-Con Construction, 1997.

Green Cathedrals, Philip J. Lowry, 1992.

Life Magazine, cover, April 1, 1946.

Missouri Republican, February 14, 1887.

Pictorial Saint Louis 1875, Camille N. Dry, 1875.

Redbirds—A Century of Cardinals' Baseball, Bob Broeg, 1988.

St. Louis Argus, May–July 1922.

St. Louis Cardinals Yearbook, 1960, 1961, 2000.

St. Louis City Directory, 1930.

St. Louis Globe-Democrat, 1875–1951.

St. Louis Post-Dispatch, 1875–2003.

St. Louis Republic, October–December 1889, January 19, 1913.

Sanborn Fire Insurance Maps, 1903–1916.

"Major League Ballparks—From the Beginning," *Senior Circuit*, Joan M. Thomas, July–December 2002.

Sporting News Complete Baseball Record Book, The Sporting News, 2002.

The Gashouse Gang and a Couple of Other Guys, J. Roy Stockton, 1945.

The National Game, Alfred H. Spink, 1911.

The Negro Leagues Book, Negro Leagues Committee of the Society for American Baseball Research, 1994.

The New York Times, January 15, 1886.

Total Baseball—Seventh Edition, Total Sports Publishing, 2001.

Through The Years At Sportsman's Park, Robert L. Tiemann. 1991.